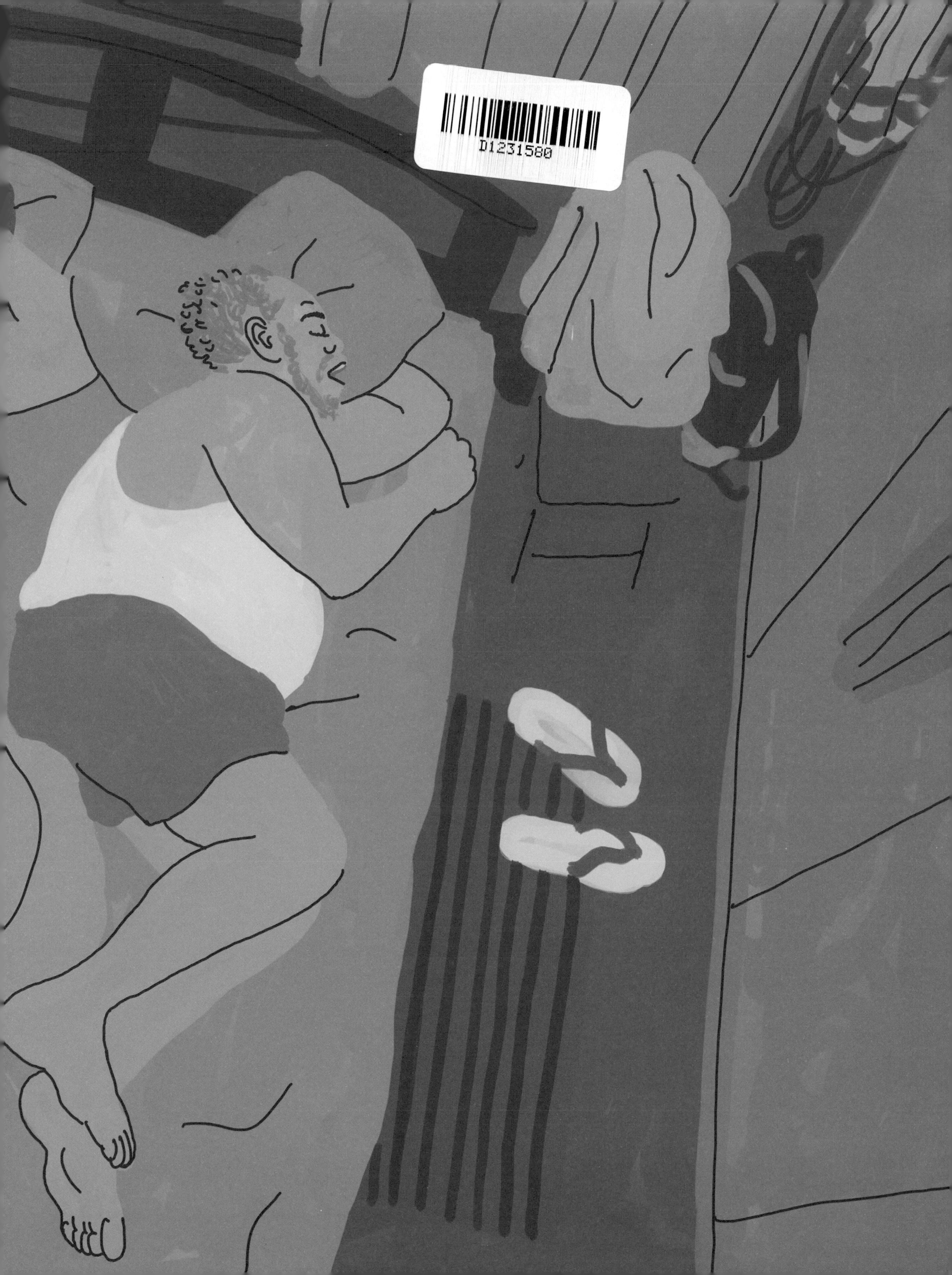

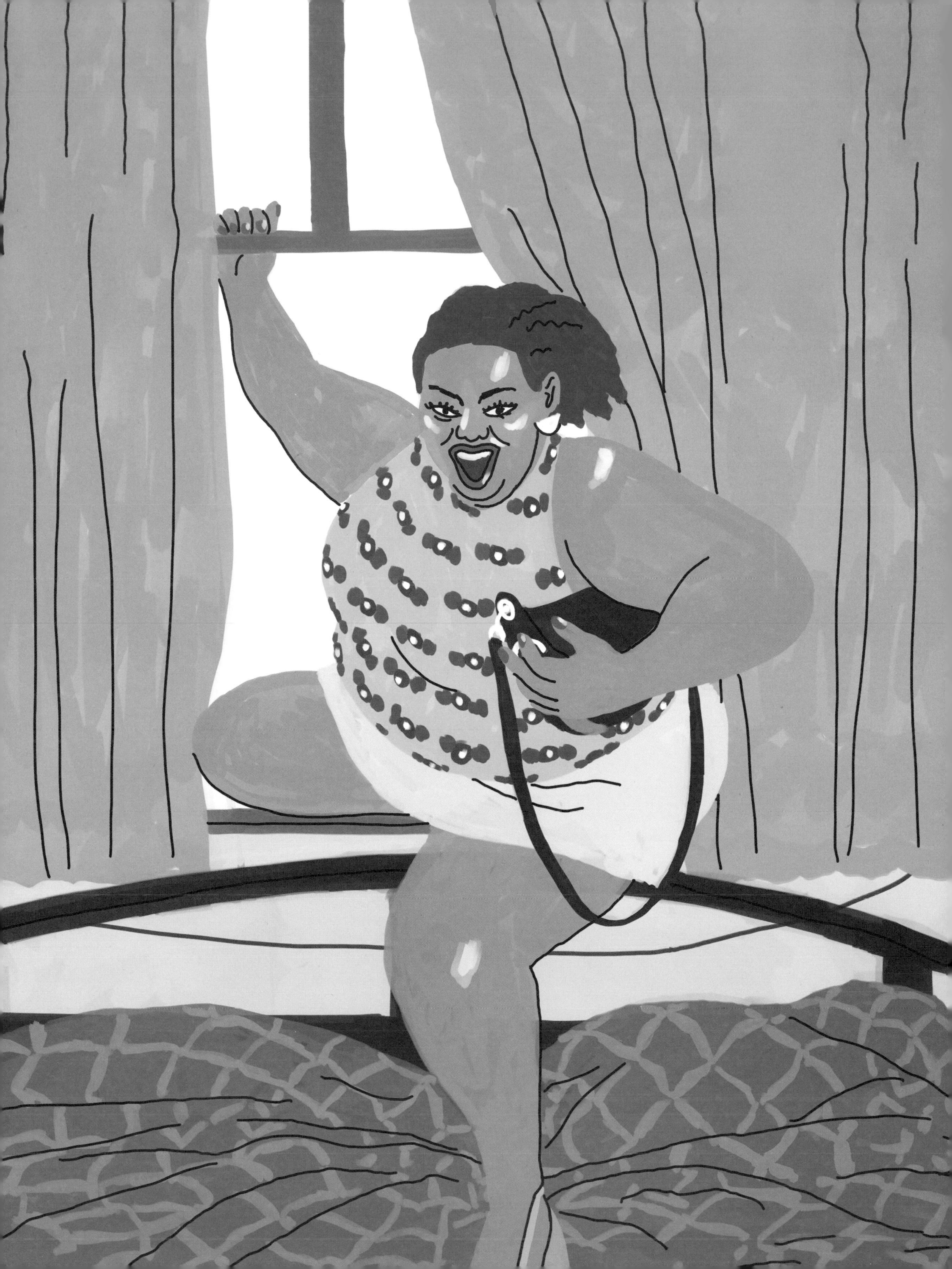

Listen, Beautiful Márcia

Listen, beautiful Márcia

marcello
quintanilha

TRANSLATED BY
ANDREA ROSENBERG

FANTAGRAPHICS

FANTAGRAPHICS BOOKS
7563 LAKE CITY WAY NE
SEATTLE, WASHINGTON 98115
WWW.FANTAGRAPHICS.COM

TRANSLATOR: ANDREA ROSENBERG
DESIGNER: KAYLA E.
PRODUCTION: PAUL BARESH & C. HWANG
PROMOTION: JACQUELENE COHEN
VP / ASSOCIATE PUBLISHER / EDITOR: ERIC REYNOLDS
PRESIDENT / PUBLISHER: GARY GROTH

ISBN 978-1-68396-777-4
LIBRARY OF CONGRESS CONTROL NUMBER 2022949000
FIRST PRINTING: MAY 2023
PRINTED IN CHINA

YES, LUCIANA,
THOSE ARE
YOUR EYELASHES.

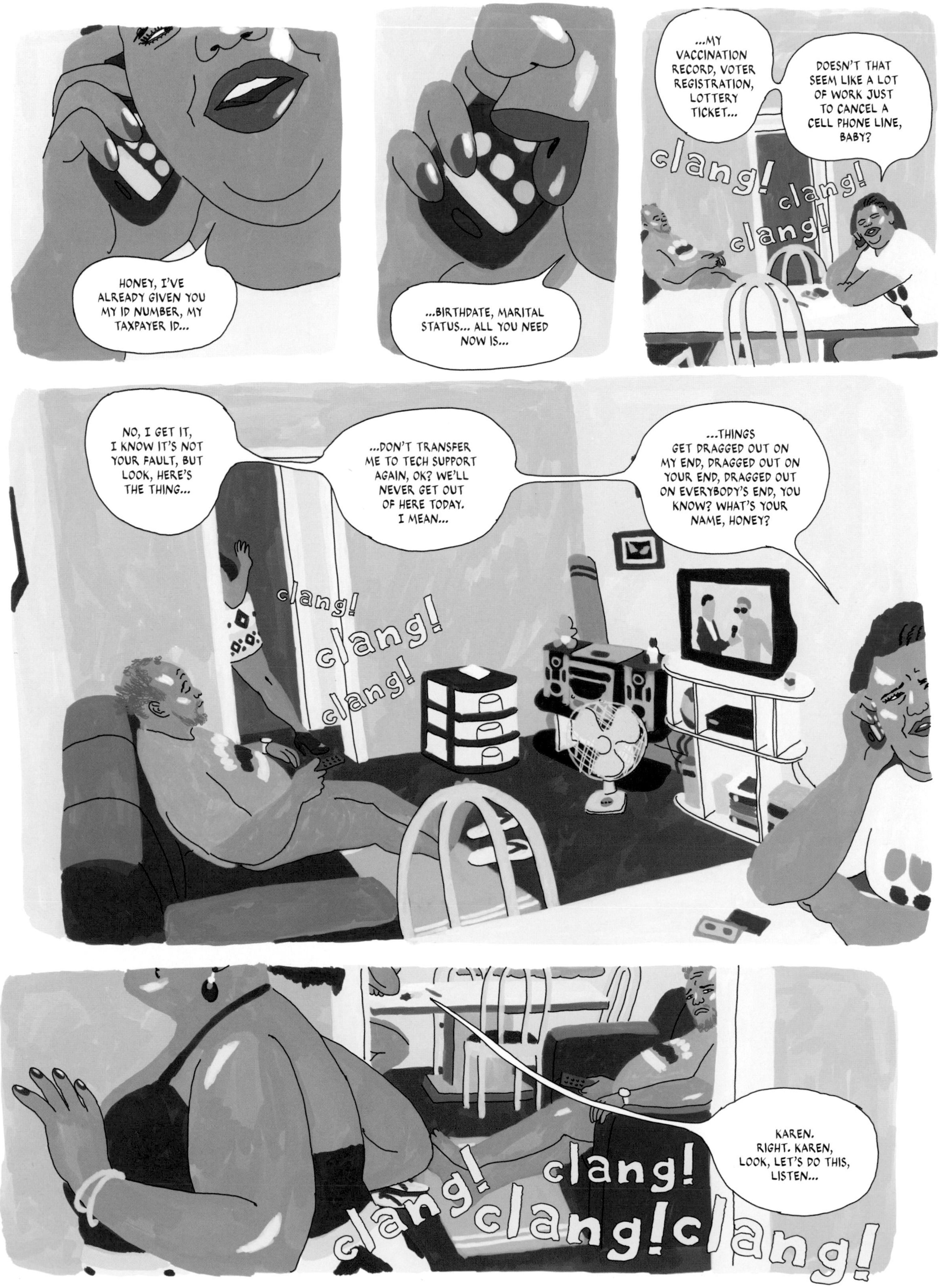
HONEY, I'VE ALREADY GIVEN YOU MY ID NUMBER, MY TAXPAYER ID...
...BIRTHDATE, MARITAL STATUS... ALL YOU NEED NOW IS...
...MY VACCINATION RECORD, VOTER REGISTRATION, LOTTERY TICKET...
DOESN'T THAT SEEM LIKE A LOT OF WORK JUST TO CANCEL A CELL PHONE LINE, BABY?
clang! clang! clang!
NO, I GET IT, I KNOW IT'S NOT YOUR FAULT, BUT LOOK, HERE'S THE THING...
...DON'T TRANSFER ME TO TECH SUPPORT AGAIN, OK? WE'LL NEVER GET OUT OF HERE TODAY. I MEAN...
...THINGS GET DRAGGED OUT ON MY END, DRAGGED OUT ON YOUR END, DRAGGED OUT ON EVERYBODY'S END, YOU KNOW? WHAT'S YOUR NAME, HONEY?
clang! clang! clang!
KAREN. RIGHT. KAREN, LOOK, LET'S DO THIS, LISTEN...
clang! clang! clang! clang! clang!

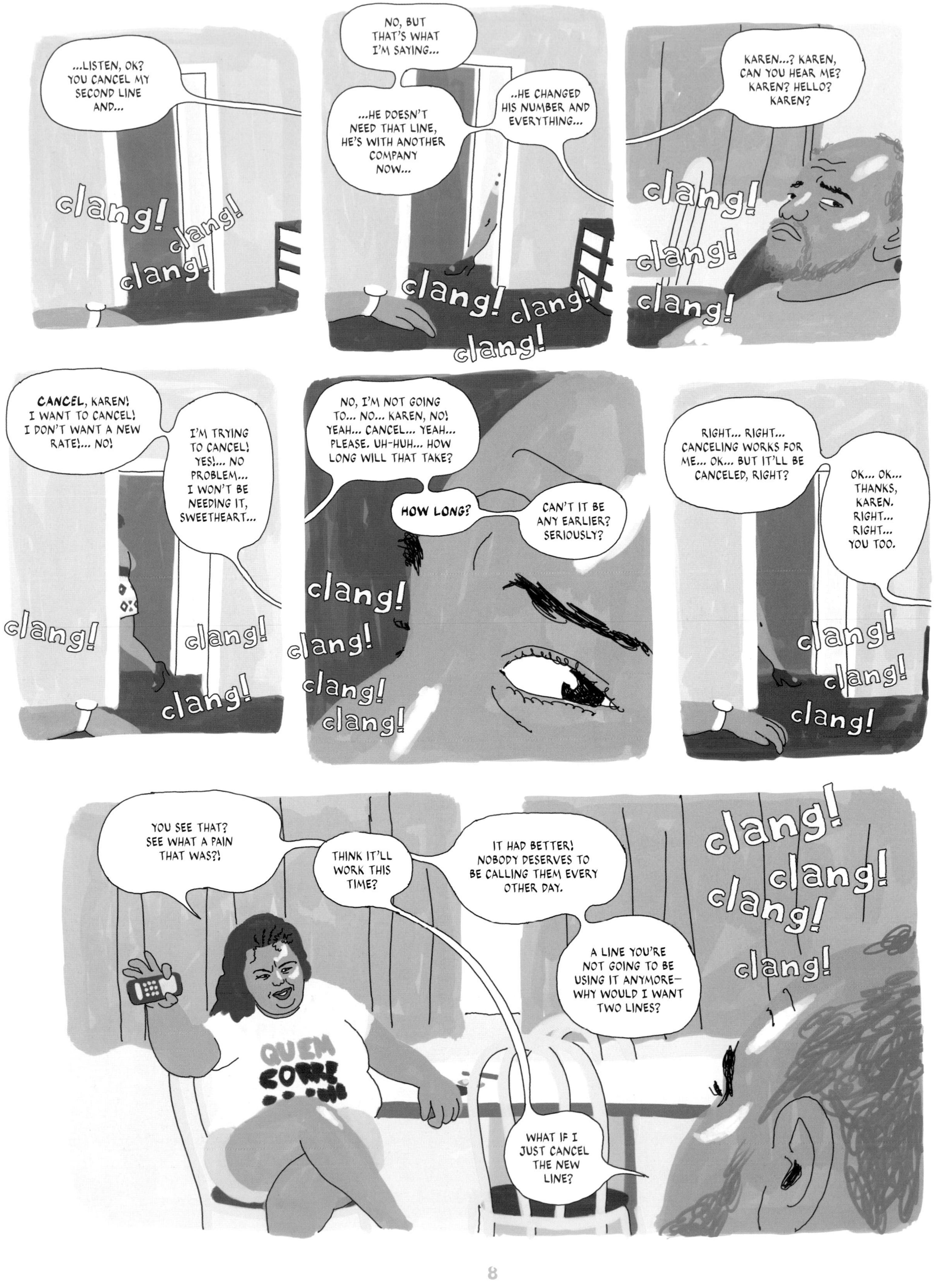
...LISTEN, OK? YOU CANCEL MY SECOND LINE AND...
clang! clang! clang!
NO, BUT THAT'S WHAT I'M SAYING...
...HE DOESN'T NEED THAT LINE, HE'S WITH ANOTHER COMPANY NOW...
..HE CHANGED HIS NUMBER AND EVERYTHING...
clang! clang! clang!
KAREN...? KAREN, CAN YOU HEAR ME? KAREN? HELLO? KAREN?
clang! clang! clang!
CANCEL, KAREN! I WANT TO CANCEL! I DON'T WANT A NEW RATE!... NO!
I'M TRYING TO CANCEL! YES!... NO PROBLEM... I WON'T BE NEEDING IT, SWEETHEART...
clang! clang! clang!
NO, I'M NOT GOING TO... NO... KAREN, NO! YEAH... CANCEL... YEAH... PLEASE. UH-HUH... HOW LONG WILL THAT TAKE?
HOW LONG?
CAN'T IT BE ANY EARLIER? SERIOUSLY?
clang! clang! clang! clang!
RIGHT... RIGHT... CANCELING WORKS FOR ME... OK... BUT IT'LL BE CANCELED, RIGHT?
OK... OK... THANKS, KAREN. RIGHT... RIGHT... YOU TOO.
clang! clang! clang!
YOU SEE THAT? SEE WHAT A PAIN THAT WAS?!
THINK IT'LL WORK THIS TIME?
IT HAD BETTER! NOBODY DESERVES TO BE CALLING THEM EVERY OTHER DAY.
clang! clang! clang! clang!
A LINE YOU'RE NOT GOING TO BE USING IT ANYMORE— WHY WOULD I WANT TWO LINES?
QUEM CORRE
WHAT IF I JUST CANCEL THE NEW LINE?

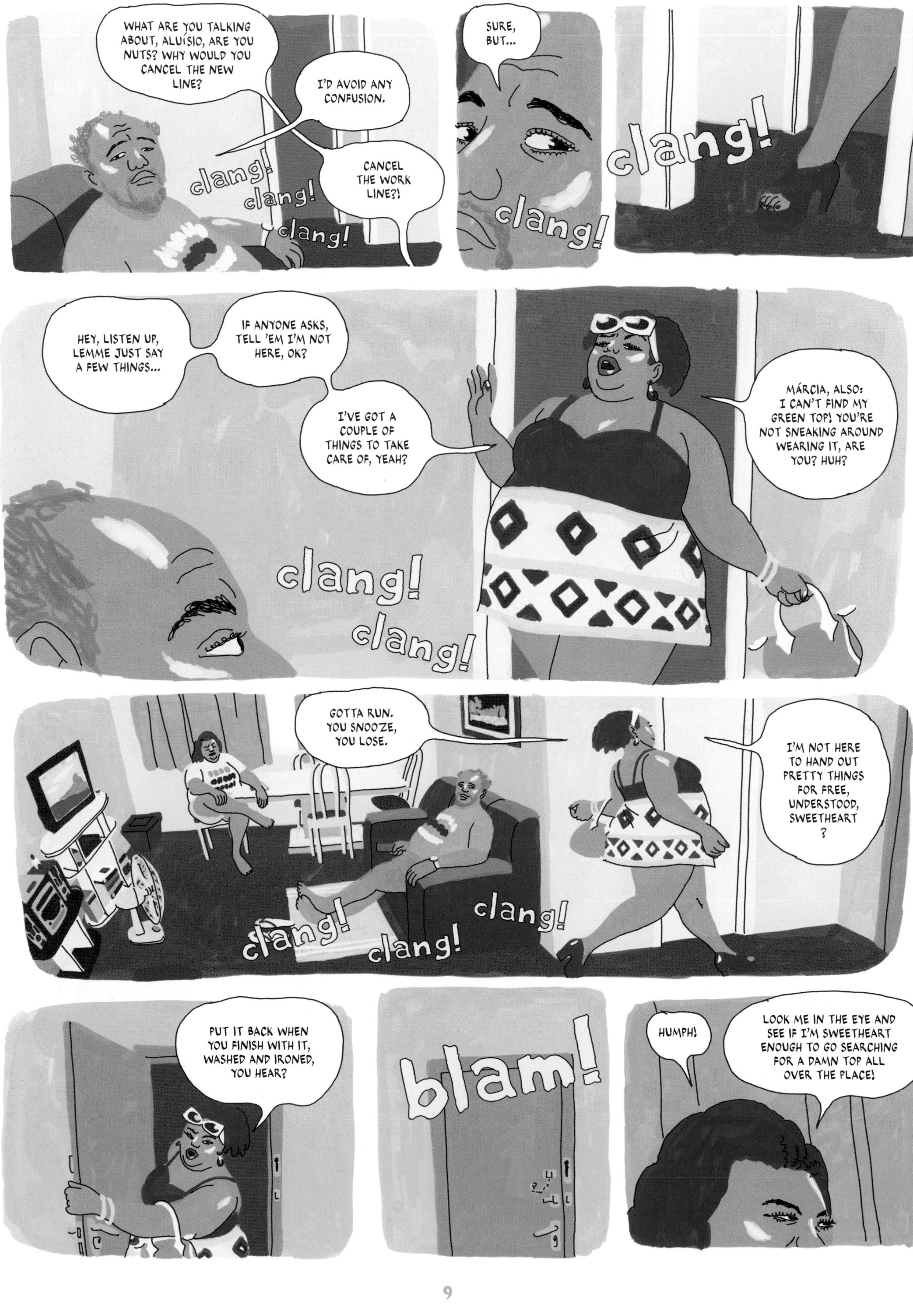
WHAT ARE YOU TALKING ABOUT, ALUÍSIO, ARE YOU NUTS? WHY WOULD YOU CANCEL THE NEW LINE?
I'D AVOID ANY CONFUSION.
CANCEL THE WORK LINE?!
clang!
clang!
clang!
SURE, BUT...
clang!
clang!
HEY, LISTEN UP, LEMME JUST SAY A FEW THINGS...
IF ANYONE ASKS, TELL 'EM I'M NOT HERE, OK?
I'VE GOT A COUPLE OF THINGS TO TAKE CARE OF, YEAH?
MÁRCIA, ALSO: I CAN'T FIND MY GREEN TOP! YOU'RE NOT SNEAKING AROUND WEARING IT, ARE YOU? HUH?
clang!
clang!
GOTTA RUN. YOU SNOOZE, YOU LOSE.
I'M NOT HERE TO HAND OUT PRETTY THINGS FOR FREE, UNDERSTOOD, SWEETHEART ?
clang!
clang!
clang!
PUT IT BACK WHEN YOU FINISH WITH IT, WASHED AND IRONED, YOU HEAR?
blam!
HUMPH!
LOOK ME IN THE EYE AND SEE IF I'M SWEETHEART ENOUGH TO GO SEARCHING FOR A DAMN TOP ALL OVER THE PLACE!

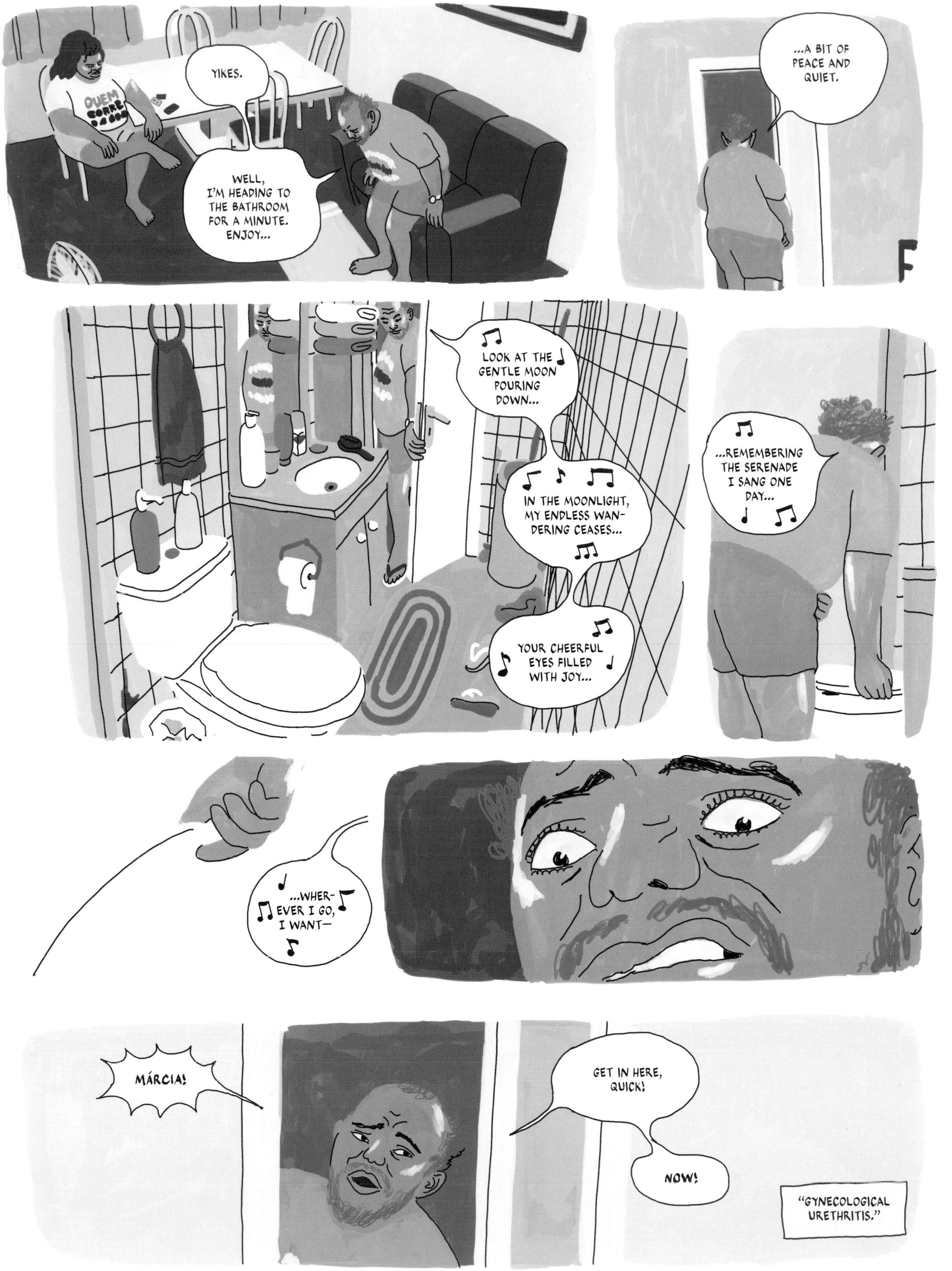
YIKES.
WELL, I'M HEADING TO THE BATHROOM FOR A MINUTE. ENJOY...
...A BIT OF PEACE AND QUIET.
LOOK AT THE GENTLE MOON POURING DOWN...
IN THE MOONLIGHT, MY ENDLESS WAN-DERING CEASES...
YOUR CHEERFUL EYES FILLED WITH JOY...
...REMEMBERING THE SERENADE I SANG ONE DAY...
...WHER-EVER I GO, I WANT—
MÁRCIA!
GET IN HERE, QUICK!
NOW!
"GYNECOLOGICAL URETHRITIS."

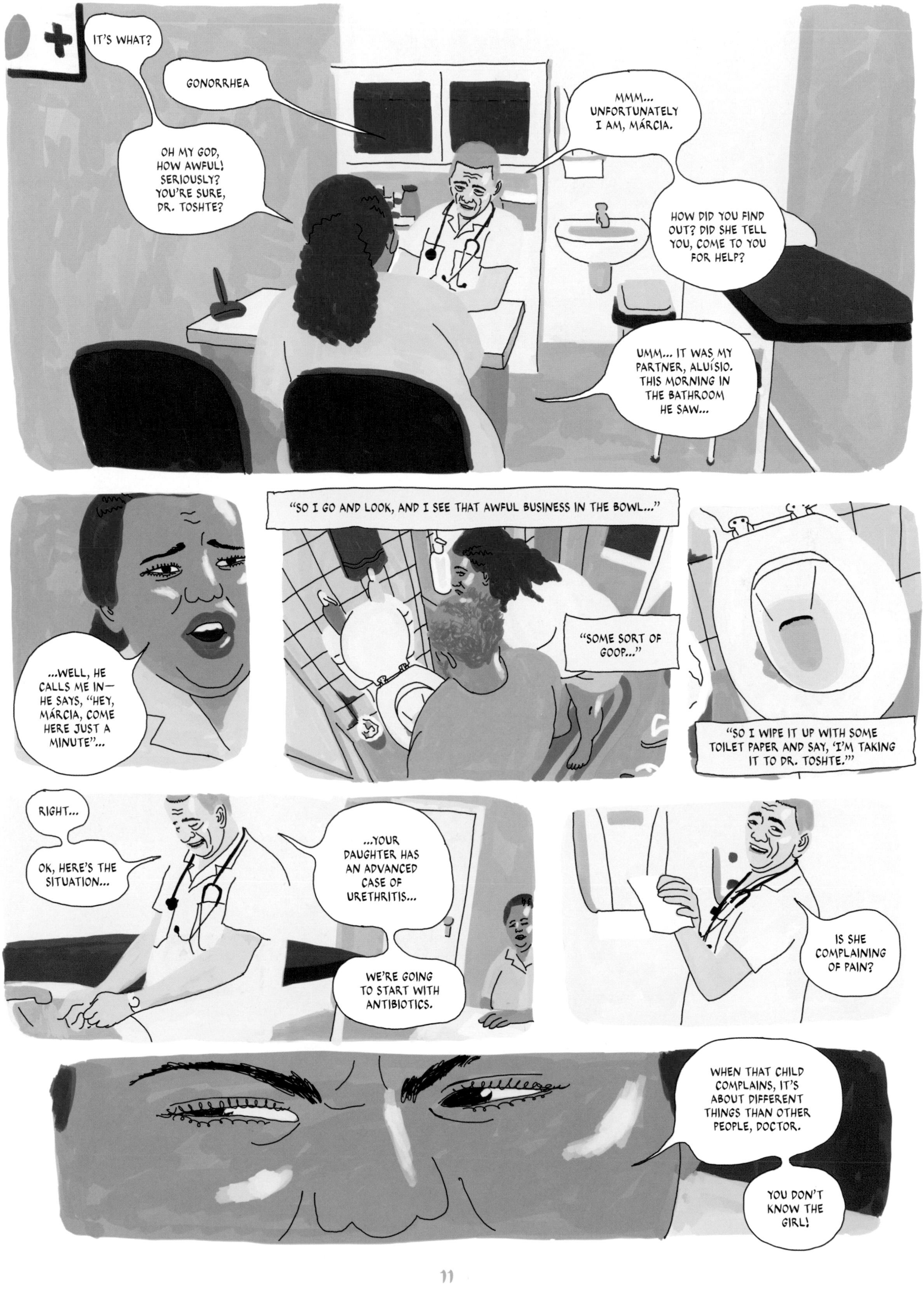
IT'S WHAT?
GONORRHEA
OH MY GOD, HOW AWFUL! SERIOUSLY? YOU'RE SURE, DR. TOSHTE?
MMM... UNFORTUNATELY I AM, MÁRCIA.
HOW DID YOU FIND OUT? DID SHE TELL YOU, COME TO YOU FOR HELP?
UMM... IT WAS MY PARTNER, ALUÍSIO. THIS MORNING IN THE BATHROOM HE SAW...
...WELL, HE CALLS ME IN—HE SAYS, "HEY, MÁRCIA, COME HERE JUST A MINUTE"...
"SO I GO AND LOOK, AND I SEE THAT AWFUL BUSINESS IN THE BOWL..."
"SOME SORT OF GOOP..."
"SO I WIPE IT UP WITH SOME TOILET PAPER AND SAY, 'I'M TAKING IT TO DR. TOSHTE.'"
RIGHT...
OK, HERE'S THE SITUATION...
...YOUR DAUGHTER HAS AN ADVANCED CASE OF URETHRITIS...
WE'RE GOING TO START WITH ANTIBIOTICS.
IS SHE COMPLAINING OF PAIN?
WHEN THAT CHILD COMPLAINS, IT'S ABOUT DIFFERENT THINGS THAN OTHER PEOPLE, DOCTOR.
YOU DON'T KNOW THE GIRL!

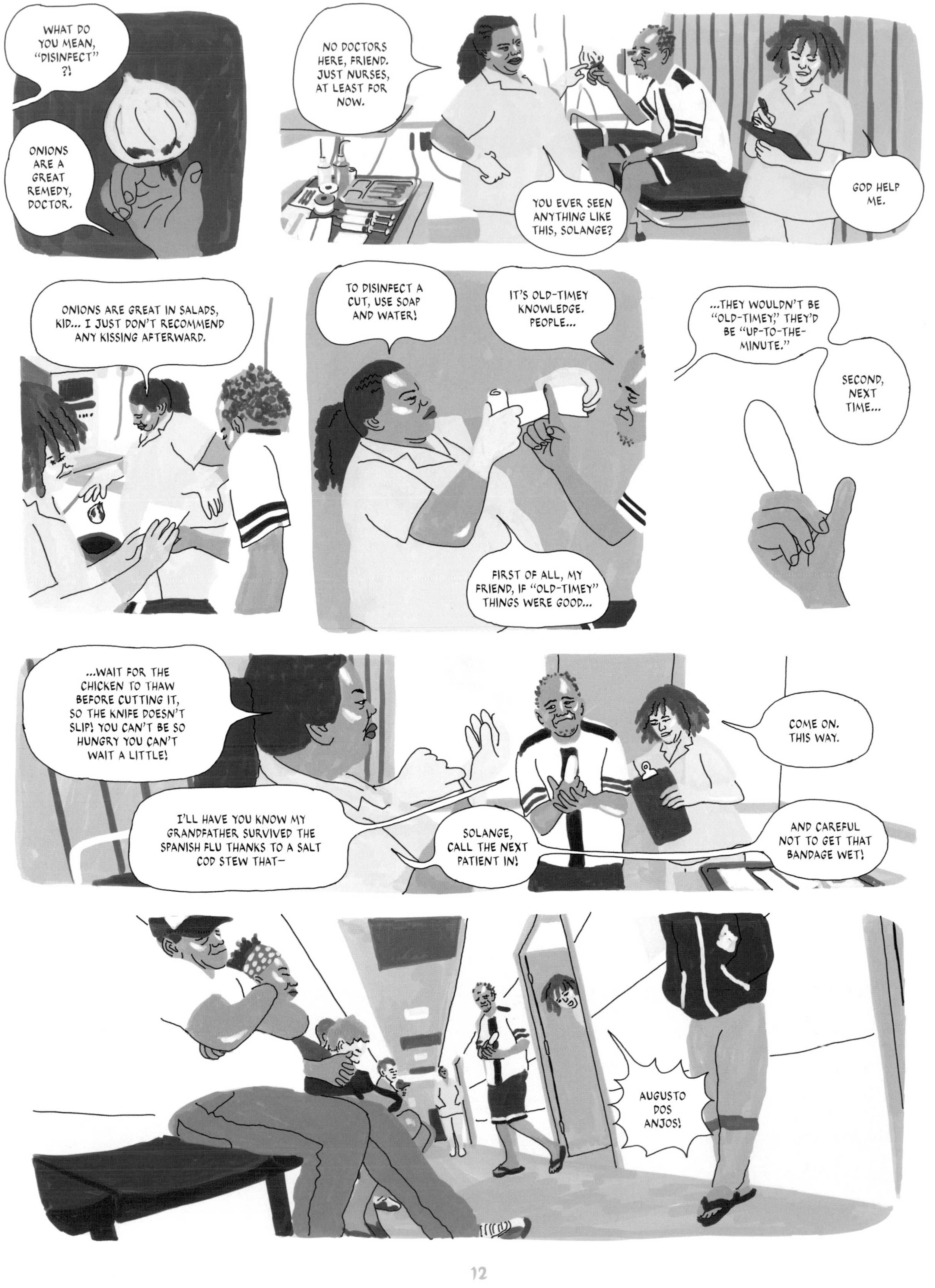
WHAT DO YOU MEAN, "DISINFECT" ?!
ONIONS ARE A GREAT REMEDY, DOCTOR.
NO DOCTORS HERE, FRIEND. JUST NURSES, AT LEAST FOR NOW.
YOU EVER SEEN ANYTHING LIKE THIS, SOLANGE?
GOD HELP ME.
ONIONS ARE GREAT IN SALADS, KID... I JUST DON'T RECOMMEND ANY KISSING AFTERWARD.
TO DISINFECT A CUT, USE SOAP AND WATER!
IT'S OLD-TIMEY KNOWLEDGE. PEOPLE...
FIRST OF ALL, MY FRIEND, IF "OLD-TIMEY" THINGS WERE GOOD...
...THEY WOULDN'T BE "OLD-TIMEY," THEY'D BE "UP-TO-THE-MINUTE."
SECOND, NEXT TIME...
...WAIT FOR THE CHICKEN TO THAW BEFORE CUTTING IT, SO THE KNIFE DOESN'T SLIP! YOU CAN'T BE SO HUNGRY YOU CAN'T WAIT A LITTLE!
I'LL HAVE YOU KNOW MY GRANDFATHER SURVIVED THE SPANISH FLU THANKS TO A SALT COD STEW THAT–
SOLANGE, CALL THE NEXT PATIENT IN!
COME ON. THIS WAY.
AND CAREFUL NOT TO GET THAT BANDAGE WET!
AUGUSTO DOS ANJOS!

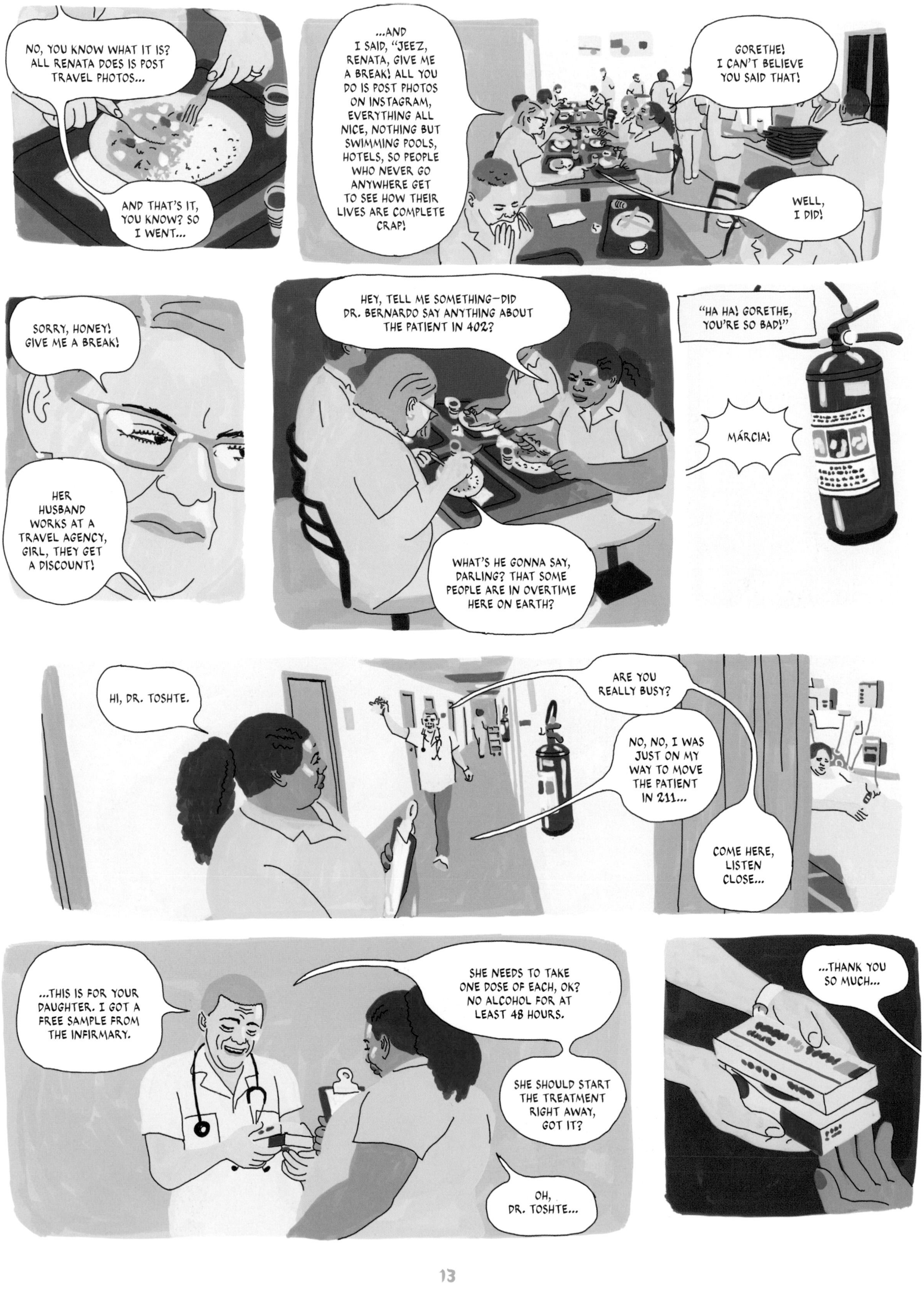
NO, YOU KNOW WHAT IT IS? ALL RENATA DOES IS POST TRAVEL PHOTOS...
AND THAT'S IT, YOU KNOW? SO I WENT...
...AND I SAID, "JEEZ, RENATA, GIVE ME A BREAK! ALL YOU DO IS POST PHOTOS ON INSTAGRAM, EVERYTHING ALL NICE, NOTHING BUT SWIMMING POOLS, HOTELS, SO PEOPLE WHO NEVER GO ANYWHERE GET TO SEE HOW THEIR LIVES ARE COMPLETE CRAP!
GORETHE! I CAN'T BELIEVE YOU SAID THAT!
WELL, I DID!
SORRY, HONEY! GIVE ME A BREAK!
HER HUSBAND WORKS AT A TRAVEL AGENCY, GIRL, THEY GET A DISCOUNT!
HEY, TELL ME SOMETHING—DID DR. BERNARDO SAY ANYTHING ABOUT THE PATIENT IN 402?
WHAT'S HE GONNA SAY, DARLING? THAT SOME PEOPLE ARE IN OVERTIME HERE ON EARTH?
"HA HA! GORETHE, YOU'RE SO BAD!"
MÁRCIA!
HI, DR. TOSHTE.
ARE YOU REALLY BUSY?
NO, NO, I WAS JUST ON MY WAY TO MOVE THE PATIENT IN 211...
COME HERE, LISTEN CLOSE...
...THIS IS FOR YOUR DAUGHTER. I GOT A FREE SAMPLE FROM THE INFIRMARY.
SHE NEEDS TO TAKE ONE DOSE OF EACH, OK? NO ALCOHOL FOR AT LEAST 48 HOURS.
SHE SHOULD START THE TREATMENT RIGHT AWAY, GOT IT?
OH, DR. TOSHTE...
...THANK YOU SO MUCH...

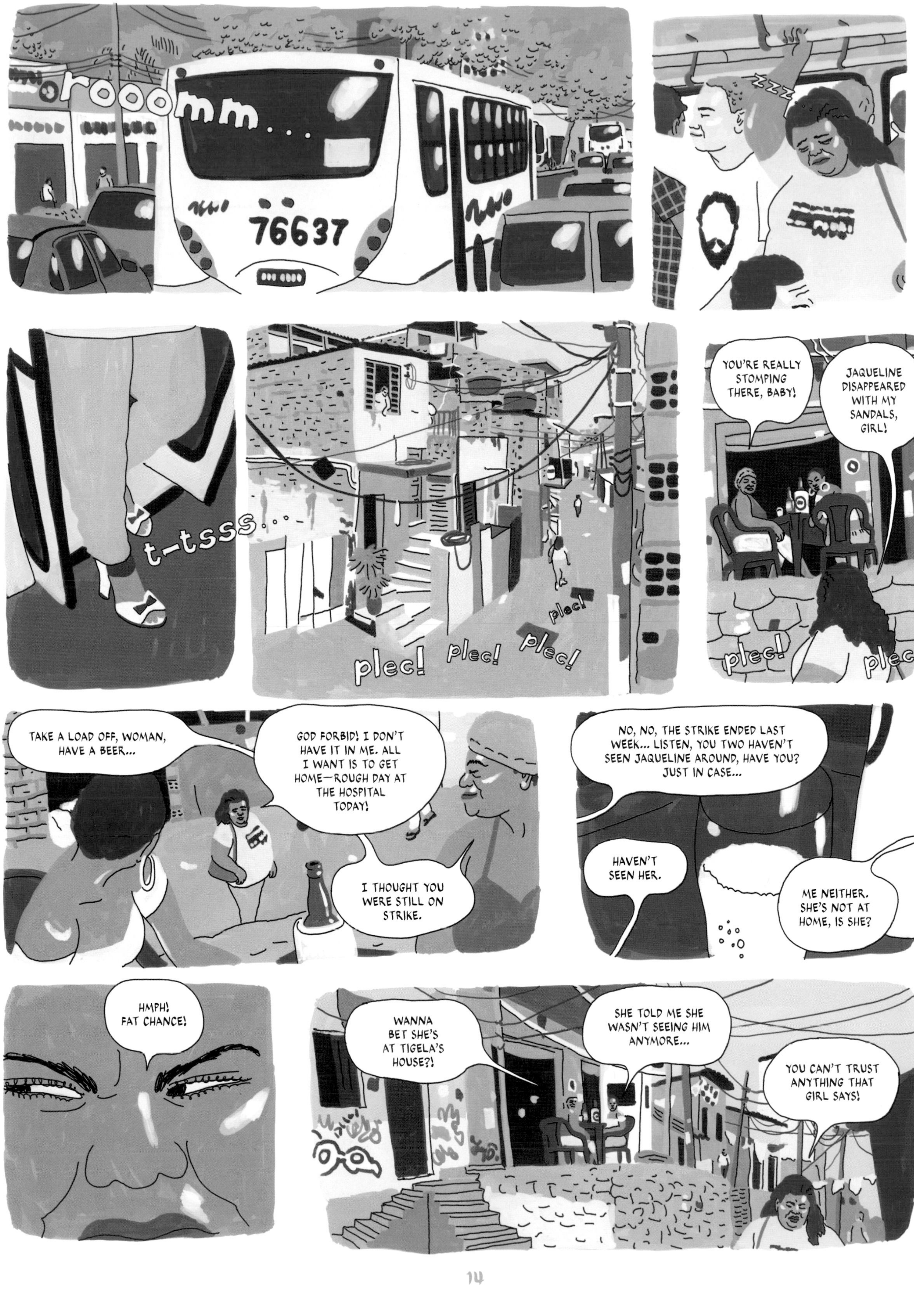
roooomm...
76637
zzz
t-tsss...
plec!
plec!
plec!
plec!
YOU'RE REALLY STOMPING THERE, BABY!
JAQUELINE DISAPPEARED WITH MY SANDALS, GIRL!
plec!
plec!
TAKE A LOAD OFF, WOMAN, HAVE A BEER...
GOD FORBID! I DON'T HAVE IT IN ME. ALL I WANT IS TO GET HOME—ROUGH DAY AT THE HOSPITAL TODAY!
I THOUGHT YOU WERE STILL ON STRIKE.
NO, NO, THE STRIKE ENDED LAST WEEK... LISTEN, YOU TWO HAVEN'T SEEN JAQUELINE AROUND, HAVE YOU? JUST IN CASE...
HAVEN'T SEEN HER.
ME NEITHER. SHE'S NOT AT HOME, IS SHE?
HMPH! FAT CHANCE!
WANNA BET SHE'S AT TIGELA'S HOUSE?!
SHE TOLD ME SHE WASN'T SEEING HIM ANYMORE...
YOU CAN'T TRUST ANYTHING THAT GIRL SAYS!

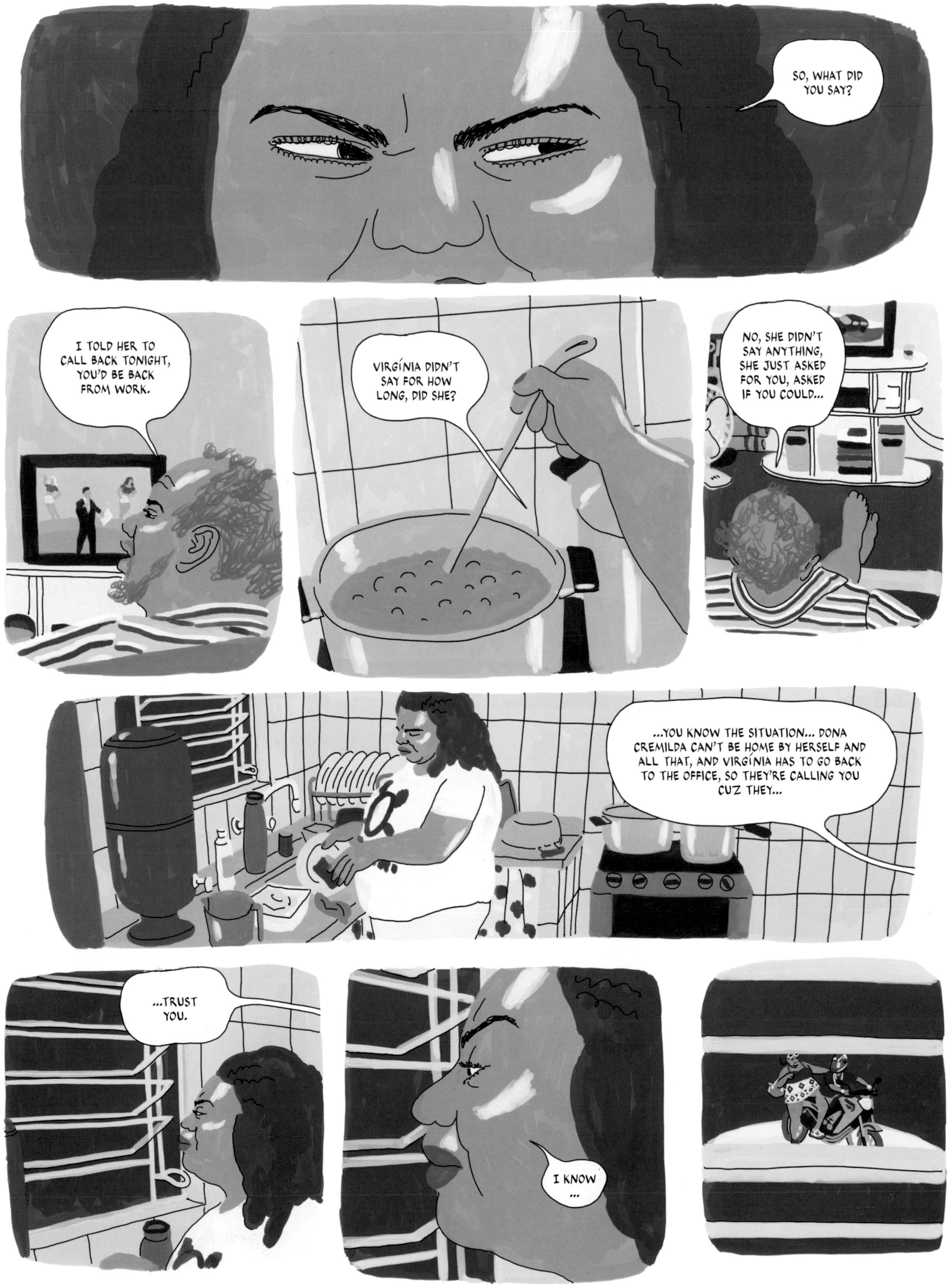
SO, WHAT DID YOU SAY?
I TOLD HER TO CALL BACK TONIGHT, YOU'D BE BACK FROM WORK.
VIRGÍNIA DIDN'T SAY FOR HOW LONG, DID SHE?
NO, SHE DIDN'T SAY ANYTHING, SHE JUST ASKED FOR YOU, ASKED IF YOU COULD...
...YOU KNOW THE SITUATION... DONA CREMILDA CAN'T BE HOME BY HERSELF AND ALL THAT, AND VIRGÍNIA HAS TO GO BACK TO THE OFFICE, SO THEY'RE CALLING YOU CUZ THEY...
...TRUST YOU.
I KNOW ...

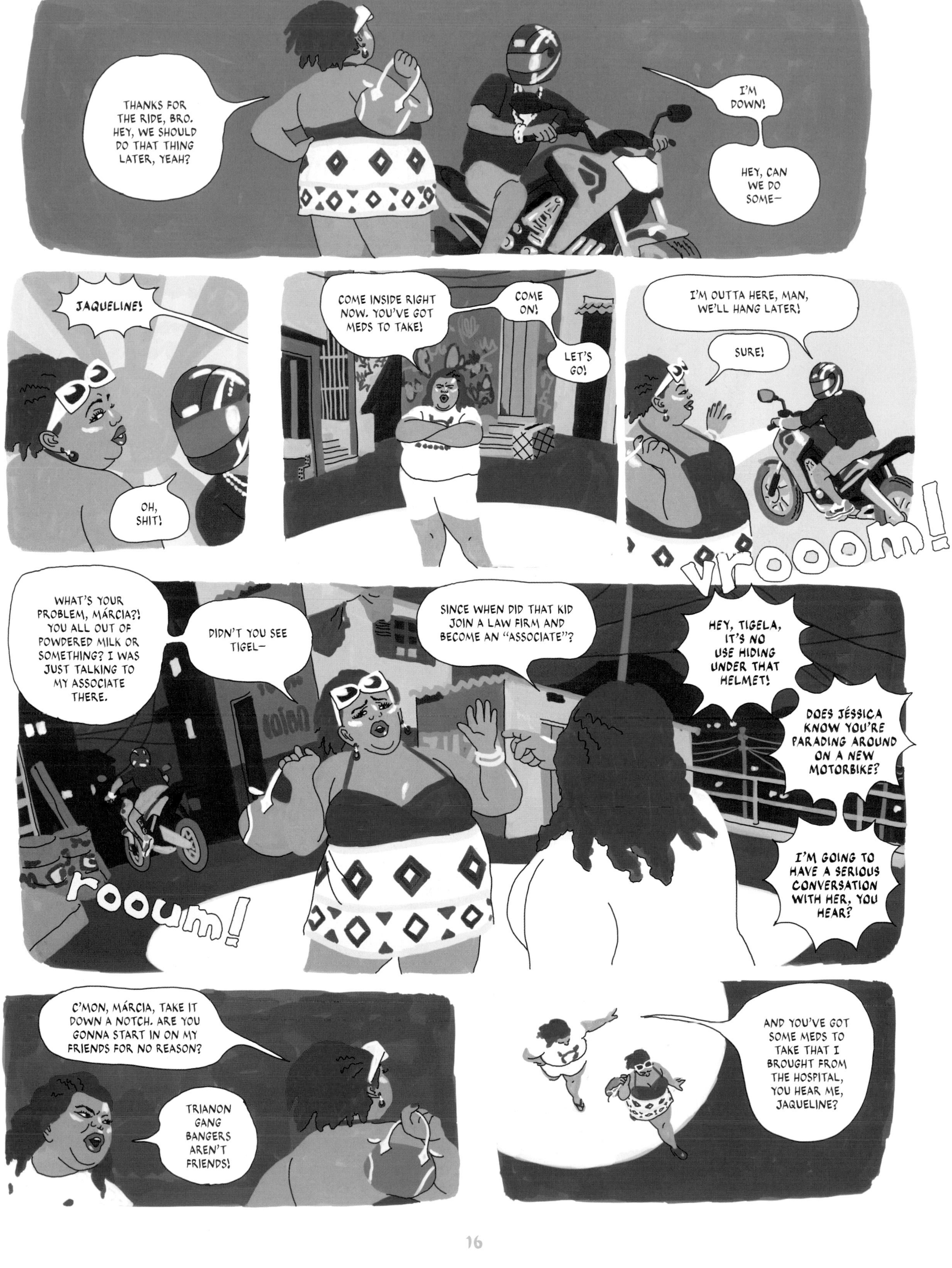
THANKS FOR THE RIDE, BRO. HEY, WE SHOULD DO THAT THING LATER, YEAH?
I'M DOWN!
HEY, CAN WE DO SOME–
JAQUELINE!
OH, SHIT!
COME INSIDE RIGHT NOW. YOU'VE GOT MEDS TO TAKE!
COME ON!
LET'S GO!
I'M OUTTA HERE, MAN, WE'LL HANG LATER!
SURE!
VROOOM!
WHAT'S YOUR PROBLEM, MÁRCIA?! YOU ALL OUT OF POWDERED MILK OR SOMETHING? I WAS JUST TALKING TO MY ASSOCIATE THERE.
DIDN'T YOU SEE TIGEL–
SINCE WHEN DID THAT KID JOIN A LAW FIRM AND BECOME AN "ASSOCIATE"?
HEY, TIGELA, IT'S NO USE HIDING UNDER THAT HELMET!
DOES JÉSSICA KNOW YOU'RE PARADING AROUND ON A NEW MOTORBIKE?
I'M GOING TO HAVE A SERIOUS CONVERSATION WITH HER, YOU HEAR?
ROOUM!
C'MON, MÁRCIA, TAKE IT DOWN A NOTCH. ARE YOU GONNA START IN ON MY FRIENDS FOR NO REASON?
TRIANON GANG BANGERS AREN'T FRIENDS!
AND YOU'VE GOT SOME MEDS TO TAKE THAT I BROUGHT FROM THE HOSPITAL, YOU HEAR ME, JAQUELINE?

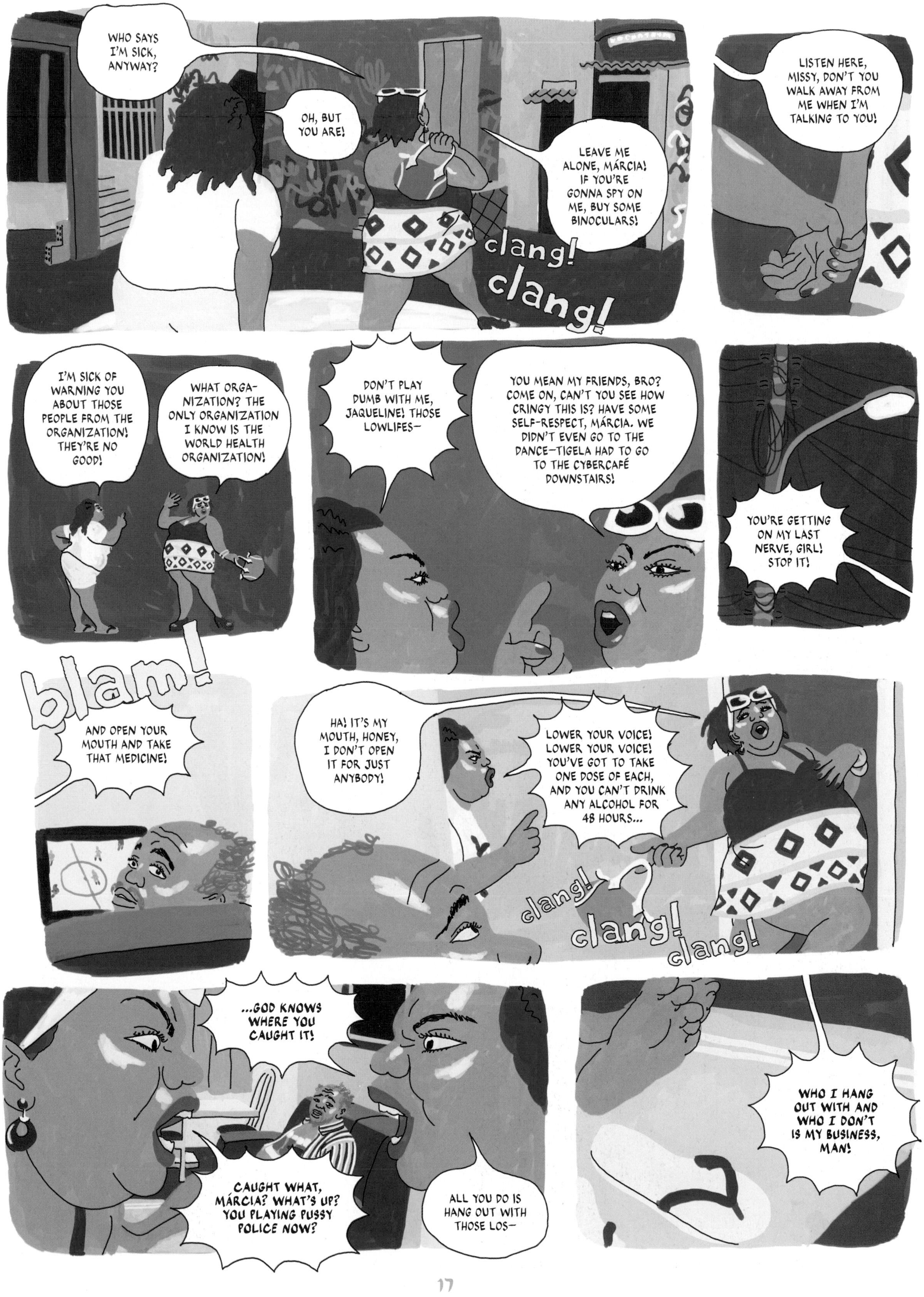
WHO SAYS I'M SICK, ANYWAY?
OH, BUT YOU ARE!
LEAVE ME ALONE, MÁRCIA! IF YOU'RE GONNA SPY ON ME, BUY SOME BINOCULARS!
clang! clang!
LISTEN HERE, MISSY, DON'T YOU WALK AWAY FROM ME WHEN I'M TALKING TO YOU!
I'M SICK OF WARNING YOU ABOUT THOSE PEOPLE FROM THE ORGANIZATION! THEY'RE NO GOOD!
WHAT ORGA-NIZATION? THE ONLY ORGANIZATION I KNOW IS THE WORLD HEALTH ORGANIZATION!
DON'T PLAY DUMB WITH ME, JAQUELINE! THOSE LOWLIFES—
YOU MEAN MY FRIENDS, BRO? COME ON, CAN'T YOU SEE HOW CRINGY THIS IS? HAVE SOME SELF-RESPECT, MÁRCIA. WE DIDN'T EVEN GO TO THE DANCE—TIGELA HAD TO GO TO THE CYBERCAFÉ DOWNSTAIRS!
YOU'RE GETTING ON MY LAST NERVE, GIRL! STOP IT!
blam!
AND OPEN YOUR MOUTH AND TAKE THAT MEDICINE!
HA! IT'S MY MOUTH, HONEY, I DON'T OPEN IT FOR JUST ANYBODY!
LOWER YOUR VOICE! LOWER YOUR VOICE! YOU'VE GOT TO TAKE ONE DOSE OF EACH, AND YOU CAN'T DRINK ANY ALCOHOL FOR 48 HOURS...
clang! clang! clang!
...GOD KNOWS WHERE YOU CAUGHT IT!
CAUGHT WHAT, MÁRCIA? WHAT'S UP? YOU PLAYING PUSSY POLICE NOW?
ALL YOU DO IS HANG OUT WITH THOSE LOS—
WHO I HANG OUT WITH AND WHO I DON'T IS MY BUSINESS, MAN!

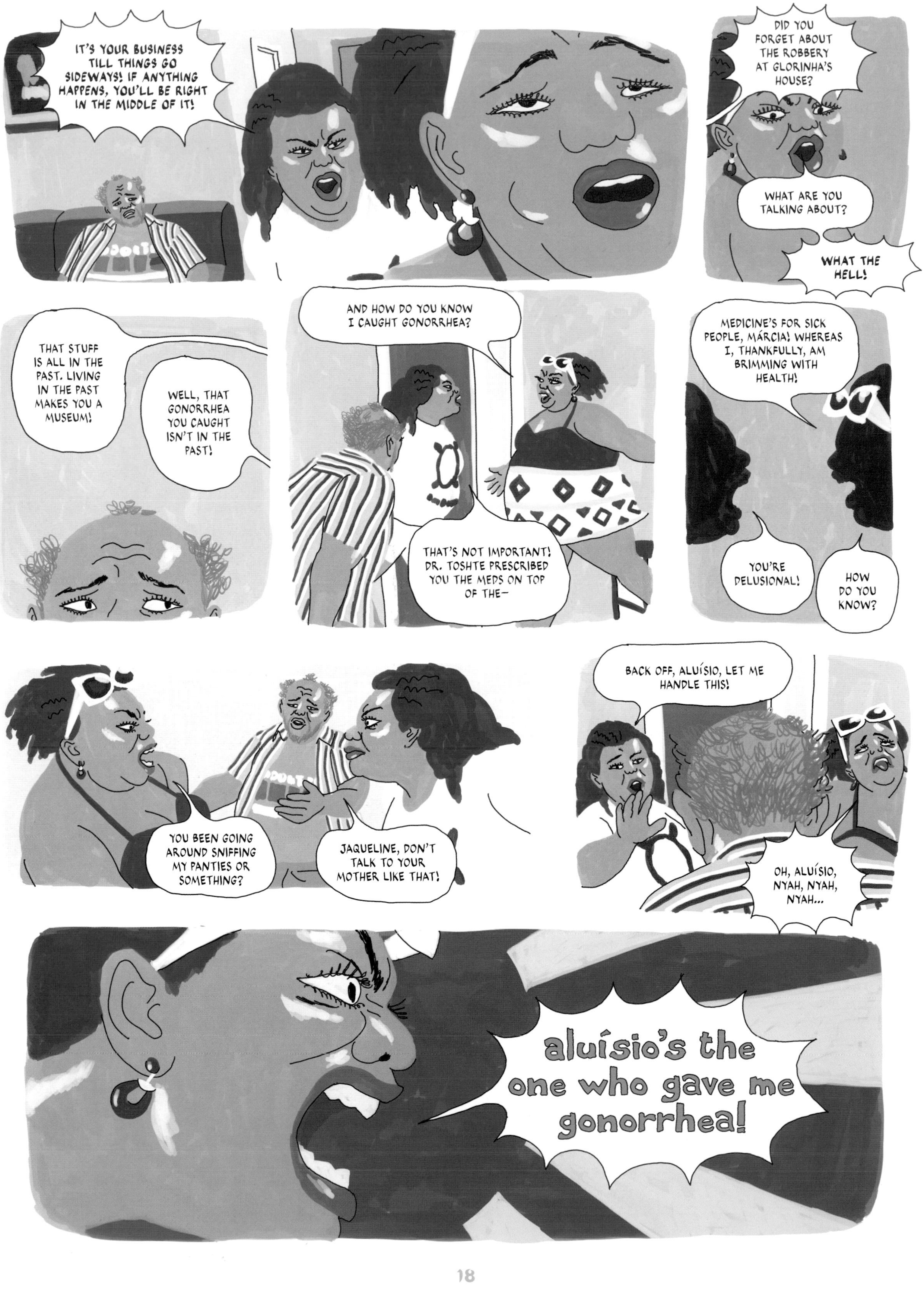
IT'S YOUR BUSINESS TILL THINGS GO SIDEWAYS! IF ANYTHING HAPPENS, YOU'LL BE RIGHT IN THE MIDDLE OF IT!
DID YOU FORGET ABOUT THE ROBBERY AT GLORINHA'S HOUSE?
WHAT ARE YOU TALKING ABOUT?
WHAT THE HELL!
THAT STUFF IS ALL IN THE PAST. LIVING IN THE PAST MAKES YOU A MUSEUM!
WELL, THAT GONORRHEA YOU CAUGHT ISN'T IN THE PAST!
AND HOW DO YOU KNOW I CAUGHT GONORRHEA?
THAT'S NOT IMPORTANT! DR. TOSHTE PRESCRIBED YOU THE MEDS ON TOP OF THE–
MEDICINE'S FOR SICK PEOPLE, MÁRCIA! WHEREAS I, THANKFULLY, AM BRIMMING WITH HEALTH!
YOU'RE DELUSIONAL!
HOW DO YOU KNOW?
YOU BEEN GOING AROUND SNIFFING MY PANTIES OR SOMETHING?
JAQUELINE, DON'T TALK TO YOUR MOTHER LIKE THAT!
BACK OFF, ALUÍSIO, LET ME HANDLE THIS!
OH, ALUÍSIO, NYAH, NYAH, NYAH...
aluísio's the one who gave me gonorrhea!

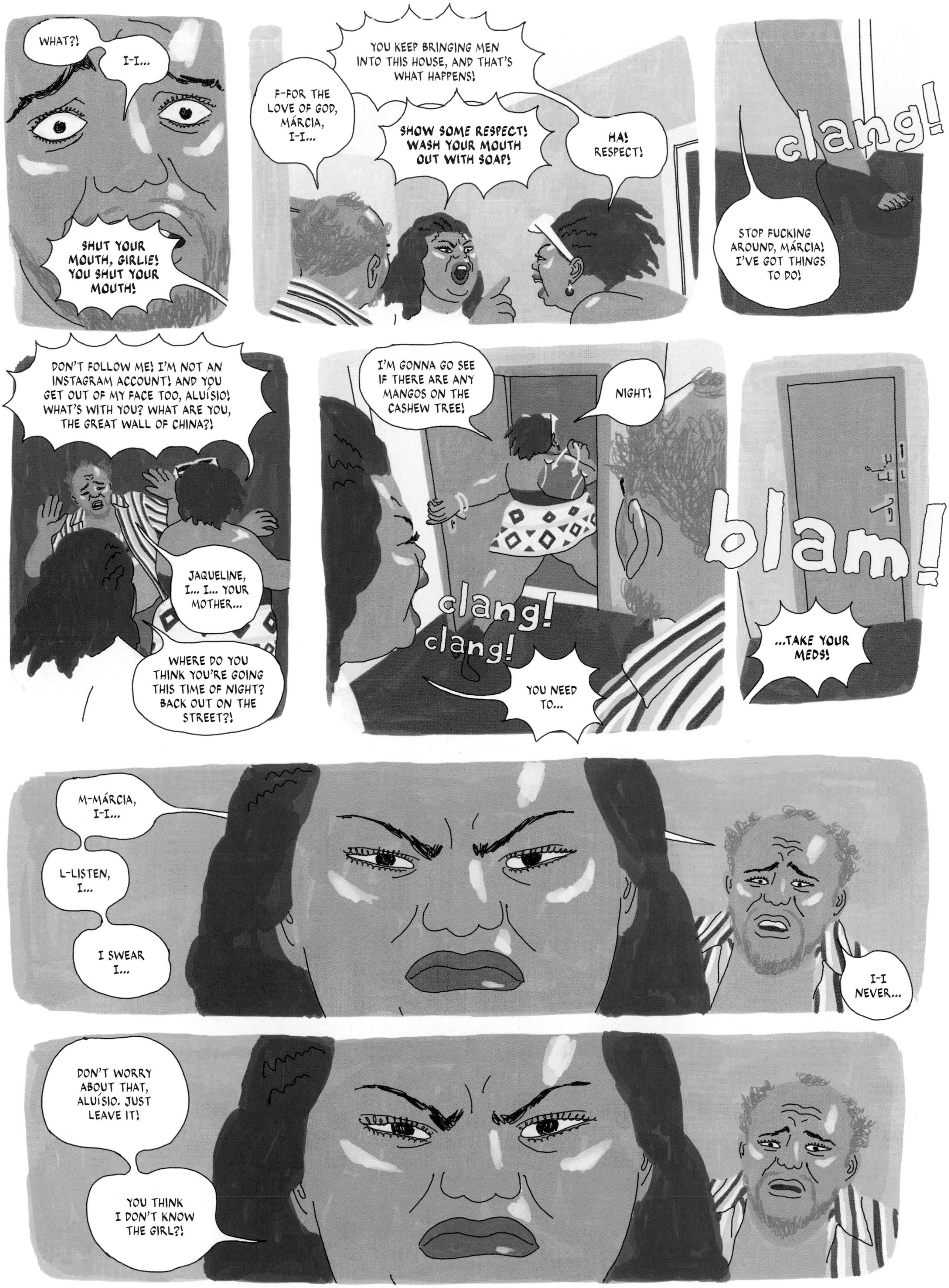
WHAT?!
I-I...
SHUT YOUR MOUTH, GIRLIE! YOU SHUT YOUR MOUTH!
YOU KEEP BRINGING MEN INTO THIS HOUSE, AND THAT'S WHAT HAPPENS!
F-FOR THE LOVE OF GOD, MÁRCIA, I-I...
SHOW SOME RESPECT! WASH YOUR MOUTH OUT WITH SOAP!
HA! RESPECT!
clang!
STOP FUCKING AROUND, MÁRCIA! I'VE GOT THINGS TO DO!
DON'T FOLLOW ME! I'M NOT AN INSTAGRAM ACCOUNT! AND YOU GET OUT OF MY FACE TOO, ALUÍSIO! WHAT'S WITH YOU? WHAT ARE YOU, THE GREAT WALL OF CHINA?!
JAQUELINE, I... I... YOUR MOTHER...
WHERE DO YOU THINK YOU'RE GOING THIS TIME OF NIGHT? BACK OUT ON THE STREET?!
I'M GONNA GO SEE IF THERE ARE ANY MANGOS ON THE CASHEW TREE!
NIGHT!
clang!
clang!
YOU NEED TO...
blam!
...TAKE YOUR MEDS!
M-MÁRCIA, I-I...
L-LISTEN, I...
I SWEAR I...
I-I NEVER...
DON'T WORRY ABOUT THAT, ALUÍSIO. JUST LEAVE IT!
YOU THINK I DON'T KNOW THE GIRL?!

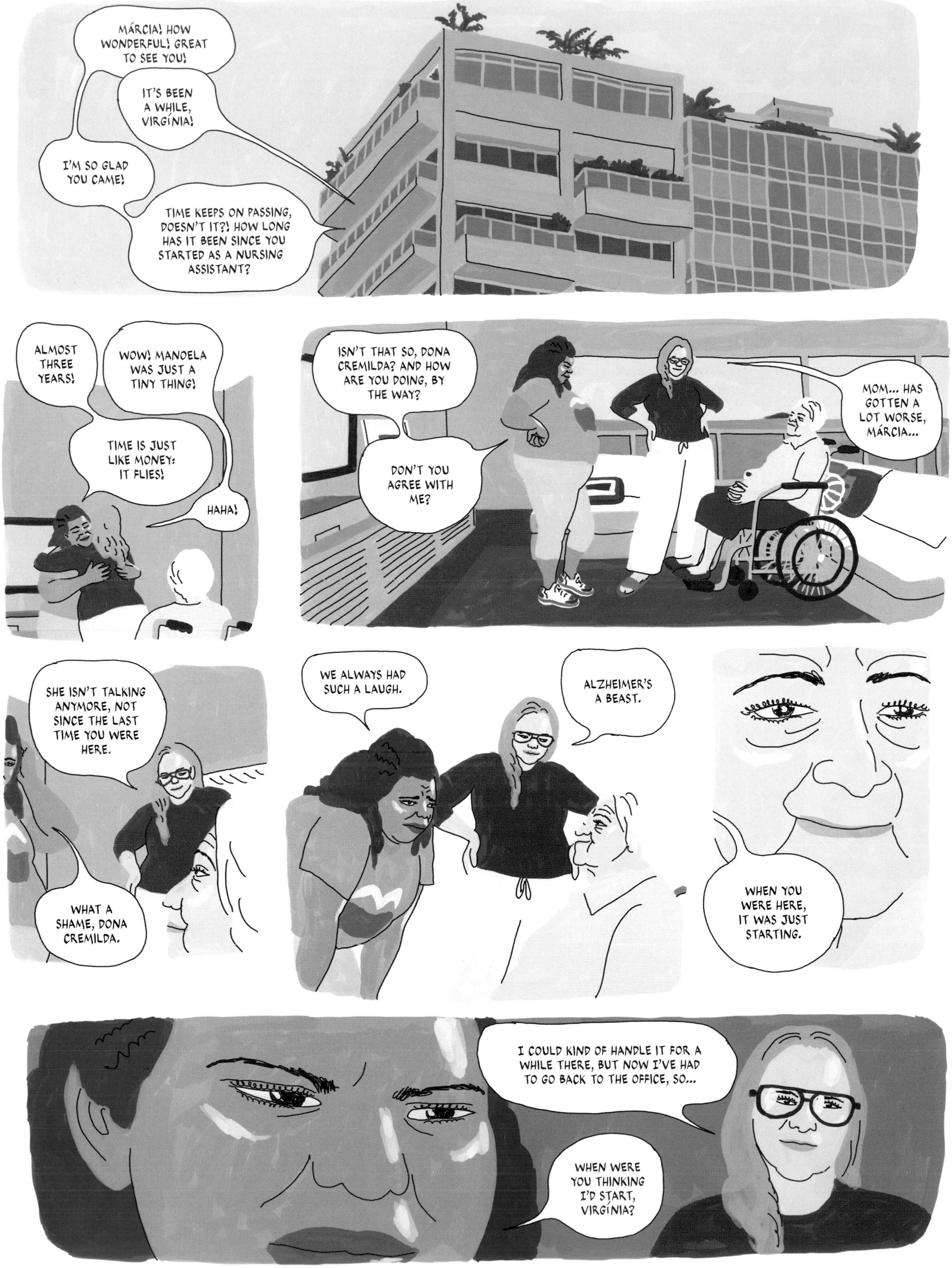
MÁRCIA! HOW WONDERFUL! GREAT TO SEE YOU!
IT'S BEEN A WHILE, VIRGÍNIA!
I'M SO GLAD YOU CAME!
TIME KEEPS ON PASSING, DOESN'T IT?! HOW LONG HAS IT BEEN SINCE YOU STARTED AS A NURSING ASSISTANT?
ALMOST THREE YEARS!
WOW! MANOELA WAS JUST A TINY THING!
TIME IS JUST LIKE MONEY: IT FLIES!
HAHA!
ISN'T THAT SO, DONA CREMILDA? AND HOW ARE YOU DOING, BY THE WAY?
DON'T YOU AGREE WITH ME?
MOM... HAS GOTTEN A LOT WORSE, MÁRCIA...
SHE ISN'T TALKING ANYMORE, NOT SINCE THE LAST TIME YOU WERE HERE.
WHAT A SHAME, DONA CREMILDA.
WE ALWAYS HAD SUCH A LAUGH.
ALZHEIMER'S A BEAST.
WHEN YOU WERE HERE, IT WAS JUST STARTING.
I COULD KIND OF HANDLE IT FOR A WHILE THERE, BUT NOW I'VE HAD TO GO BACK TO THE OFFICE, SO...
WHEN WERE YOU THINKING I'D START, VIRGÍNIA?

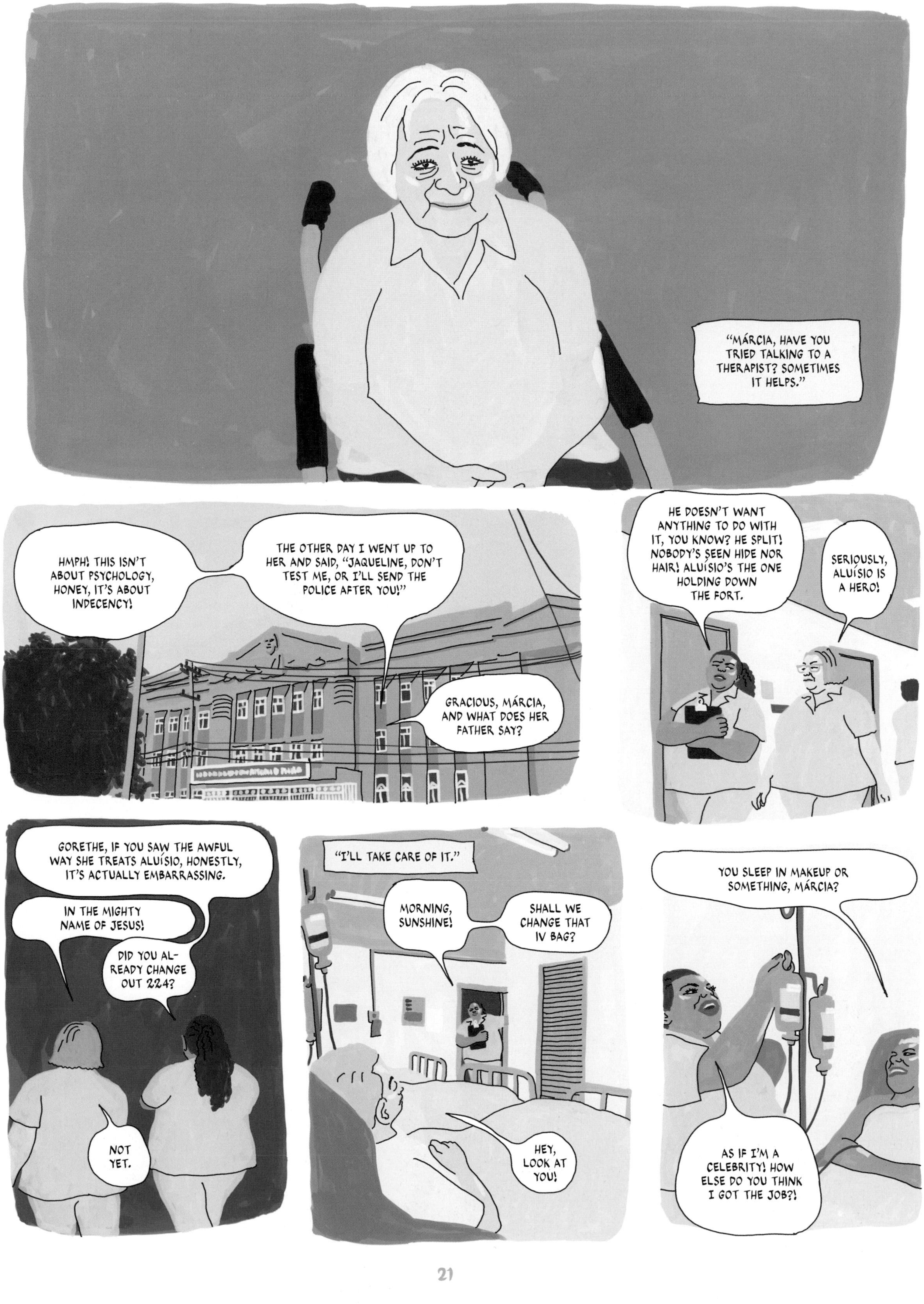
"MÁRCIA, HAVE YOU TRIED TALKING TO A THERAPIST? SOMETIMES IT HELPS."
HMPH! THIS ISN'T ABOUT PSYCHOLOGY, HONEY, IT'S ABOUT INDECENCY!
THE OTHER DAY I WENT UP TO HER AND SAID, "JAQUELINE, DON'T TEST ME, OR I'LL SEND THE POLICE AFTER YOU!"
GRACIOUS, MÁRCIA, AND WHAT DOES HER FATHER SAY?
HE DOESN'T WANT ANYTHING TO DO WITH IT, YOU KNOW? HE SPLIT! NOBODY'S SEEN HIDE NOR HAIR! ALUÍSIO'S THE ONE HOLDING DOWN THE FORT.
SERIOUSLY, ALUÍSIO IS A HERO!
GORETHE, IF YOU SAW THE AWFUL WAY SHE TREATS ALUÍSIO, HONESTLY, IT'S ACTUALLY EMBARRASSING.
IN THE MIGHTY NAME OF JESUS!
DID YOU ALREADY CHANGE OUT 224?
NOT YET.
"I'LL TAKE CARE OF IT."
MORNING, SUNSHINE!
SHALL WE CHANGE THAT IV BAG?
HEY, LOOK AT YOU!
YOU SLEEP IN MAKEUP OR SOMETHING, MÁRCIA?
AS IF I'M A CELEBRITY! HOW ELSE DO YOU THINK I GOT THE JOB?!

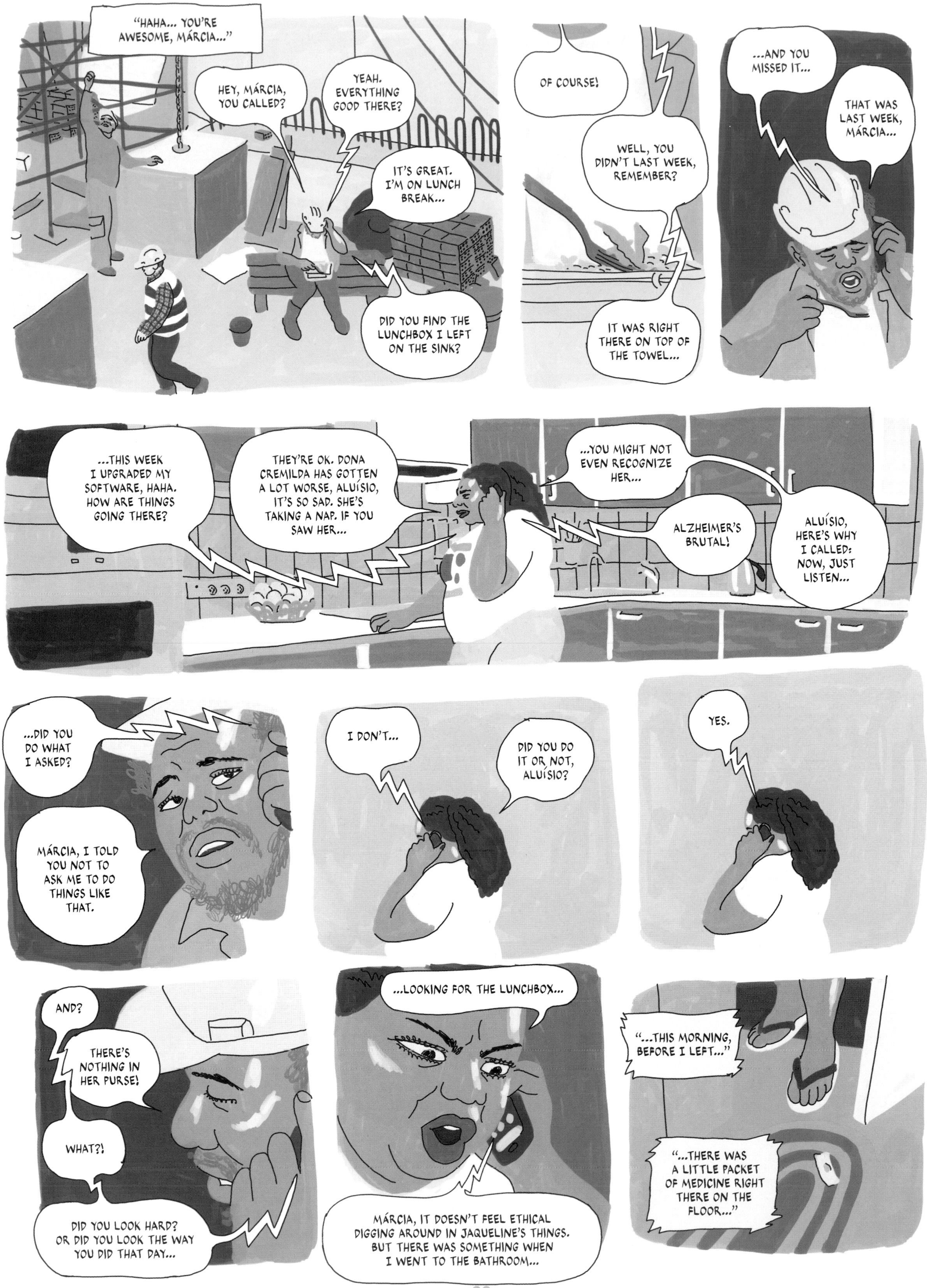
"HAHA... YOU'RE AWESOME, MÁRCIA..."
HEY, MÁRCIA, YOU CALLED?
YEAH. EVERYTHING GOOD THERE?
IT'S GREAT. I'M ON LUNCH BREAK...
DID YOU FIND THE LUNCHBOX I LEFT ON THE SINK?
OF COURSE!
WELL, YOU DIDN'T LAST WEEK, REMEMBER?
IT WAS RIGHT THERE ON TOP OF THE TOWEL...
...AND YOU MISSED IT...
THAT WAS LAST WEEK, MÁRCIA...
...THIS WEEK I UPGRADED MY SOFTWARE, HAHA. HOW ARE THINGS GOING THERE?
THEY'RE OK. DONA CREMILDA HAS GOTTEN A LOT WORSE, ALUÍSIO, IT'S SO SAD. SHE'S TAKING A NAP. IF YOU SAW HER...
...YOU MIGHT NOT EVEN RECOGNIZE HER...
ALZHEIMER'S BRUTAL!
ALUÍSIO, HERE'S WHY I CALLED: NOW, JUST LISTEN...
...DID YOU DO WHAT I ASKED?
MÁRCIA, I TOLD YOU NOT TO ASK ME TO DO THINGS LIKE THAT.
I DON'T...
DID YOU DO IT OR NOT, ALUÍSIO?
YES.
AND?
THERE'S NOTHING IN HER PURSE!
WHAT?!
DID YOU LOOK HARD? OR DID YOU LOOK THE WAY YOU DID THAT DAY...
...LOOKING FOR THE LUNCHBOX...
MÁRCIA, IT DOESN'T FEEL ETHICAL DIGGING AROUND IN JAQUELINE'S THINGS. BUT THERE WAS SOMETHING WHEN I WENT TO THE BATHROOM...
"...THIS MORNING, BEFORE I LEFT..."
"...THERE WAS A LITTLE PACKET OF MEDICINE RIGHT THERE ON THE FLOOR..."

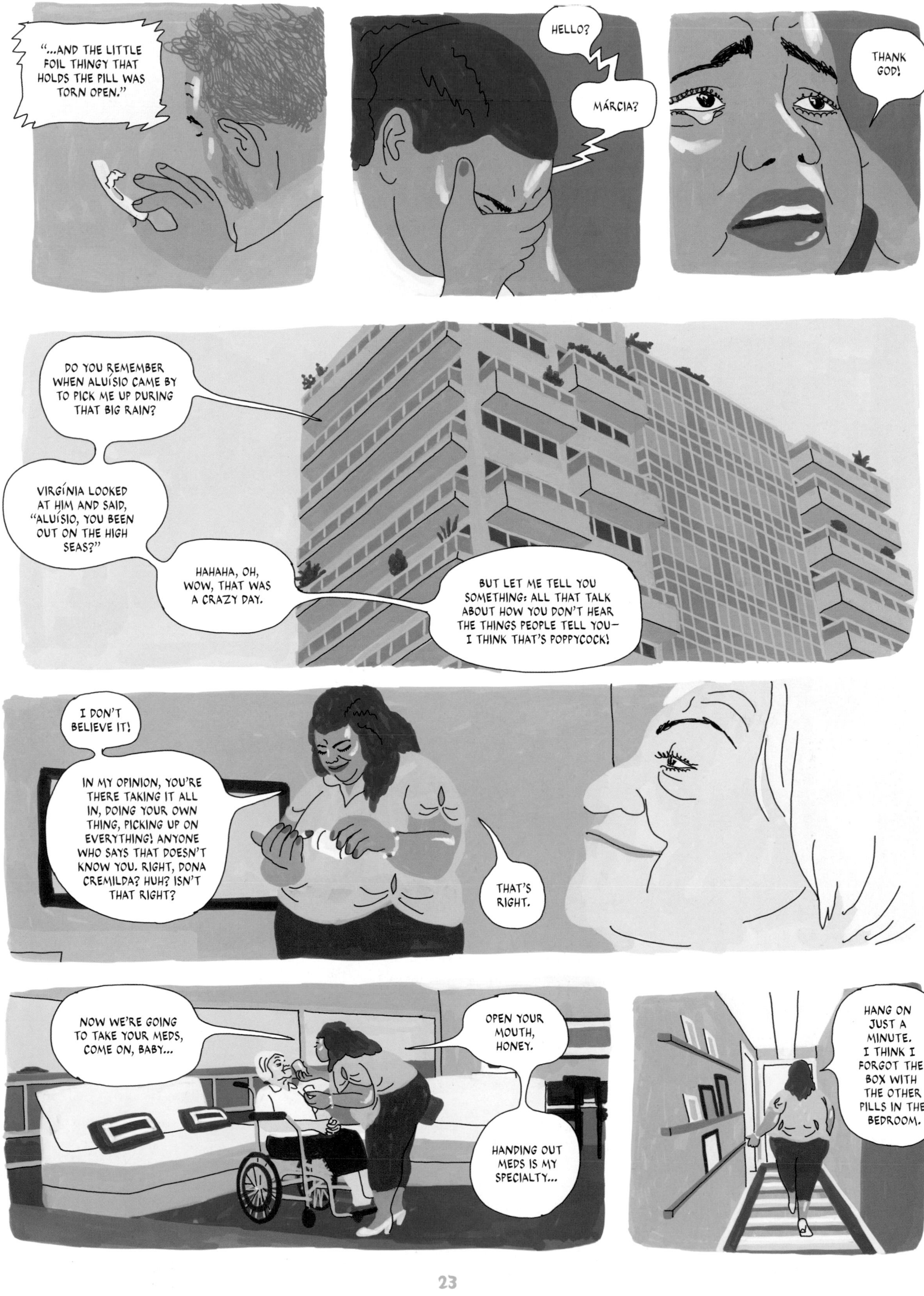
"...AND THE LITTLE FOIL THINGY THAT HOLDS THE PILL WAS TORN OPEN."
HELLO?
MÁRCIA?
THANK GOD!
DO YOU REMEMBER WHEN ALUÍSIO CAME BY TO PICK ME UP DURING THAT BIG RAIN?
VIRGÍNIA LOOKED AT HIM AND SAID, "ALUÍSIO, YOU BEEN OUT ON THE HIGH SEAS?"
HAHAHA, OH, WOW, THAT WAS A CRAZY DAY.
BUT LET ME TELL YOU SOMETHING: ALL THAT TALK ABOUT HOW YOU DON'T HEAR THE THINGS PEOPLE TELL YOU— I THINK THAT'S POPPYCOCK!
I DON'T BELIEVE IT!
IN MY OPINION, YOU'RE THERE TAKING IT ALL IN, DOING YOUR OWN THING, PICKING UP ON EVERYTHING! ANYONE WHO SAYS THAT DOESN'T KNOW YOU. RIGHT, DONA CREMILDA? HUH? ISN'T THAT RIGHT?
THAT'S RIGHT.
NOW WE'RE GOING TO TAKE YOUR MEDS, COME ON, BABY...
OPEN YOUR MOUTH, HONEY.
HANDING OUT MEDS IS MY SPECIALTY...
HANG ON JUST A MINUTE. I THINK I FORGOT THE BOX WITH THE OTHER PILLS IN THE BEDROOM.

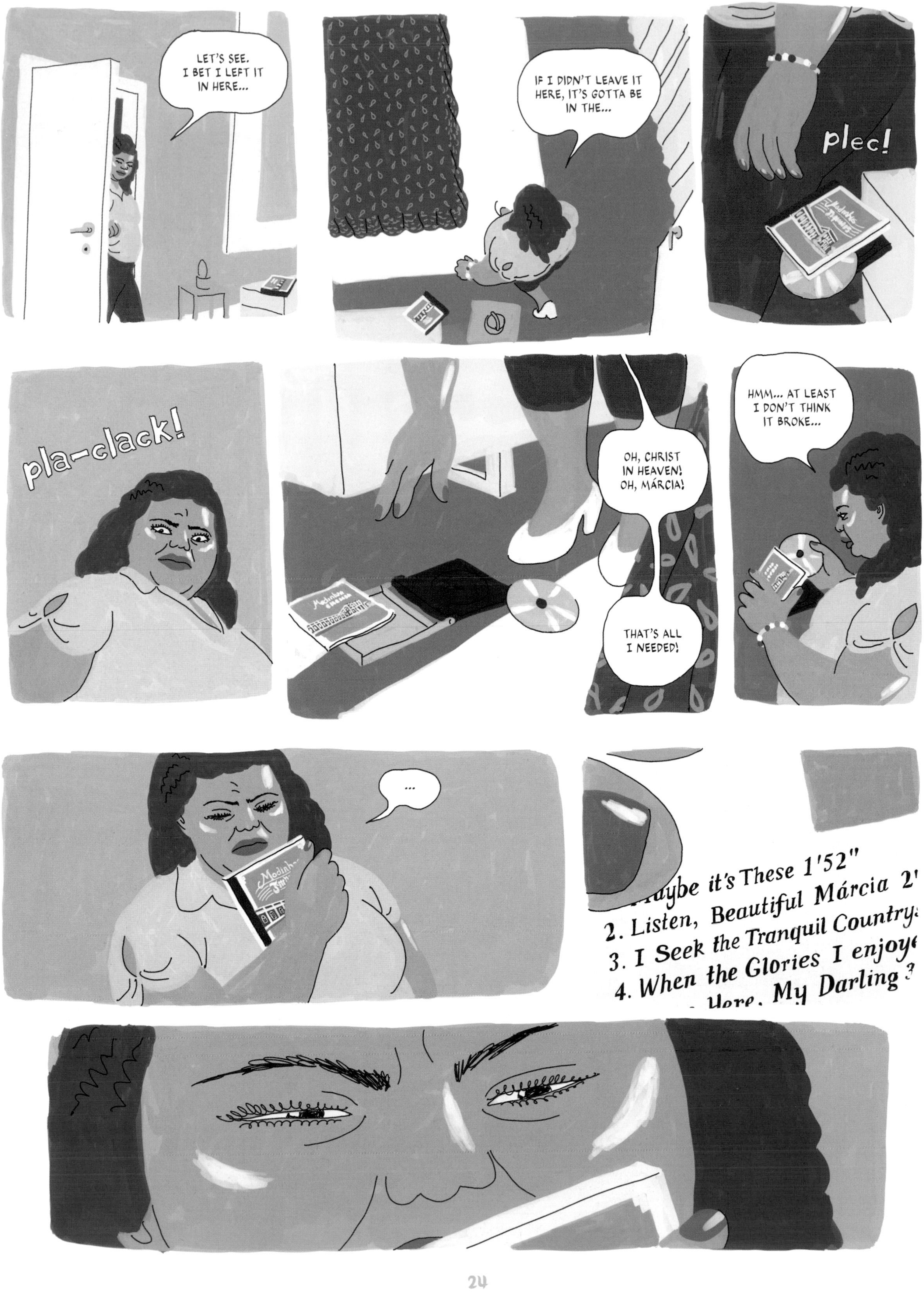
LET'S SEE. I BET I LEFT IT IN HERE...
IF I DIDN'T LEAVE IT HERE, IT'S GOTTA BE IN THE...
plec!
pla-clack!
OH, CHRIST IN HEAVEN! OH, MÁRCIA!
THAT'S ALL I NEEDED!
HMM... AT LEAST I DON'T THINK IT BROKE...
...
Maybe it's These 1'52"
2. Listen, Beautiful Márcia
3. I Seek the Tranquil Country
4. When the Glories I enjoye
Here, My Darling

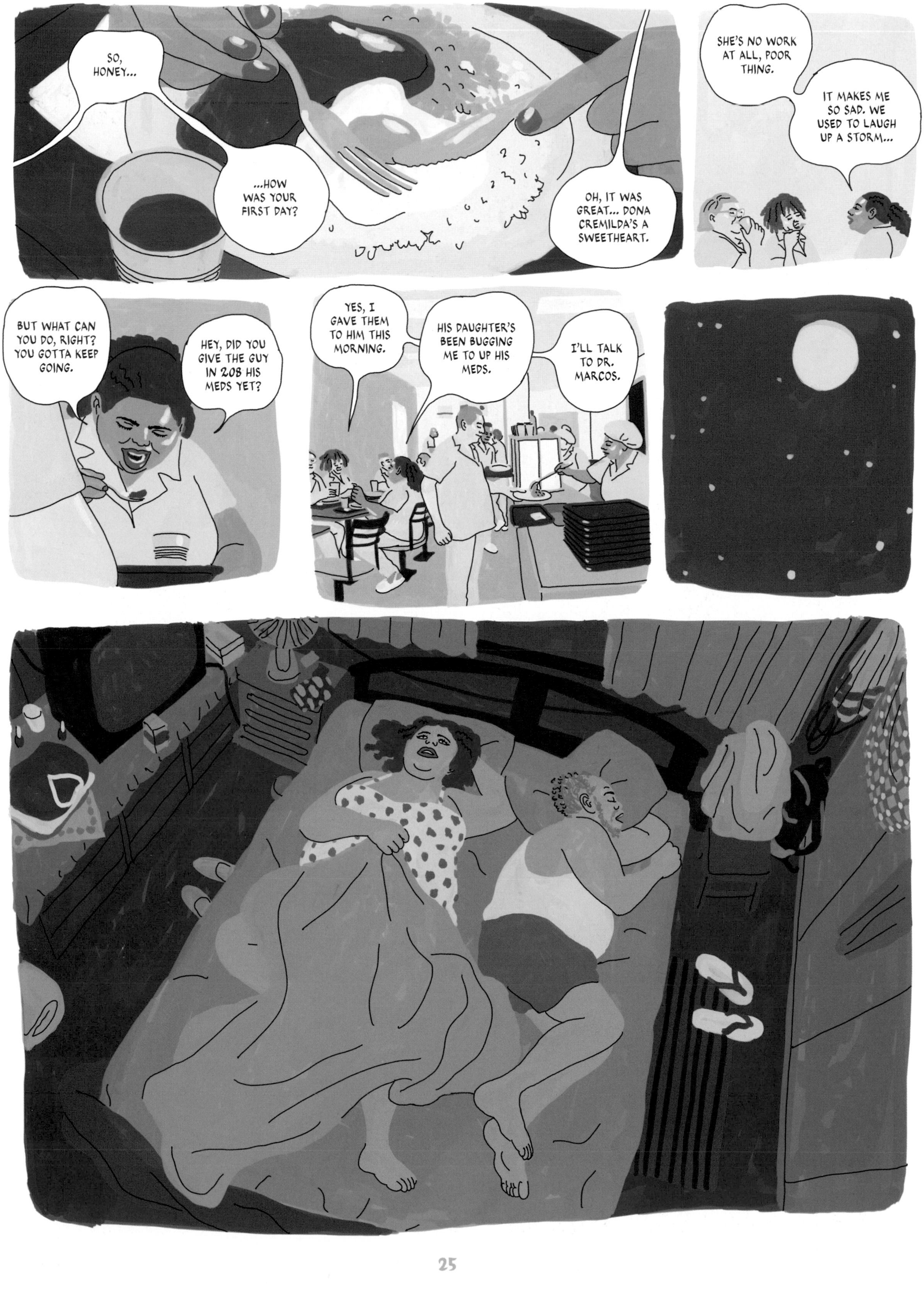
SO, HONEY...
...HOW WAS YOUR FIRST DAY?
OH, IT WAS GREAT... DONA CREMILDA'S A SWEETHEART.
SHE'S NO WORK AT ALL, POOR THING.
IT MAKES ME SO SAD. WE USED TO LAUGH UP A STORM...
BUT WHAT CAN YOU DO, RIGHT? YOU GOTTA KEEP GOING.
HEY, DID YOU GIVE THE GUY IN 208 HIS MEDS YET?
YES, I GAVE THEM TO HIM THIS MORNING.
HIS DAUGHTER'S BEEN BUGGING ME TO UP HIS MEDS.
I'LL TALK TO DR. MARCOS.

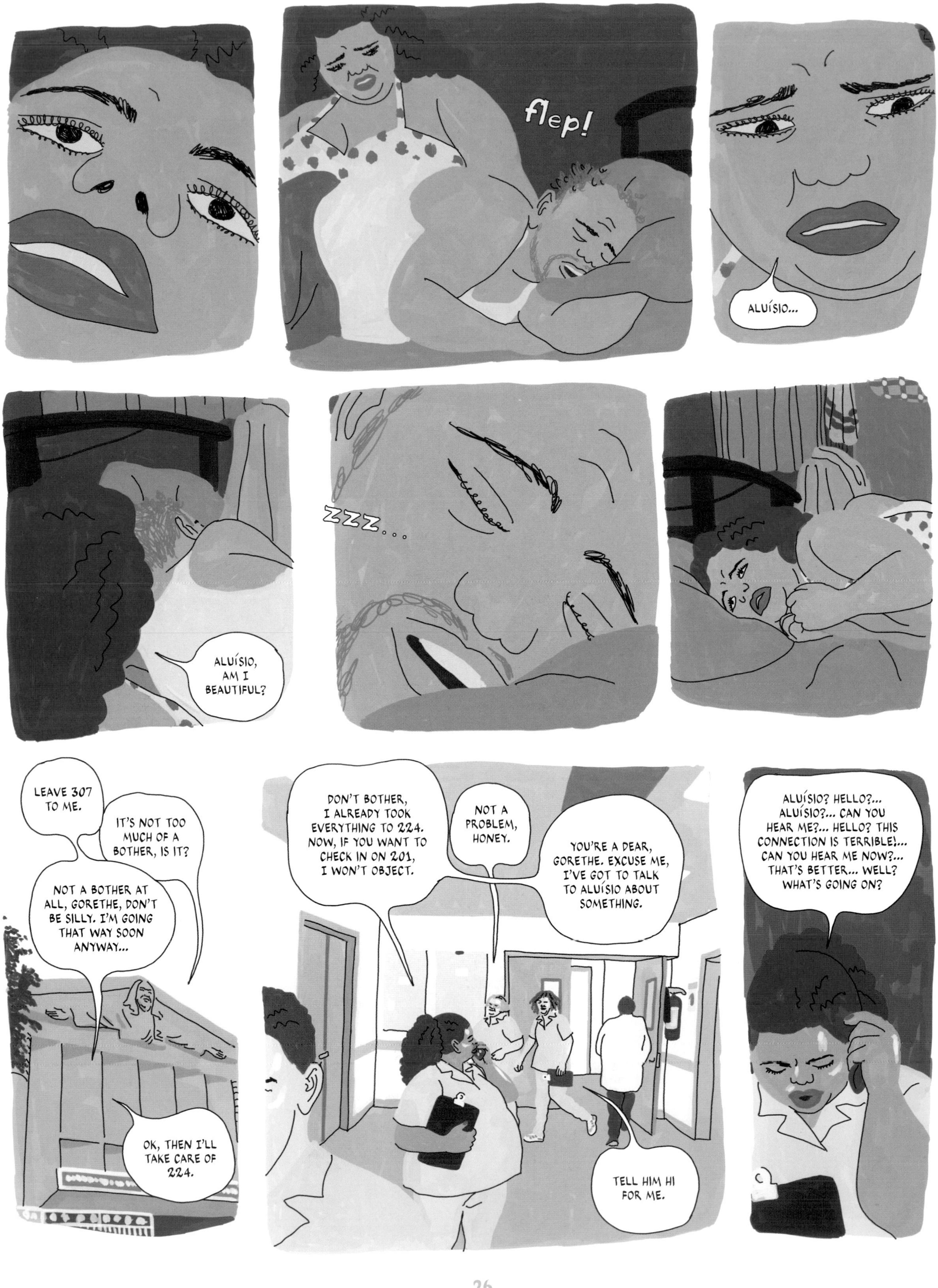
flep!
ALUÍSIO...
ALUÍSIO, AM I BEAUTIFUL?
ZZZ...
LEAVE 307 TO ME.
IT'S NOT TOO MUCH OF A BOTHER, IS IT?
NOT A BOTHER AT ALL, GORETHE, DON'T BE SILLY. I'M GOING THAT WAY SOON ANYWAY...
OK, THEN I'LL TAKE CARE OF 224.
DON'T BOTHER, I ALREADY TOOK EVERYTHING TO 224. NOW, IF YOU WANT TO CHECK IN ON 201, I WON'T OBJECT.
NOT A PROBLEM, HONEY.
YOU'RE A DEAR, GORETHE. EXCUSE ME, I'VE GOT TO TALK TO ALUÍSIO ABOUT SOMETHING.
TELL HIM HI FOR ME.
ALUÍSIO? HELLO?... ALUÍSIO?... CAN YOU HEAR ME?... HELLO? THIS CONNECTION IS TERRIBLE!... CAN YOU HEAR ME NOW?... THAT'S BETTER... WELL? WHAT'S GOING ON?

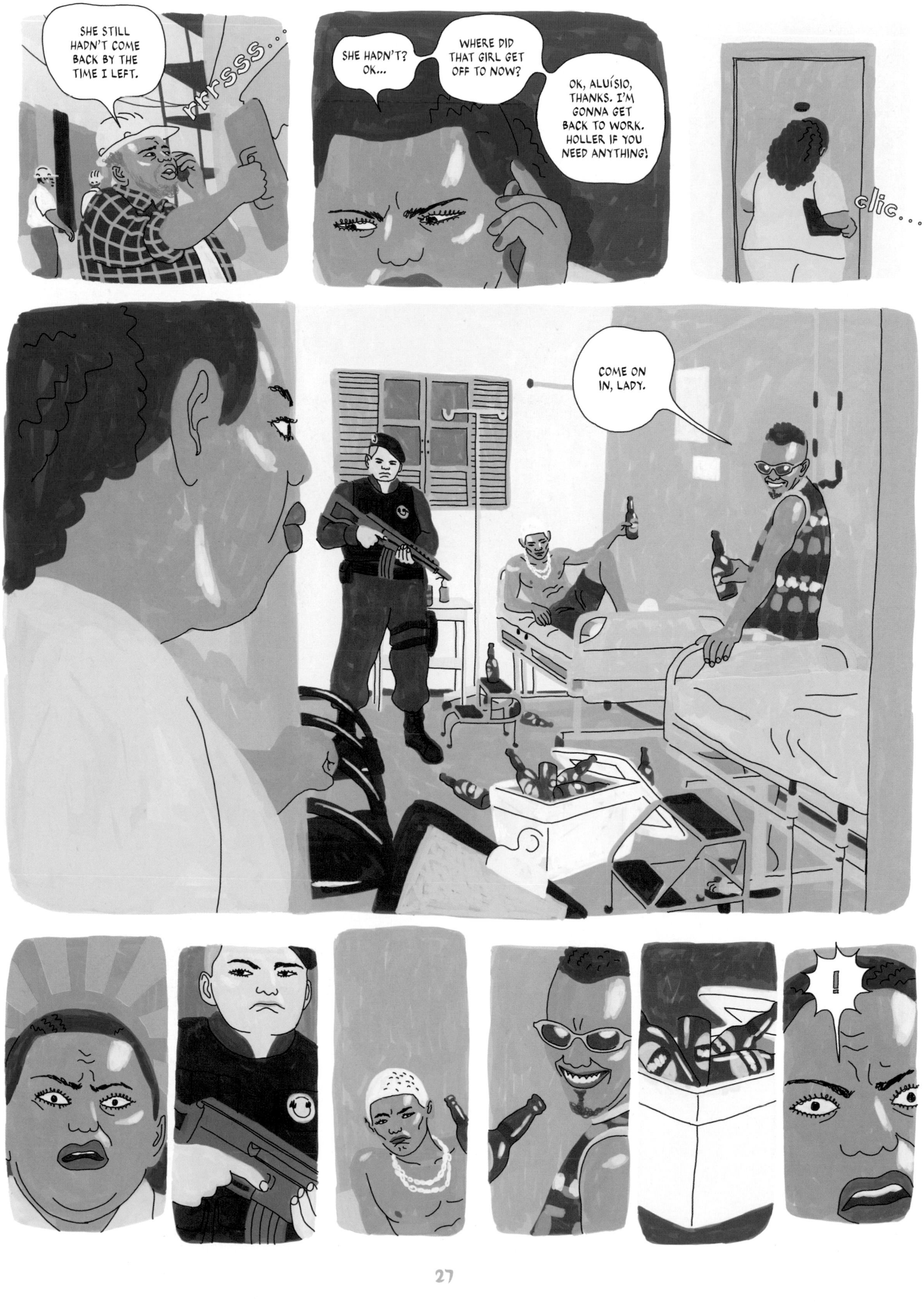
SHE STILL HADN'T COME BACK BY THE TIME I LEFT.
rrrsss...
SHE HADN'T? OK...
WHERE DID THAT GIRL GET OFF TO NOW?
OK, ALUÍSIO, THANKS. I'M GONNA GET BACK TO WORK. HOLLER IF YOU NEED ANYTHING!
clic...
COME ON IN, LADY.
!

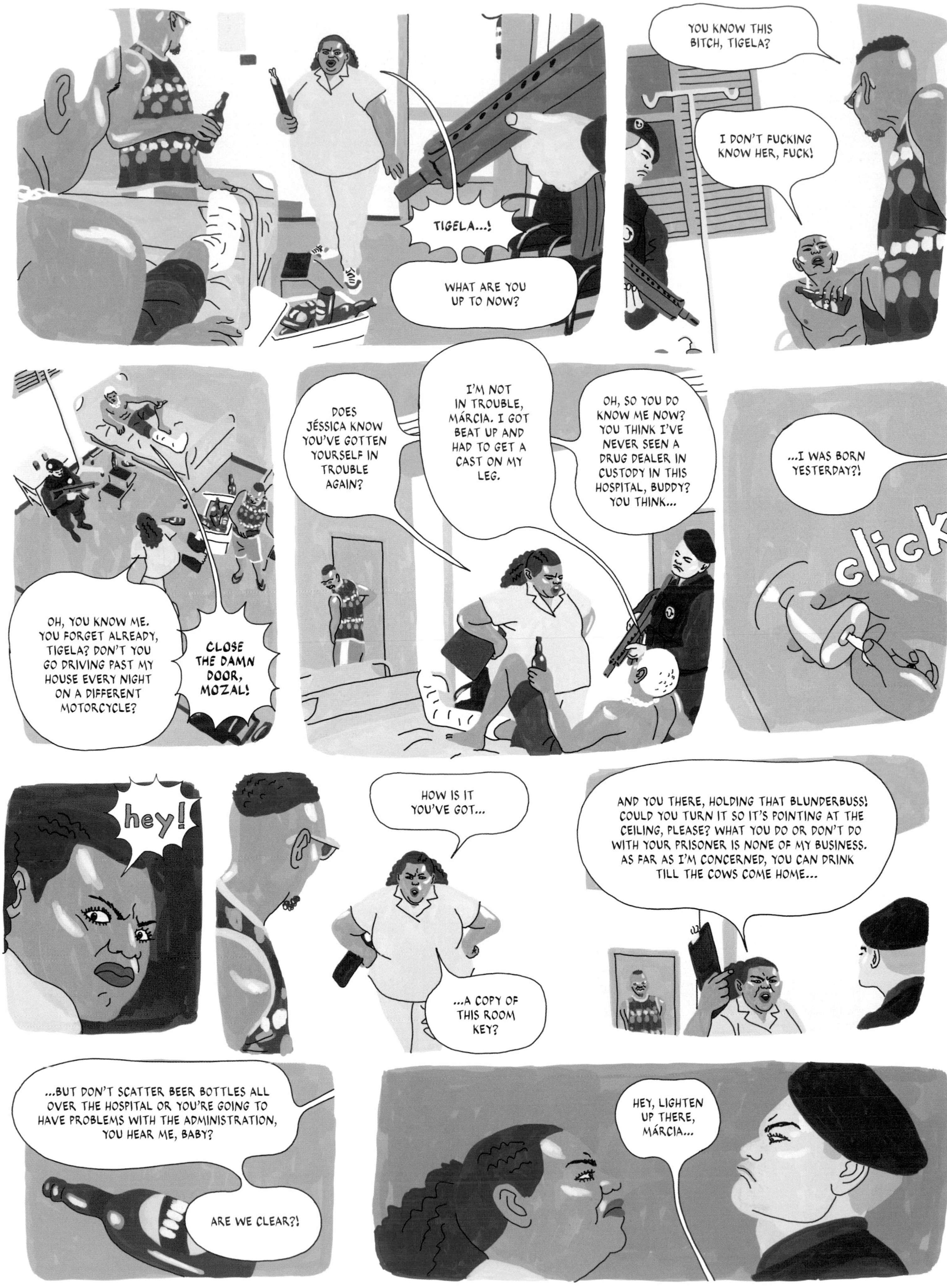
TIGELA...!
WHAT ARE YOU UP TO NOW?
YOU KNOW THIS BITCH, TIGELA?
I DON'T FUCKING KNOW HER, FUCK!
OH, YOU KNOW ME. YOU FORGET ALREADY, TIGELA? DON'T YOU GO DRIVING PAST MY HOUSE EVERY NIGHT ON A DIFFERENT MOTORCYCLE?
CLOSE THE DAMN DOOR, MOZAL!
DOES JÉSSICA KNOW YOU'VE GOTTEN YOURSELF IN TROUBLE AGAIN?
I'M NOT IN TROUBLE, MÁRCIA. I GOT BEAT UP AND HAD TO GET A CAST ON MY LEG.
OH, SO YOU DO KNOW ME NOW? YOU THINK I'VE NEVER SEEN A DRUG DEALER IN CUSTODY IN THIS HOSPITAL, BUDDY? YOU THINK...
...I WAS BORN YESTERDAY?!
click!
hey!
HOW IS IT YOU'VE GOT...
...A COPY OF THIS ROOM KEY?
AND YOU THERE, HOLDING THAT BLUNDERBUSS! COULD YOU TURN IT SO IT'S POINTING AT THE CEILING, PLEASE? WHAT YOU DO OR DON'T DO WITH YOUR PRISONER IS NONE OF MY BUSINESS. AS FAR AS I'M CONCERNED, YOU CAN DRINK TILL THE COWS COME HOME...
...BUT DON'T SCATTER BEER BOTTLES ALL OVER THE HOSPITAL OR YOU'RE GOING TO HAVE PROBLEMS WITH THE ADMINISTRATION, YOU HEAR ME, BABY?
ARE WE CLEAR?!
HEY, LIGHTEN UP THERE, MÁRCIA...

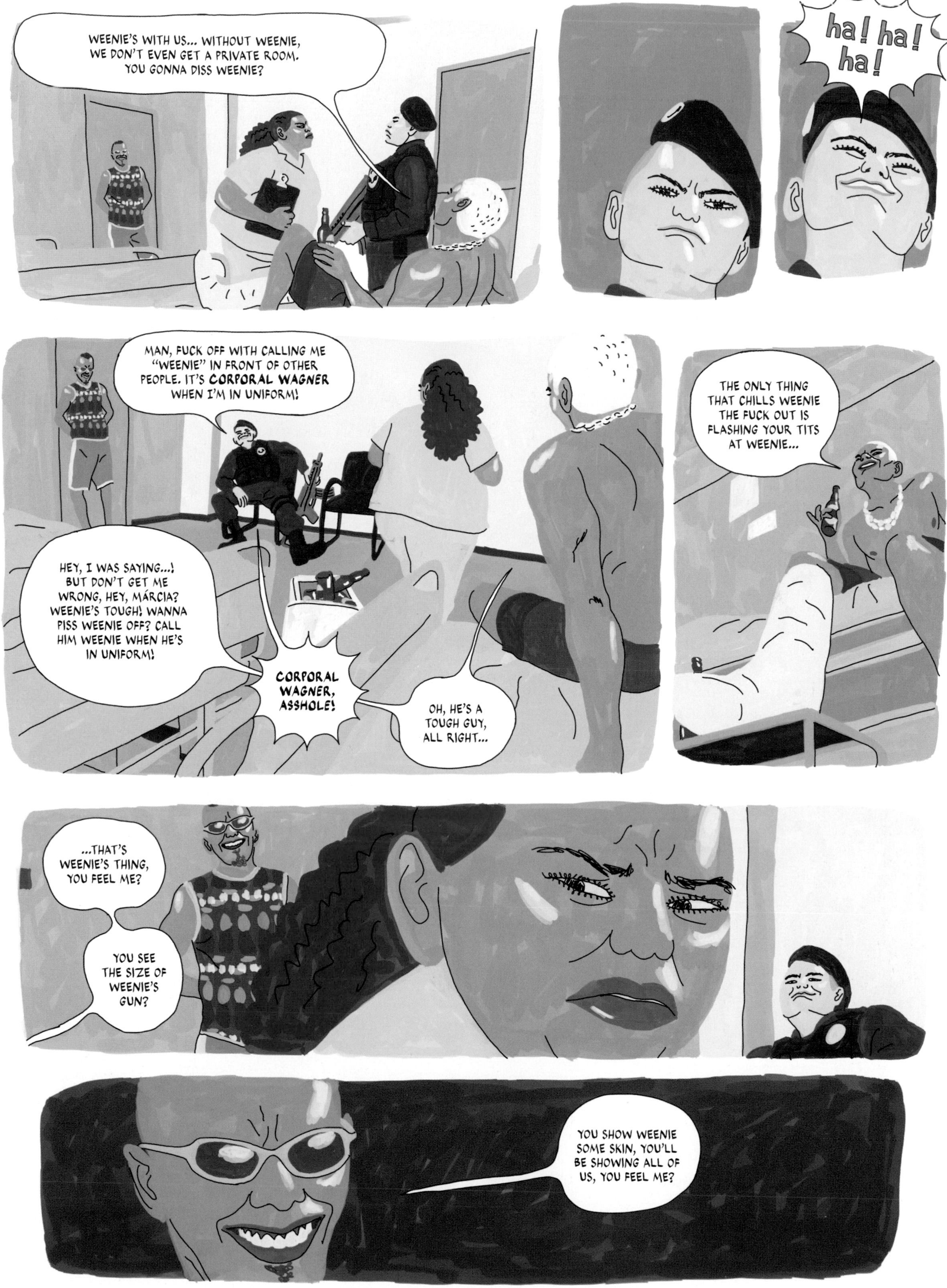
WEENIE'S WITH US... WITHOUT WEENIE, WE DON'T EVEN GET A PRIVATE ROOM. YOU GONNA DISS WEENIE?
ha! ha! ha!
MAN, FUCK OFF WITH CALLING ME "WEENIE" IN FRONT OF OTHER PEOPLE. IT'S CORPORAL WAGNER WHEN I'M IN UNIFORM!
HEY, I WAS SAYING...! BUT DON'T GET ME WRONG, HEY, MÁRCIA? WEENIE'S TOUGH! WANNA PISS WEENIE OFF? CALL HIM WEENIE WHEN HE'S IN UNIFORM!
CORPORAL WAGNER, ASSHOLE!
OH, HE'S A TOUGH GUY, ALL RIGHT...
THE ONLY THING THAT CHILLS WEENIE THE FUCK OUT IS FLASHING YOUR TITS AT WEENIE...
...THAT'S WEENIE'S THING, YOU FEEL ME?
YOU SEE THE SIZE OF WEENIE'S GUN?
YOU SHOW WEENIE SOME SKIN, YOU'LL BE SHOWING ALL OF US, YOU FEEL ME?

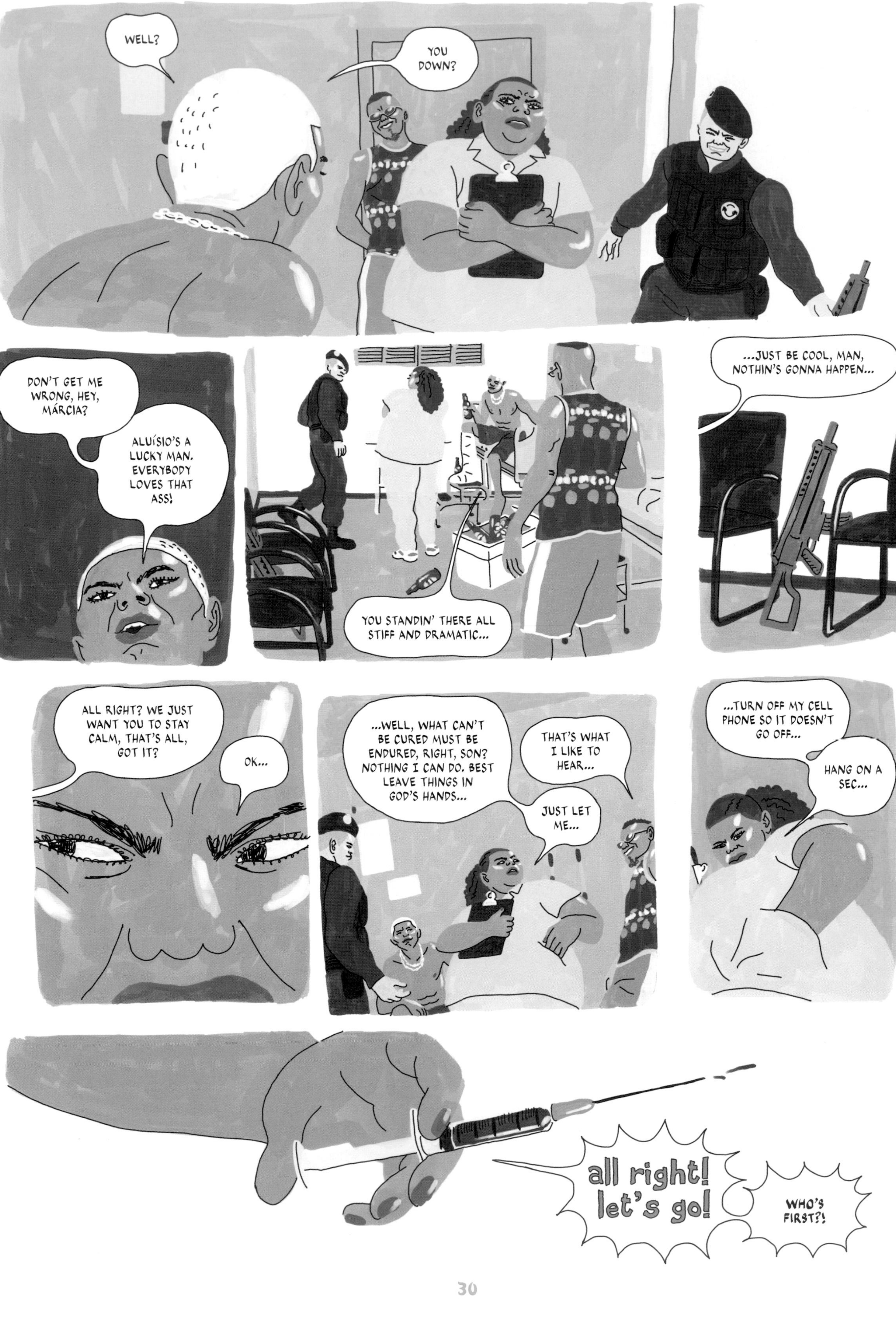
WELL?
YOU DOWN?
DON'T GET ME WRONG, HEY, MÁRCIA?
ALUÍSIO'S A LUCKY MAN. EVERYBODY LOVES THAT ASS!
YOU STANDIN' THERE ALL STIFF AND DRAMATIC...
...JUST BE COOL, MAN, NOTHIN'S GONNA HAPPEN...
ALL RIGHT? WE JUST WANT YOU TO STAY CALM, THAT'S ALL, GOT IT?
OK...
...WELL, WHAT CAN'T BE CURED MUST BE ENDURED, RIGHT, SON? NOTHING I CAN DO. BEST LEAVE THINGS IN GOD'S HANDS...
THAT'S WHAT I LIKE TO HEAR...
JUST LET ME...
...TURN OFF MY CELL PHONE SO IT DOESN'T GO OFF...
HANG ON A SEC...
all right! let's go!
WHO'S FIRST?!

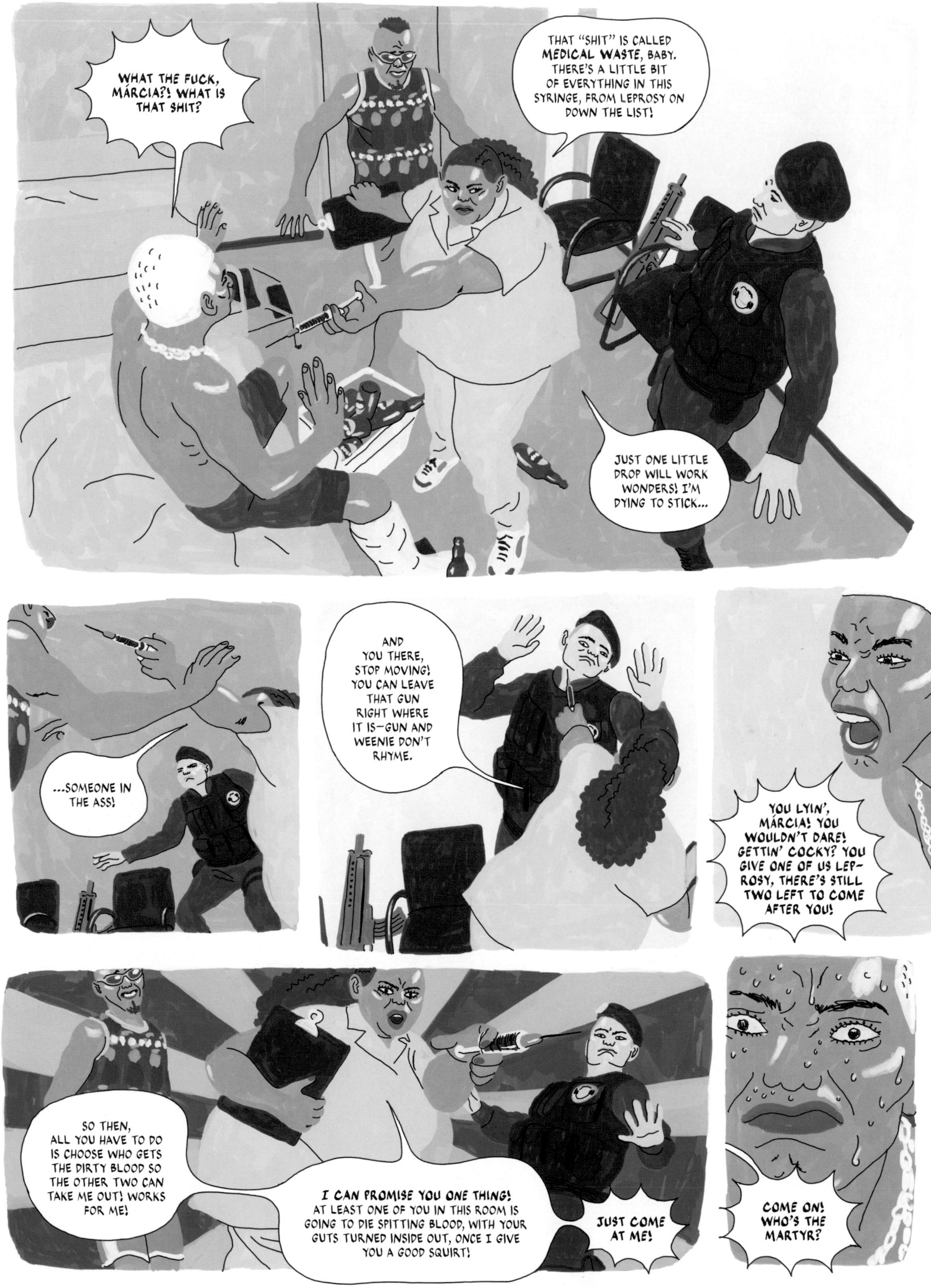
WHAT THE FUCK, MÁRCIA?! WHAT IS THAT SHIT?
THAT "SHIT" IS CALLED MEDICAL WASTE, BABY. THERE'S A LITTLE BIT OF EVERYTHING IN THIS SYRINGE, FROM LEPROSY ON DOWN THE LIST!
JUST ONE LITTLE DROP WILL WORK WONDERS! I'M DYING TO STICK...
...SOMEONE IN THE ASS!
AND YOU THERE, STOP MOVING! YOU CAN LEAVE THAT GUN RIGHT WHERE IT IS—GUN AND WEENIE DON'T RHYME.
YOU LYIN', MÁRCIA! YOU WOULDN'T DARE! GETTIN' COCKY? YOU GIVE ONE OF US LEP-ROSY, THERE'S STILL TWO LEFT TO COME AFTER YOU!
SO THEN, ALL YOU HAVE TO DO IS CHOOSE WHO GETS THE DIRTY BLOOD SO THE OTHER TWO CAN TAKE ME OUT! WORKS FOR ME!
I CAN PROMISE YOU ONE THING! AT LEAST ONE OF YOU IN THIS ROOM IS GOING TO DIE SPITTING BLOOD, WITH YOUR GUTS TURNED INSIDE OUT, ONCE I GIVE YOU A GOOD SQUIRT!
JUST COME AT ME!
COME ON! WHO'S THE MARTYR?

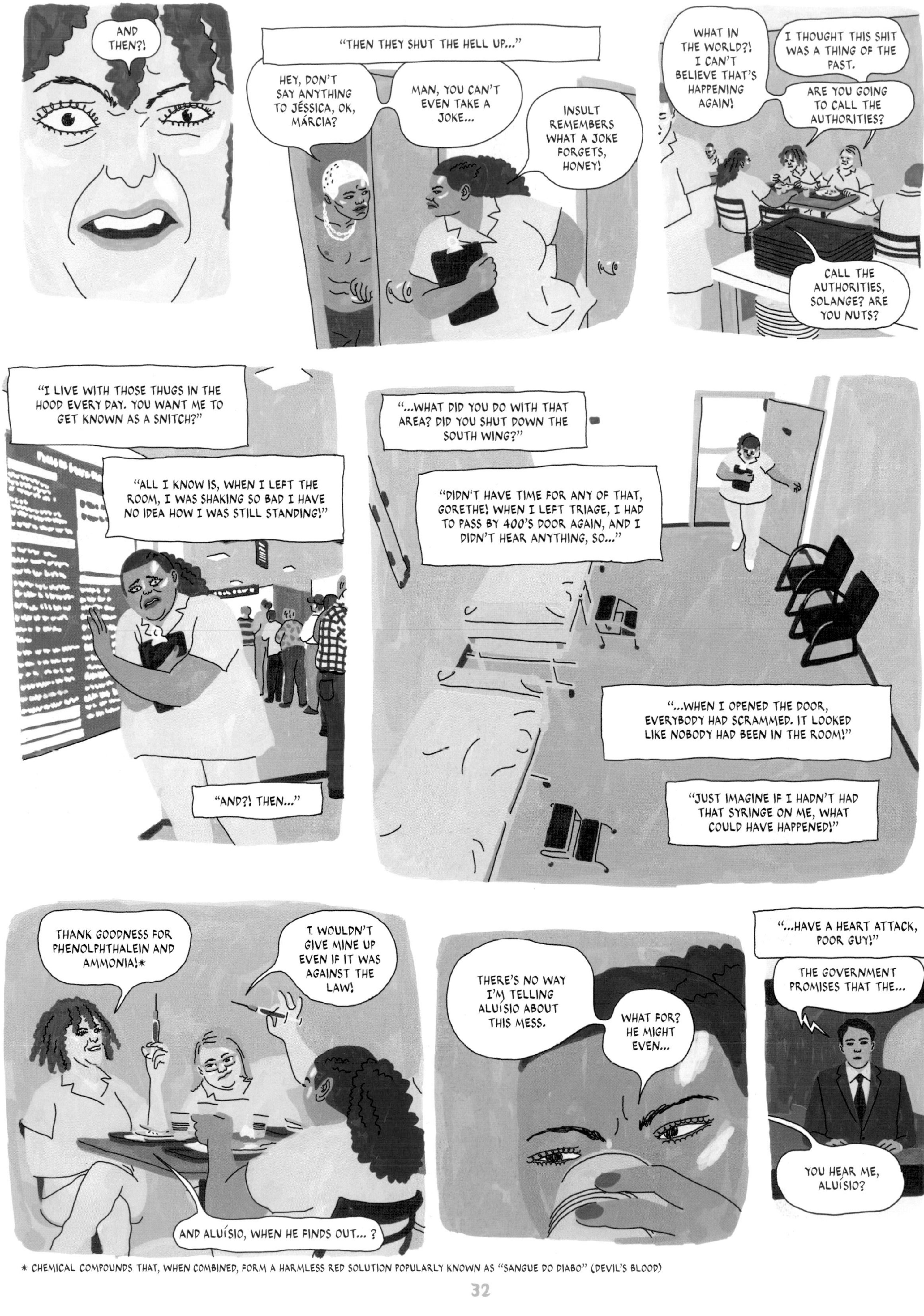
AND THEN?!
"THEN THEY SHUT THE HELL UP..."
HEY, DON'T SAY ANYTHING TO JÉSSICA, OK, MÁRCIA?
MAN, YOU CAN'T EVEN TAKE A JOKE...
INSULT REMEMBERS WHAT A JOKE FORGETS, HONEY!
WHAT IN THE WORLD?! I CAN'T BELIEVE THAT'S HAPPENING AGAIN!
I THOUGHT THIS SHIT WAS A THING OF THE PAST.
ARE YOU GOING TO CALL THE AUTHORITIES?
CALL THE AUTHORITIES, SOLANGE? ARE YOU NUTS?
"I LIVE WITH THOSE THUGS IN THE HOOD EVERY DAY. YOU WANT ME TO GET KNOWN AS A SNITCH?"
"ALL I KNOW IS, WHEN I LEFT THE ROOM, I WAS SHAKING SO BAD I HAVE NO IDEA HOW I WAS STILL STANDING!"
"AND?! THEN..."
"...WHAT DID YOU DO WITH THAT AREA? DID YOU SHUT DOWN THE SOUTH WING?"
"DIDN'T HAVE TIME FOR ANY OF THAT, GORETHE! WHEN I LEFT TRIAGE, I HAD TO PASS BY 400'S DOOR AGAIN, AND I DIDN'T HEAR ANYTHING, SO..."
"...WHEN I OPENED THE DOOR, EVERYBODY HAD SCRAMMED. IT LOOKED LIKE NOBODY HAD BEEN IN THE ROOM!"
"JUST IMAGINE IF I HADN'T HAD THAT SYRINGE ON ME, WHAT COULD HAVE HAPPENED!"
THANK GOODNESS FOR PHENOLPHTHALEIN AND AMMONIA!*
I WOULDN'T GIVE MINE UP EVEN IF IT WAS AGAINST THE LAW!
AND ALUÍSIO, WHEN HE FINDS OUT... ?
THERE'S NO WAY I'M TELLING ALUÍSIO ABOUT THIS MESS.
WHAT FOR? HE MIGHT EVEN...
"...HAVE A HEART ATTACK, POOR GUY!"
THE GOVERNMENT PROMISES THAT THE...
YOU HEAR ME, ALUÍSIO?

* CHEMICAL COMPOUNDS THAT, WHEN COMBINED, FORM A HARMLESS RED SOLUTION POPULARLY KNOWN AS "SANGUE DO DIABO" (DEVIL'S BLOOD)

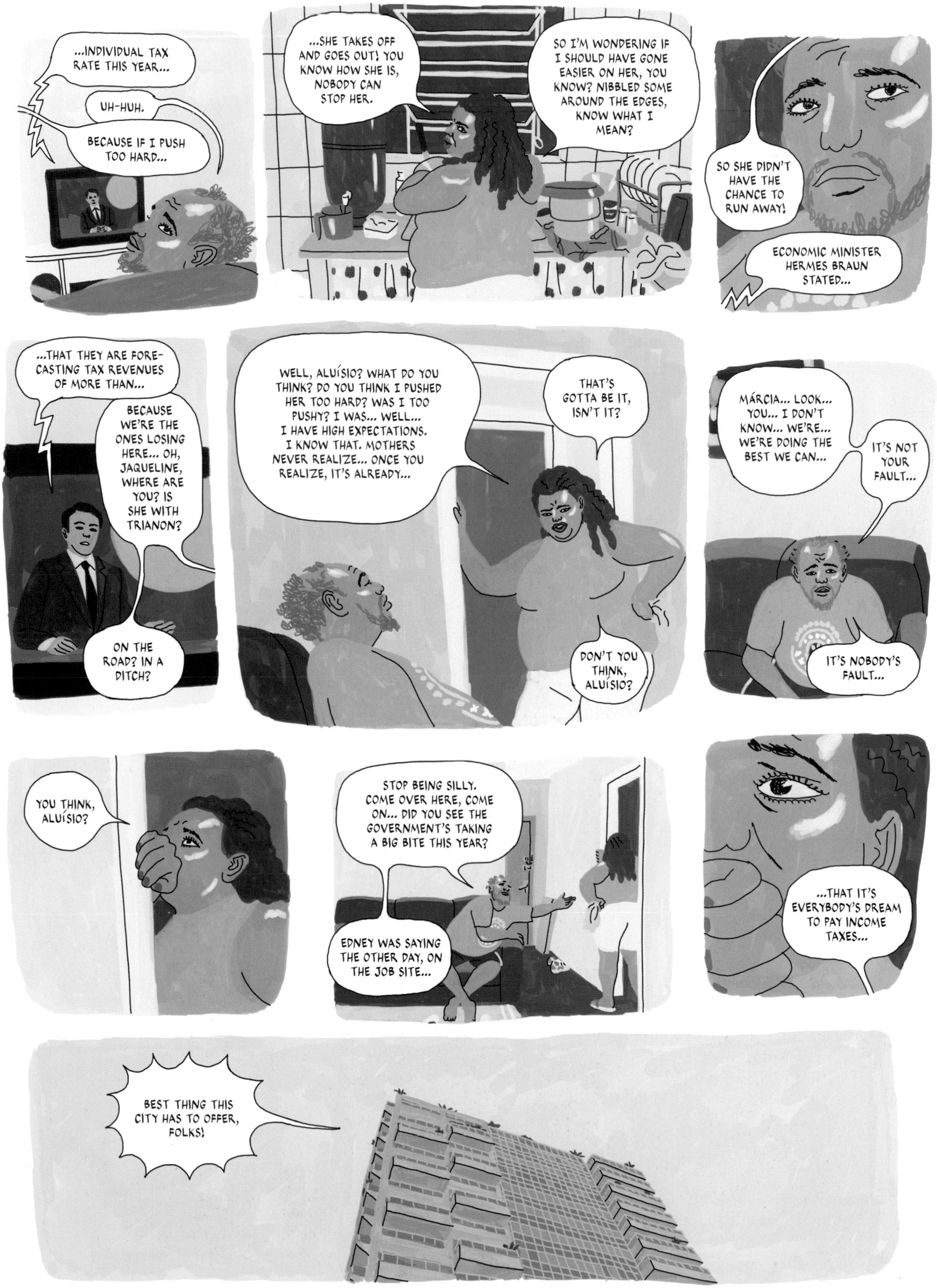
...INDIVIDUAL TAX RATE THIS YEAR...
UH-HUH.
BECAUSE IF I PUSH TOO HARD...
...SHE TAKES OFF AND GOES OUT! YOU KNOW HOW SHE IS, NOBODY CAN STOP HER.
SO I'M WONDERING IF I SHOULD HAVE GONE EASIER ON HER, YOU KNOW? NIBBLED SOME AROUND THE EDGES, KNOW WHAT I MEAN?
SO SHE DIDN'T HAVE THE CHANCE TO RUN AWAY!
ECONOMIC MINISTER HERMES BRAUN STATED...
...THAT THEY ARE FORE-CASTING TAX REVENUES OF MORE THAN...
BECAUSE WE'RE THE ONES LOSING HERE... OH, JAQUELINE, WHERE ARE YOU? IS SHE WITH TRIANON?
ON THE ROAD? IN A DITCH?
WELL, ALUÍSIO? WHAT DO YOU THINK? DO YOU THINK I PUSHED HER TOO HARD? WAS I TOO PUSHY? I WAS... WELL... I HAVE HIGH EXPECTATIONS. I KNOW THAT. MOTHERS NEVER REALIZE... ONCE YOU REALIZE, IT'S ALREADY...
THAT'S GOTTA BE IT, ISN'T IT?
DON'T YOU THINK, ALUÍSIO?
MÁRCIA... LOOK... YOU... I DON'T KNOW... WE'RE... WE'RE DOING THE BEST WE CAN...
IT'S NOT YOUR FAULT...
IT'S NOBODY'S FAULT...
YOU THINK, ALUÍSIO?
STOP BEING SILLY. COME OVER HERE, COME ON... DID YOU SEE THE GOVERNMENT'S TAKING A BIG BITE THIS YEAR?
EDNEY WAS SAYING THE OTHER DAY, ON THE JOB SITE...
...THAT IT'S EVERYBODY'S DREAM TO PAY INCOME TAXES...
BEST THING THIS CITY HAS TO OFFER, FOLKS!

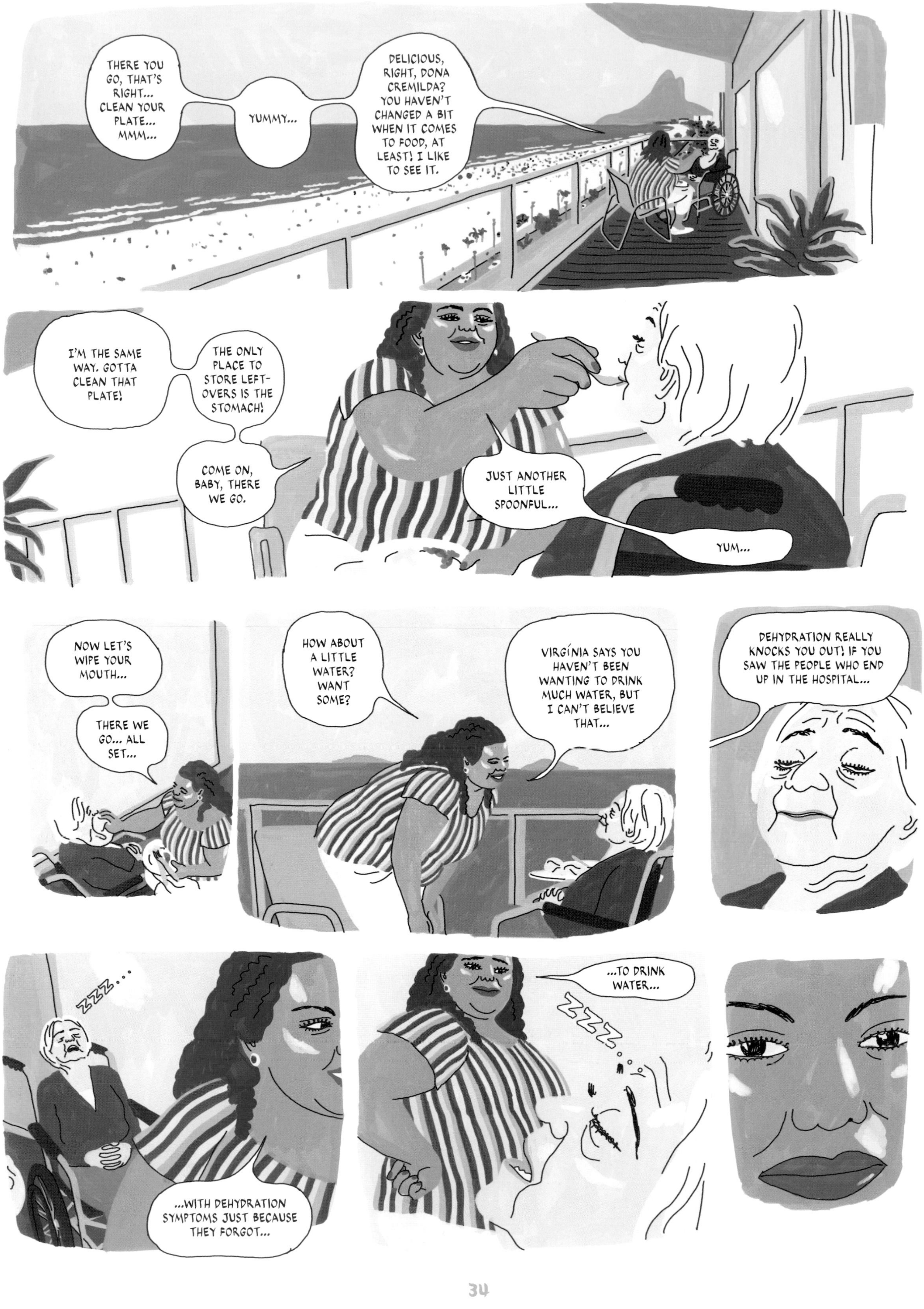
THERE YOU GO, THAT'S RIGHT... CLEAN YOUR PLATE... MMM...
YUMMY...
DELICIOUS, RIGHT, DONA CREMILDA? YOU HAVEN'T CHANGED A BIT WHEN IT COMES TO FOOD, AT LEAST! I LIKE TO SEE IT.
I'M THE SAME WAY. GOTTA CLEAN THAT PLATE!
THE ONLY PLACE TO STORE LEFT-OVERS IS THE STOMACH!
COME ON, BABY, THERE WE GO.
JUST ANOTHER LITTLE SPOONFUL...
YUM...
NOW LET'S WIPE YOUR MOUTH...
THERE WE GO... ALL SET...
HOW ABOUT A LITTLE WATER? WANT SOME?
VIRGÍNIA SAYS YOU HAVEN'T BEEN WANTING TO DRINK MUCH WATER, BUT I CAN'T BELIEVE THAT...
DEHYDRATION REALLY KNOCKS YOU OUT! IF YOU SAW THE PEOPLE WHO END UP IN THE HOSPITAL...
ZZZ...
...WITH DEHYDRATION SYMPTOMS JUST BECAUSE THEY FORGOT...
...TO DRINK WATER...
ZZZ

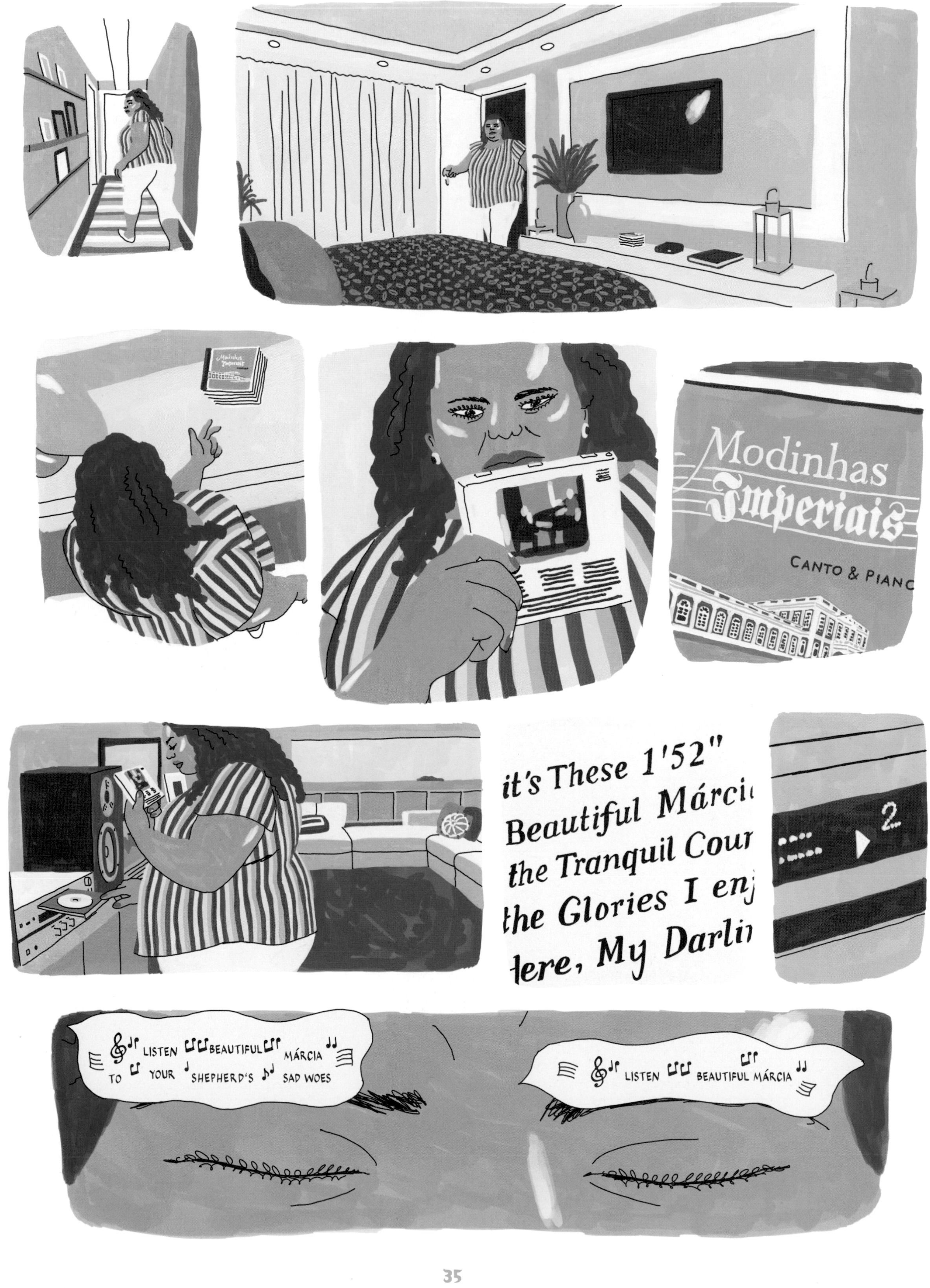
Modinhas Imperiais
CANTO & PIANC
it's These 1'52"
Beautiful Márci
the Tranquil Cour
the Glories I enj
lere, My Darlin
2
LISTEN BEAUTIFUL MÁRCIA TO YOUR SHEPHERD'S SAD WOES
LISTEN BEAUTIFUL MÁRCIA

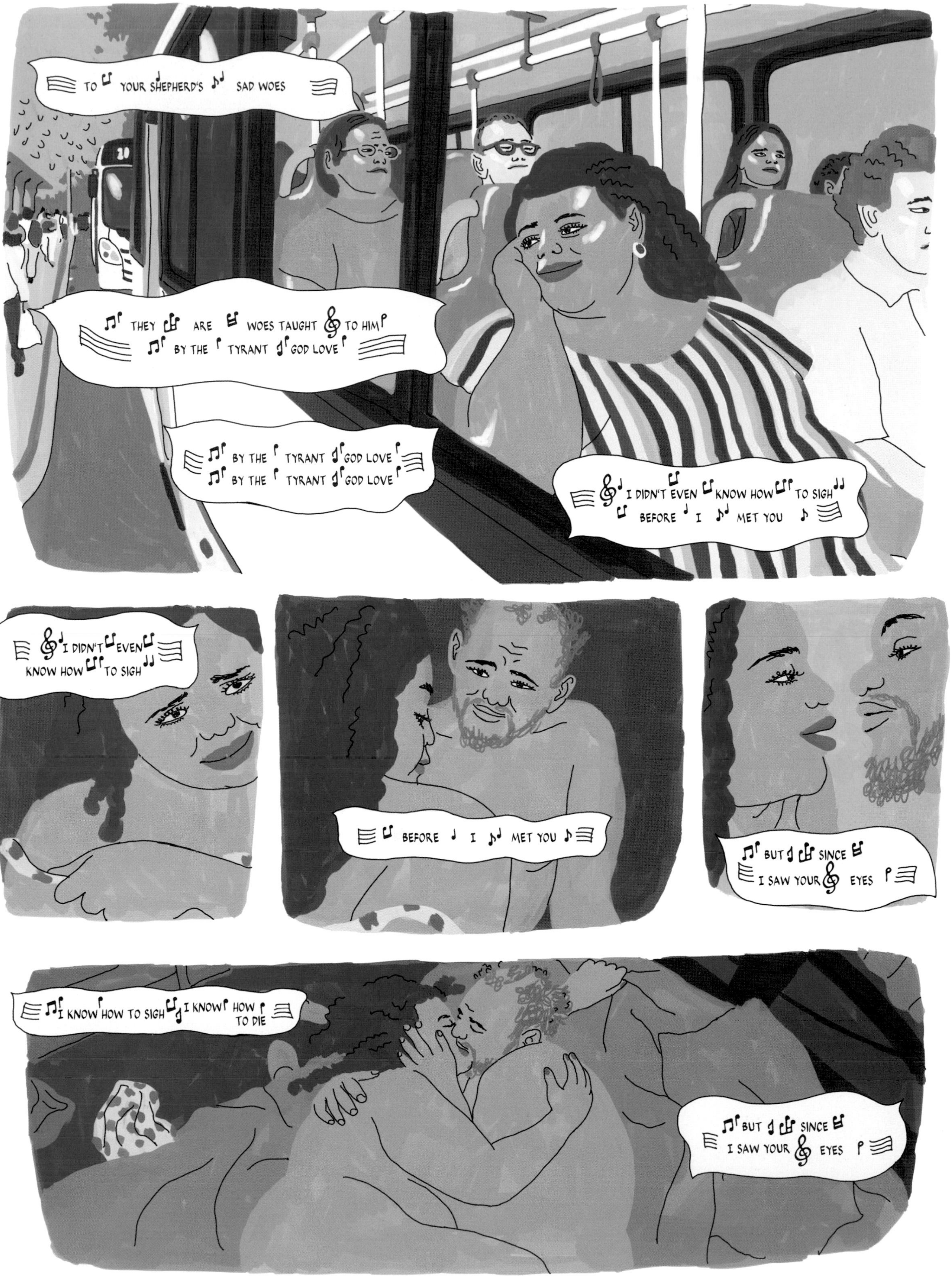

TO YOUR SHEPHERD'S SAD WOES
THEY ARE WOES TAUGHT TO HIM BY THE TYRANT GOD LOVE
BY THE TYRANT GOD LOVE BY THE TYRANT GOD LOVE
I DIDN'T EVEN KNOW HOW TO SIGH BEFORE I MET YOU
I DIDN'T EVEN KNOW HOW TO SIGH
BEFORE I MET YOU
BUT SINCE I SAW YOUR EYES
I KNOW HOW TO SIGH I KNOW HOW TO DIE
BUT SINCE I SAW YOUR EYES

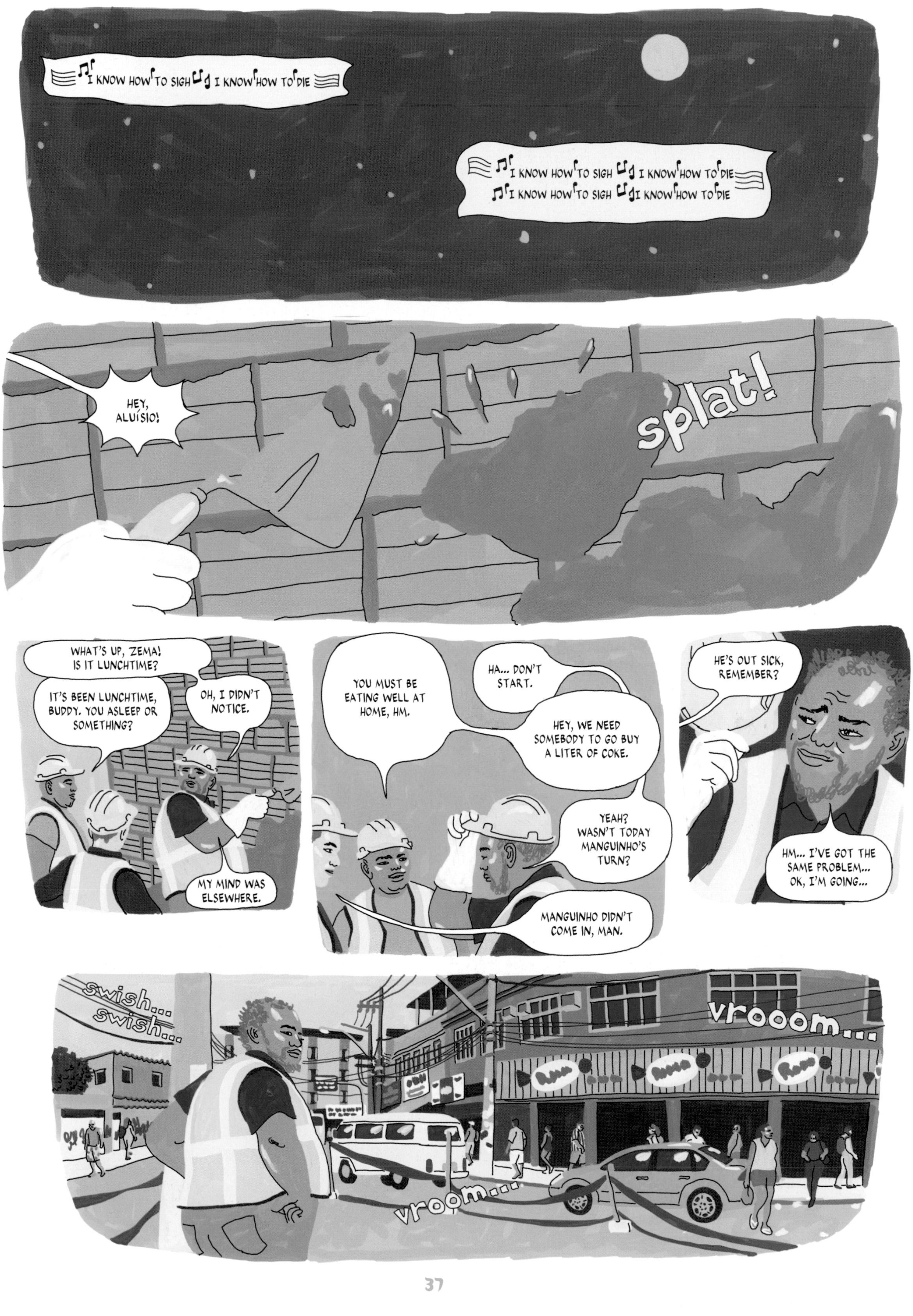
I KNOW HOW TO SIGH I KNOW HOW TO DIE
I KNOW HOW TO SIGH I KNOW HOW TO DIE
I KNOW HOW TO SIGH I KNOW HOW TO DIE
HEY, ALUÍSIO!
splat!
WHAT'S UP, ZEMA! IS IT LUNCHTIME?
IT'S BEEN LUNCHTIME, BUDDY. YOU ASLEEP OR SOMETHING?
OH, I DIDN'T NOTICE.
MY MIND WAS ELSEWHERE.
YOU MUST BE EATING WELL AT HOME, HM.
HA... DON'T START.
HEY, WE NEED SOMEBODY TO GO BUY A LITER OF COKE.
YEAH? WASN'T TODAY MANGUINHO'S TURN?
MANGUINHO DIDN'T COME IN, MAN.
HE'S OUT SICK, REMEMBER?
HM... I'VE GOT THE SAME PROBLEM... OK, I'M GOING...
swish... swish...
vrooom...
vroom...

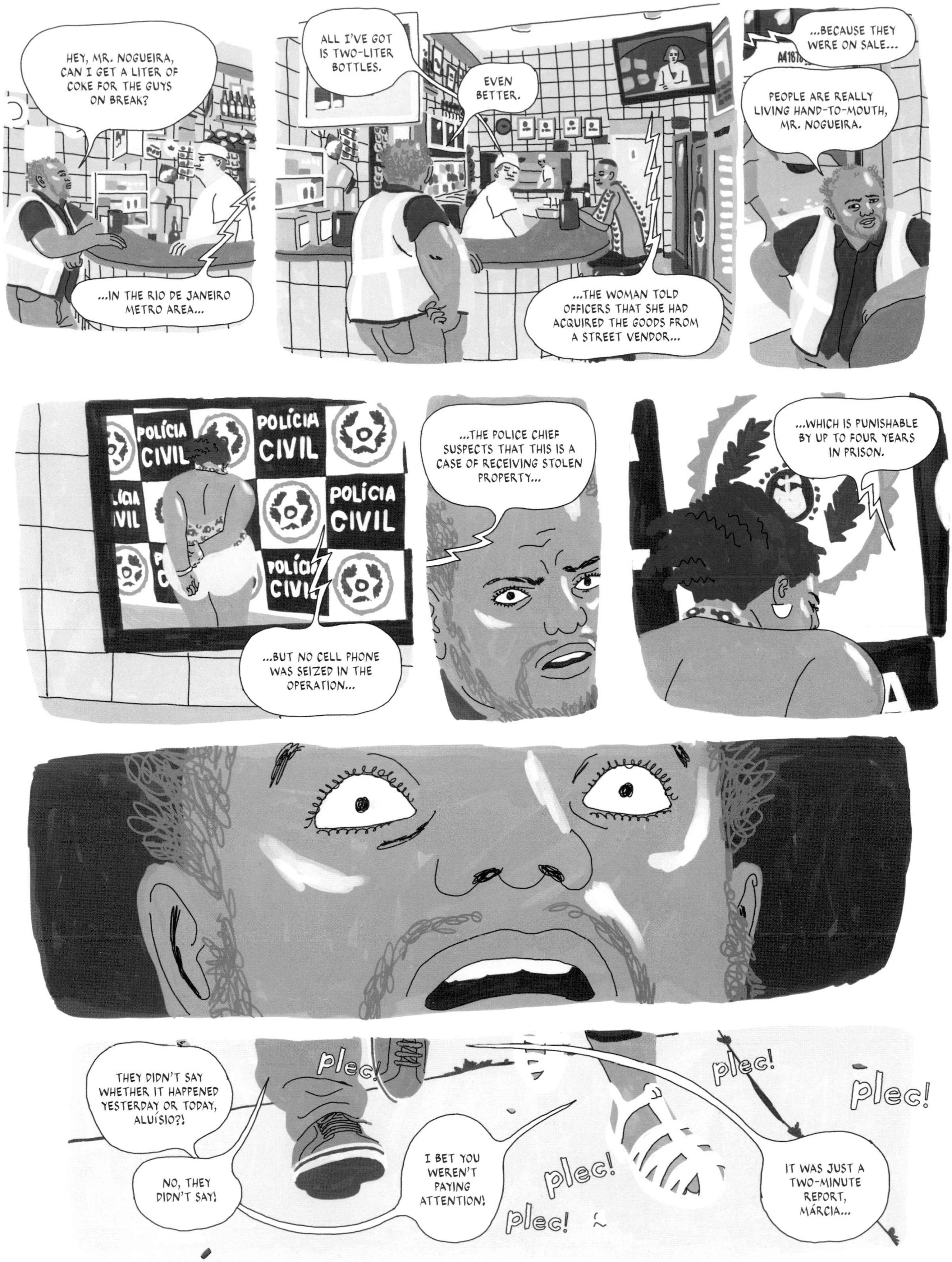
HEY, MR. NOGUEIRA, CAN I GET A LITER OF COKE FOR THE GUYS ON BREAK?
...IN THE RIO DE JANEIRO METRO AREA...
ALL I'VE GOT IS TWO-LITER BOTTLES.
EVEN BETTER.
...THE WOMAN TOLD OFFICERS THAT SHE HAD ACQUIRED THE GOODS FROM A STREET VENDOR...
...BECAUSE THEY WERE ON SALE...
PEOPLE ARE REALLY LIVING HAND-TO-MOUTH, MR. NOGUEIRA.
POLÍCIA CIVIL
...BUT NO CELL PHONE WAS SEIZED IN THE OPERATION...
...THE POLICE CHIEF SUSPECTS THAT THIS IS A CASE OF RECEIVING STOLEN PROPERTY...
...WHICH IS PUNISHABLE BY UP TO FOUR YEARS IN PRISON.
THEY DIDN'T SAY WHETHER IT HAPPENED YESTERDAY OR TODAY, ALUÍSIO?!
NO, THEY DIDN'T SAY!
I BET YOU WEREN'T PAYING ATTENTION!
IT WAS JUST A TWO-MINUTE REPORT, MÁRCIA...
plec!
plec!
plec!
plec!
plec!

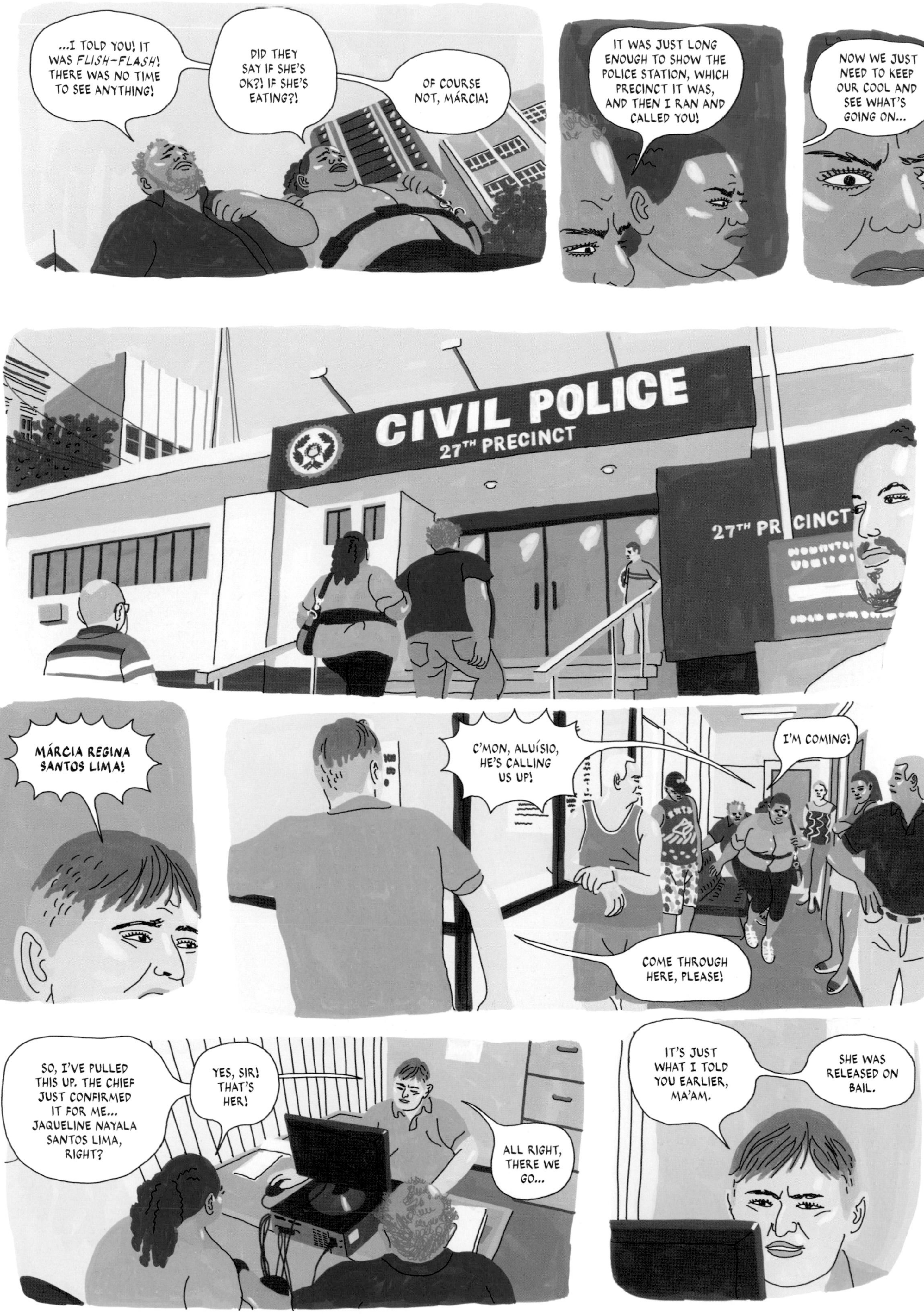
...I TOLD YOU! IT WAS *FLISH-FLASH*! THERE WAS NO TIME TO SEE ANYTHING!
DID THEY SAY IF SHE'S OK?! IF SHE'S EATING?!
OF COURSE NOT, MÁRCIA!
IT WAS JUST LONG ENOUGH TO SHOW THE POLICE STATION, WHICH PRECINCT IT WAS, AND THEN I RAN AND CALLED YOU!
NOW WE JUST NEED TO KEEP OUR COOL AND SEE WHAT'S GOING ON...
CIVIL POLICE
27TH PRECINCT
27TH PRECINCT
MÁRCIA REGINA SANTOS LIMA!
C'MON, ALUÍSIO, HE'S CALLING US UP!
I'M COMING!
COME THROUGH HERE, PLEASE!
SO, I'VE PULLED THIS UP. THE CHIEF JUST CONFIRMED IT FOR ME... JAQUELINE NAYALA SANTOS LIMA, RIGHT?
YES, SIR! THAT'S HER!
ALL RIGHT, THERE WE GO...
IT'S JUST WHAT I TOLD YOU EARLIER, MA'AM.
SHE WAS RELEASED ON BAIL.

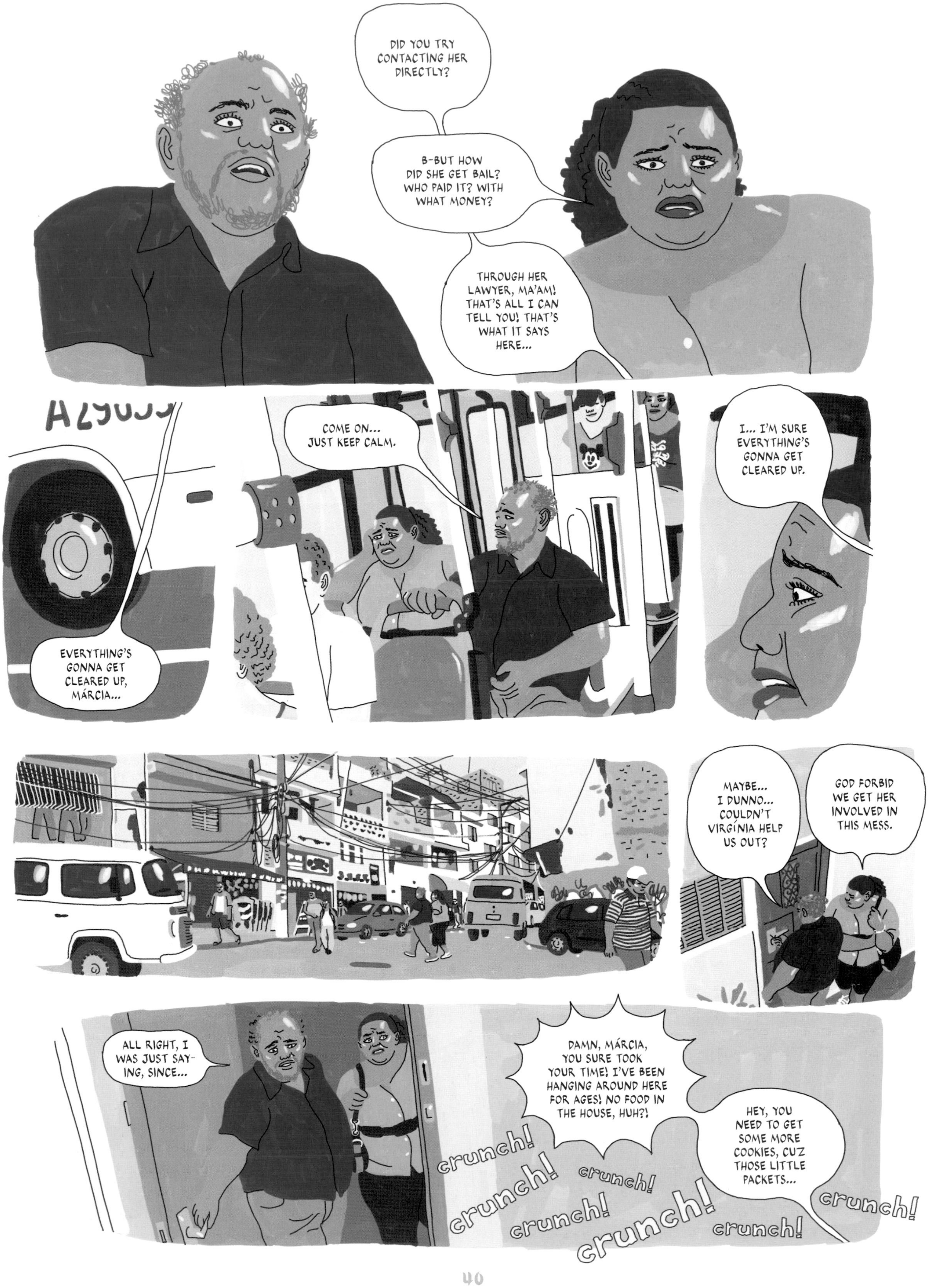
DID YOU TRY CONTACTING HER DIRECTLY?
B-BUT HOW DID SHE GET BAIL? WHO PAID IT? WITH WHAT MONEY?
THROUGH HER LAWYER, MA'AM! THAT'S ALL I CAN TELL YOU! THAT'S WHAT IT SAYS HERE...
EVERYTHING'S GONNA GET CLEARED UP, MÁRCIA...
COME ON... JUST KEEP CALM.
I... I'M SURE EVERYTHING'S GONNA GET CLEARED UP.
MAYBE... I DUNNO... COULDN'T VIRGÍNIA HELP US OUT?
GOD FORBID WE GET HER INVOLVED IN THIS MESS.
ALL RIGHT, I WAS JUST SAYING, SINCE...
DAMN, MÁRCIA, YOU SURE TOOK YOUR TIME! I'VE BEEN HANGING AROUND HERE FOR AGES! NO FOOD IN THE HOUSE, HUH?!
HEY, YOU NEED TO GET SOME MORE COOKIES, CUZ THOSE LITTLE PACKETS...
crunch! crunch! crunch! crunch! crunch! crunch! crunch! crunch!

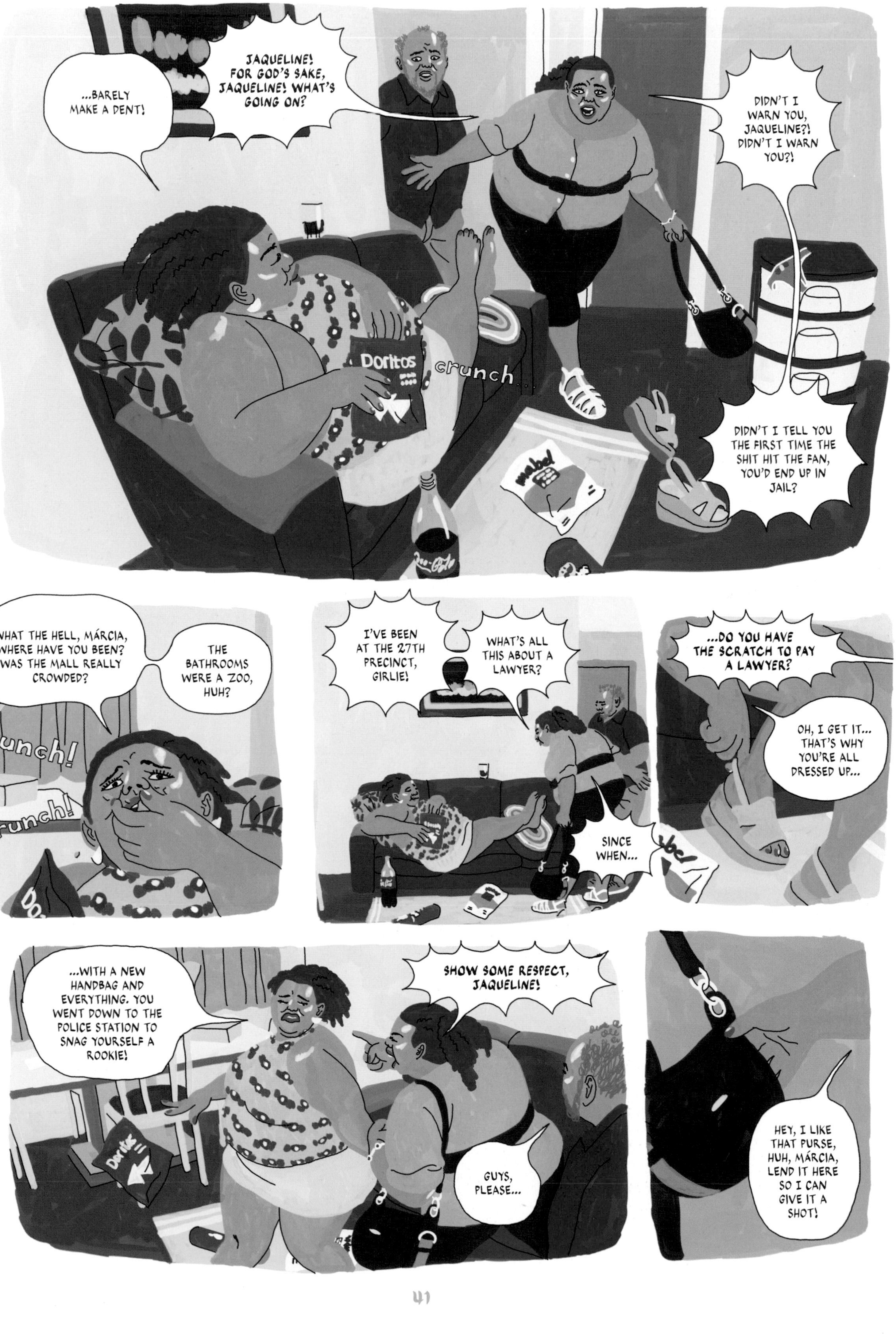

...BARELY MAKE A DENT!
JAQUELINE! FOR GOD'S SAKE, JAQUELINE! WHAT'S GOING ON?
DIDN'T I WARN YOU, JAQUELINE?! DIDN'T I WARN YOU?!
Doritos
crunch...
DIDN'T I TELL YOU THE FIRST TIME THE SHIT HIT THE FAN, YOU'D END UP IN JAIL?
WHAT THE HELL, MÁRCIA, WHERE HAVE YOU BEEN? WAS THE MALL REALLY CROWDED?
THE BATHROOMS WERE A ZOO, HUH?
crunch!
crunch!
I'VE BEEN AT THE 27TH PRECINCT, GIRLIE!
WHAT'S ALL THIS ABOUT A LAWYER?
SINCE WHEN...
...DO YOU HAVE THE SCRATCH TO PAY A LAWYER?
OH, I GET IT... THAT'S WHY YOU'RE ALL DRESSED UP...
...WITH A NEW HANDBAG AND EVERYTHING. YOU WENT DOWN TO THE POLICE STATION TO SNAG YOURSELF A ROOKIE!
SHOW SOME RESPECT, JAQUELINE!
GUYS, PLEASE...
HEY, I LIKE THAT PURSE, HUH, MÁRCIA, LEND IT HERE SO I CAN GIVE IT A SHOT!

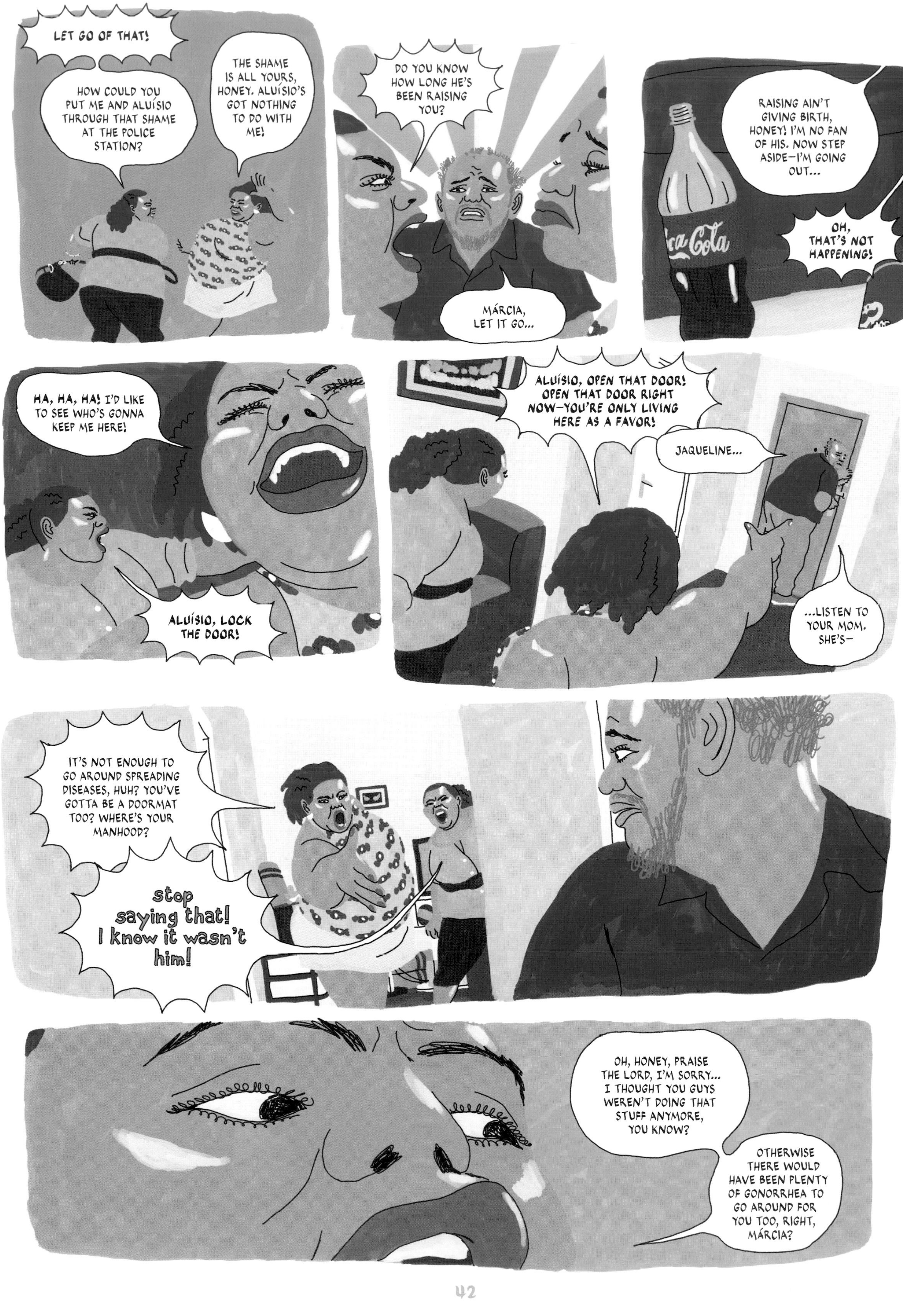

LET GO OF THAT!
HOW COULD YOU PUT ME AND ALUÍSIO THROUGH THAT SHAME AT THE POLICE STATION?
THE SHAME IS ALL YOURS, HONEY. ALUÍSIO'S GOT NOTHING TO DO WITH ME!
DO YOU KNOW HOW LONG HE'S BEEN RAISING YOU?
MÁRCIA, LET IT GO...
RAISING AIN'T GIVING BIRTH, HONEY! I'M NO FAN OF HIS. NOW STEP ASIDE—I'M GOING OUT...
Coca-Cola
OH, THAT'S NOT HAPPENING!
HA, HA, HA! I'D LIKE TO SEE WHO'S GONNA KEEP ME HERE!
ALUÍSIO, LOCK THE DOOR!
ALUÍSIO, OPEN THAT DOOR! OPEN THAT DOOR RIGHT NOW—YOU'RE ONLY LIVING HERE AS A FAVOR!
JAQUELINE...
...LISTEN TO YOUR MOM. SHE'S—
IT'S NOT ENOUGH TO GO AROUND SPREADING DISEASES, HUH? YOU'VE GOTTA BE A DOORMAT TOO? WHERE'S YOUR MANHOOD?
stop saying that! I know it wasn't him!
OH, HONEY, PRAISE THE LORD, I'M SORRY... I THOUGHT YOU GUYS WEREN'T DOING THAT STUFF ANYMORE, YOU KNOW?
OTHERWISE THERE WOULD HAVE BEEN PLENTY OF GONORRHEA TO GO AROUND FOR YOU TOO, RIGHT, MÁRCIA?

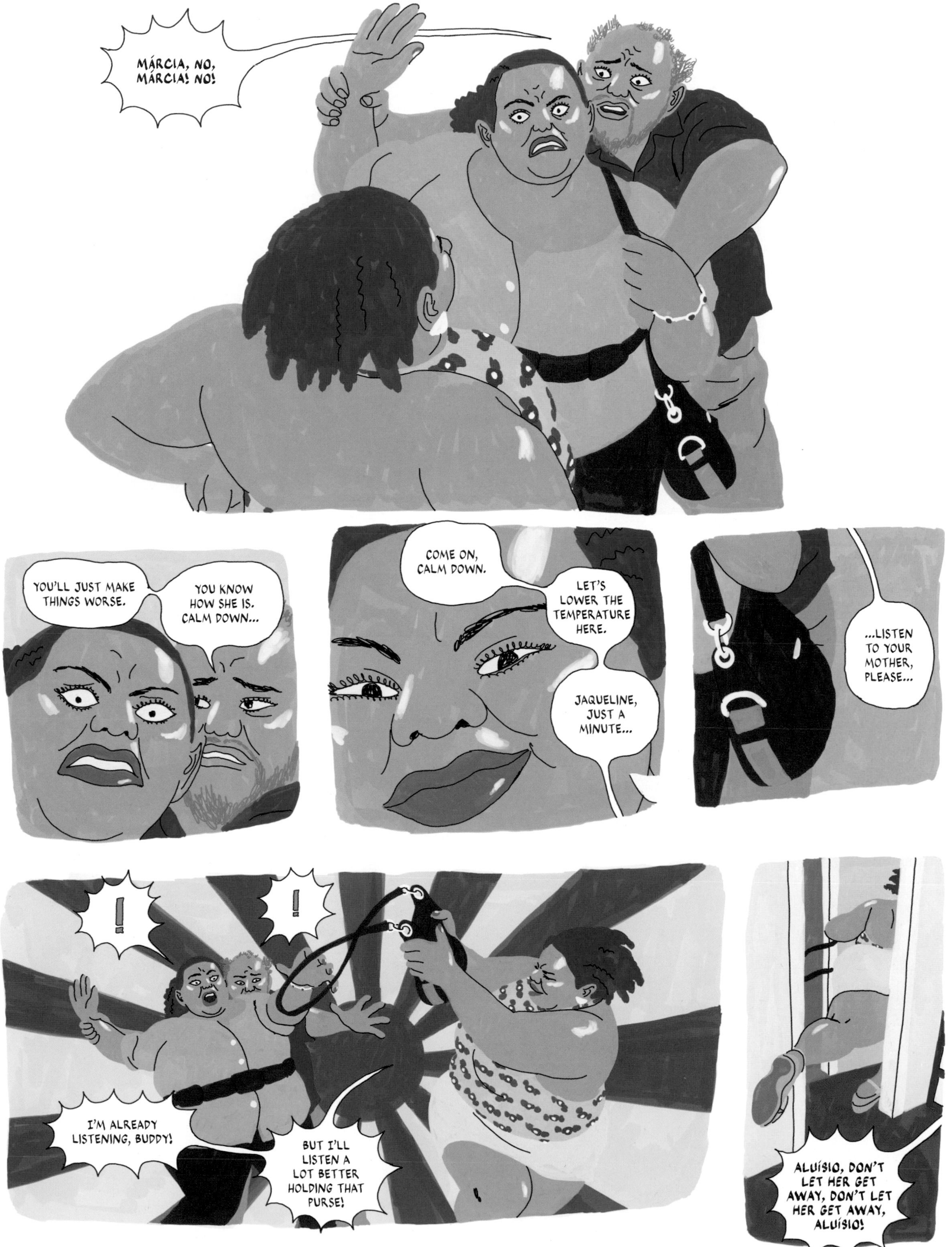
MÁRCIA, NO, MÁRCIA! NO!
YOU'LL JUST MAKE THINGS WORSE.
YOU KNOW HOW SHE IS. CALM DOWN...
COME ON, CALM DOWN.
LET'S LOWER THE TEMPERATURE HERE.
JAQUELINE, JUST A MINUTE...
...LISTEN TO YOUR MOTHER, PLEASE...
!
!
I'M ALREADY LISTENING, BUDDY!
BUT I'LL LISTEN A LOT BETTER HOLDING THAT PURSE!
ALUÍSIO, DON'T LET HER GET AWAY, DON'T LET HER GET AWAY, ALUÍSIO!

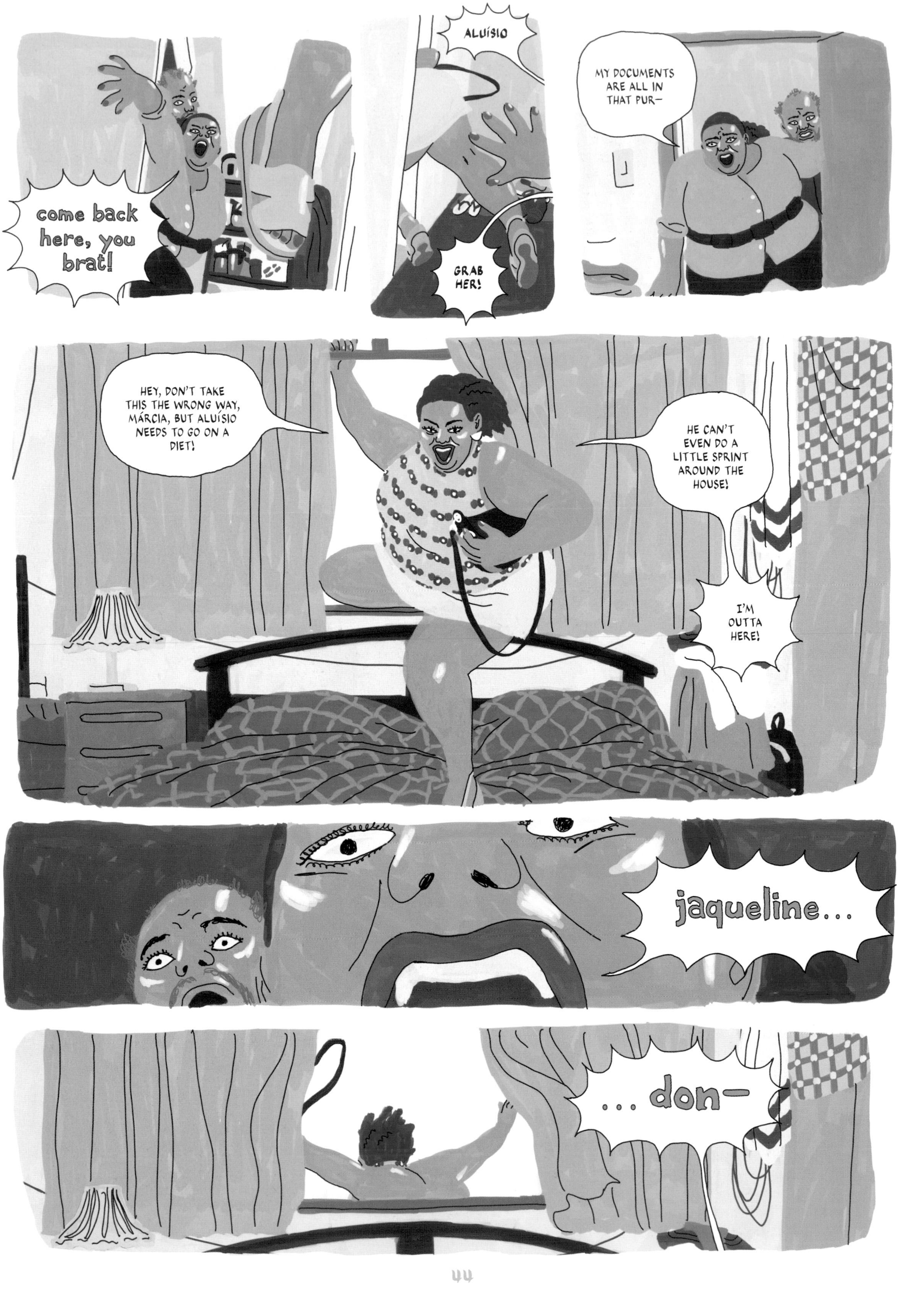
come back here, you brat!
ALUÍSIO
GRAB HER!
MY DOCUMENTS ARE ALL IN THAT PUR–
HEY, DON'T TAKE THIS THE WRONG WAY, MÁRCIA, BUT ALUÍSIO NEEDS TO GO ON A DIET!
HE CAN'T EVEN DO A LITTLE SPRINT AROUND THE HOUSE!
I'M OUTTA HERE!
jaqueline...
... don–

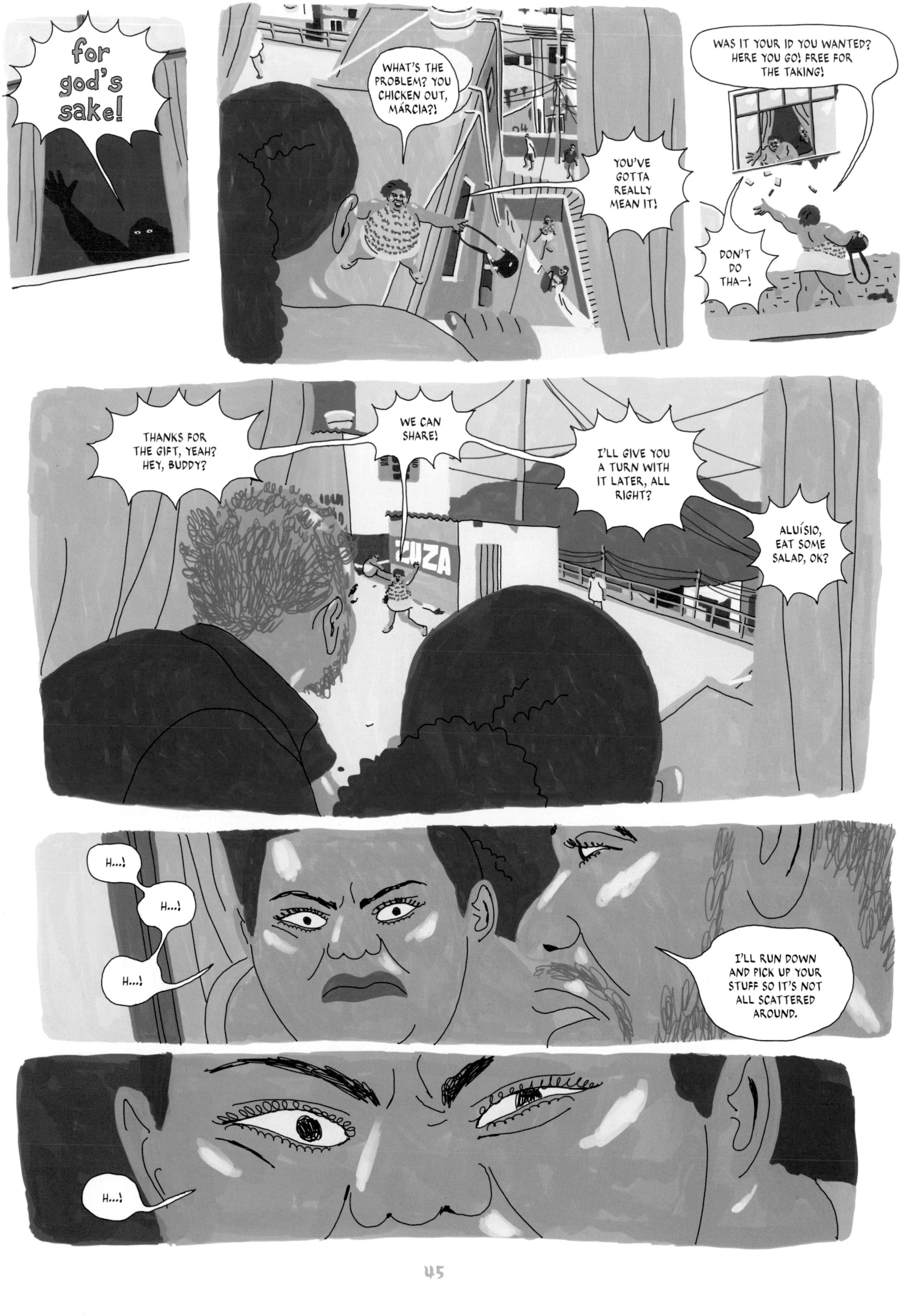
for god's sake!
WHAT'S THE PROBLEM? YOU CHICKEN OUT, MÁRCIA?!
YOU'VE GOTTA REALLY MEAN IT!
WAS IT YOUR ID YOU WANTED? HERE YOU GO! FREE FOR THE TAKING!
DON'T DO THA—!
THANKS FOR THE GIFT, YEAH? HEY, BUDDY?
WE CAN SHARE!
I'LL GIVE YOU A TURN WITH IT LATER, ALL RIGHT?
ALUÍSIO, EAT SOME SALAD, OK?
ZUZA
H...!
H...!
H...!
I'LL RUN DOWN AND PICK UP YOUR STUFF SO IT'S NOT ALL SCATTERED AROUND.
H...!

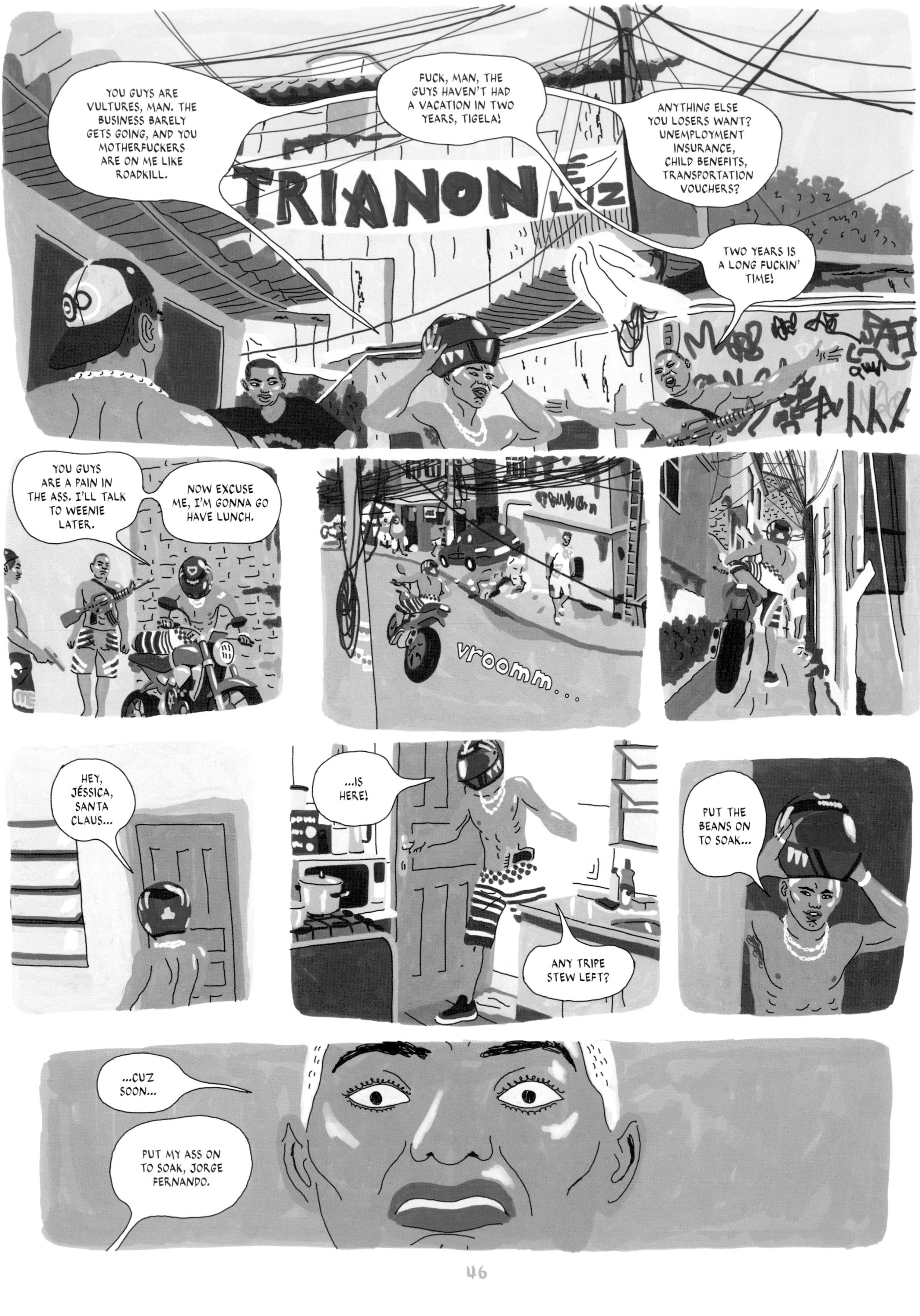
YOU GUYS ARE VULTURES, MAN. THE BUSINESS BARELY GETS GOING, AND YOU MOTHERFUCKERS ARE ON ME LIKE ROADKILL.
FUCK, MAN, THE GUYS HAVEN'T HAD A VACATION IN TWO YEARS, TIGELA!
ANYTHING ELSE YOU LOSERS WANT? UNEMPLOYMENT INSURANCE, CHILD BENEFITS, TRANSPORTATION VOUCHERS?
TRIANON
LUZ
TWO YEARS IS A LONG FUCKIN' TIME!
YOU GUYS ARE A PAIN IN THE ASS. I'LL TALK TO WEENIE LATER.
NOW EXCUSE ME, I'M GONNA GO HAVE LUNCH.
vroomm...
HEY, JÉSSICA, SANTA CLAUS...
...IS HERE!
ANY TRIPE STEW LEFT?
PUT THE BEANS ON TO SOAK...
...CUZ SOON...
PUT MY ASS ON TO SOAK, JORGE FERNANDO.

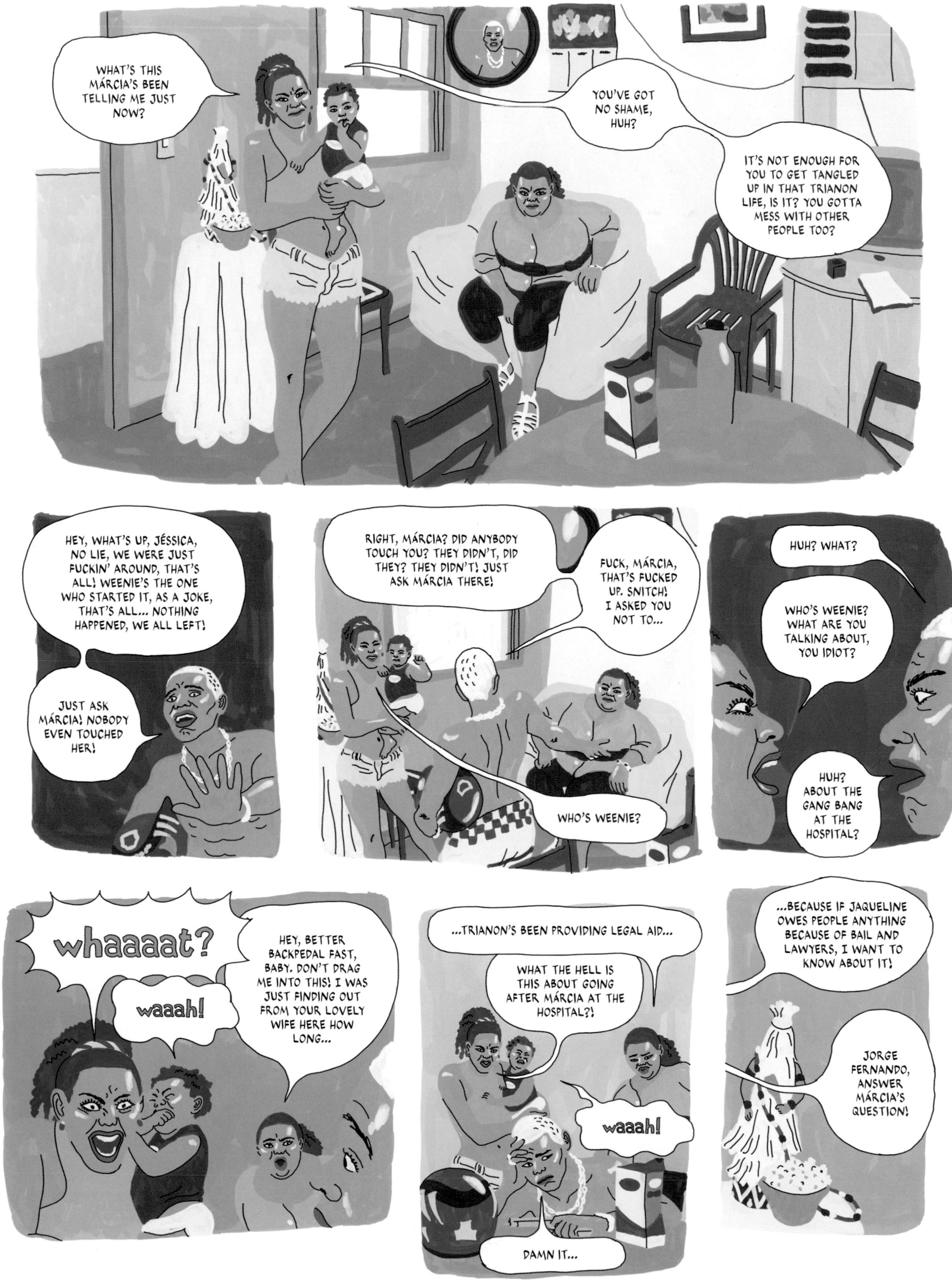
WHAT'S THIS MÁRCIA'S BEEN TELLING ME JUST NOW?
YOU'VE GOT NO SHAME, HUH?
IT'S NOT ENOUGH FOR YOU TO GET TANGLED UP IN THAT TRIANON LIFE, IS IT? YOU GOTTA MESS WITH OTHER PEOPLE TOO?
HEY, WHAT'S UP, JÉSSICA, NO LIE, WE WERE JUST FUCKIN' AROUND, THAT'S ALL! WEENIE'S THE ONE WHO STARTED IT, AS A JOKE, THAT'S ALL... NOTHING HAPPENED, WE ALL LEFT!
JUST ASK MÁRCIA! NOBODY EVEN TOUCHED HER!
RIGHT, MÁRCIA? DID ANYBODY TOUCH YOU? THEY DIDN'T, DID THEY? THEY DIDN'T! JUST ASK MÁRCIA THERE!
FUCK, MÁRCIA, THAT'S FUCKED UP. SNITCH! I ASKED YOU NOT TO...
WHO'S WEENIE?
HUH? WHAT?
WHO'S WEENIE? WHAT ARE YOU TALKING ABOUT, YOU IDIOT?
HUH? ABOUT THE GANG BANG AT THE HOSPITAL?
whaaaat?
waaah!
HEY, BETTER BACKPEDAL FAST, BABY. DON'T DRAG ME INTO THIS! I WAS JUST FINDING OUT FROM YOUR LOVELY WIFE HERE HOW LONG...
...TRIANON'S BEEN PROVIDING LEGAL AID...
WHAT THE HELL IS THIS ABOUT GOING AFTER MÁRCIA AT THE HOSPITAL?!
waaah!
DAMN IT...
...BECAUSE IF JAQUELINE OWES PEOPLE ANYTHING BECAUSE OF BAIL AND LAWYERS, I WANT TO KNOW ABOUT IT!
JORGE FERNANDO, ANSWER MÁRCIA'S QUESTION!

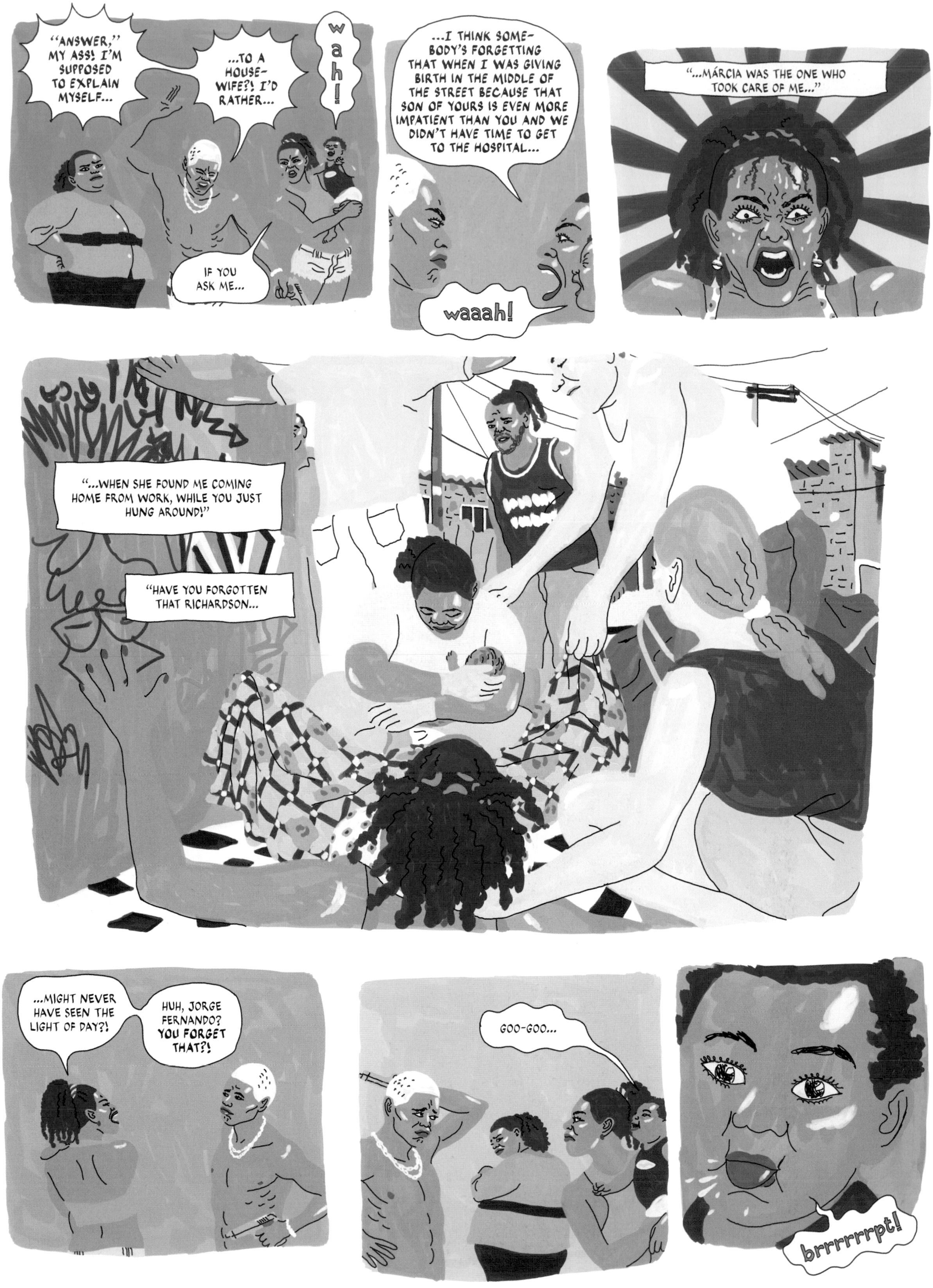
"ANSWER," MY ASS! I'M SUPPOSED TO EXPLAIN MYSELF...
...TO A HOUSE-WIFE?! I'D RATHER...
wah!
IF YOU ASK ME...
...I THINK SOME-BODY'S FORGETTING THAT WHEN I WAS GIVING BIRTH IN THE MIDDLE OF THE STREET BECAUSE THAT SON OF YOURS IS EVEN MORE IMPATIENT THAN YOU AND WE DIDN'T HAVE TIME TO GET TO THE HOSPITAL...
waaah!
"...MÁRCIA WAS THE ONE WHO TOOK CARE OF ME..."
"...WHEN SHE FOUND ME COMING HOME FROM WORK, WHILE YOU JUST HUNG AROUND!"
"HAVE YOU FORGOTTEN THAT RICHARDSON...
...MIGHT NEVER HAVE SEEN THE LIGHT OF DAY?!
HUH, JORGE FERNANDO? YOU FORGET THAT?!
GOO-GOO...
brrrrrrpt!

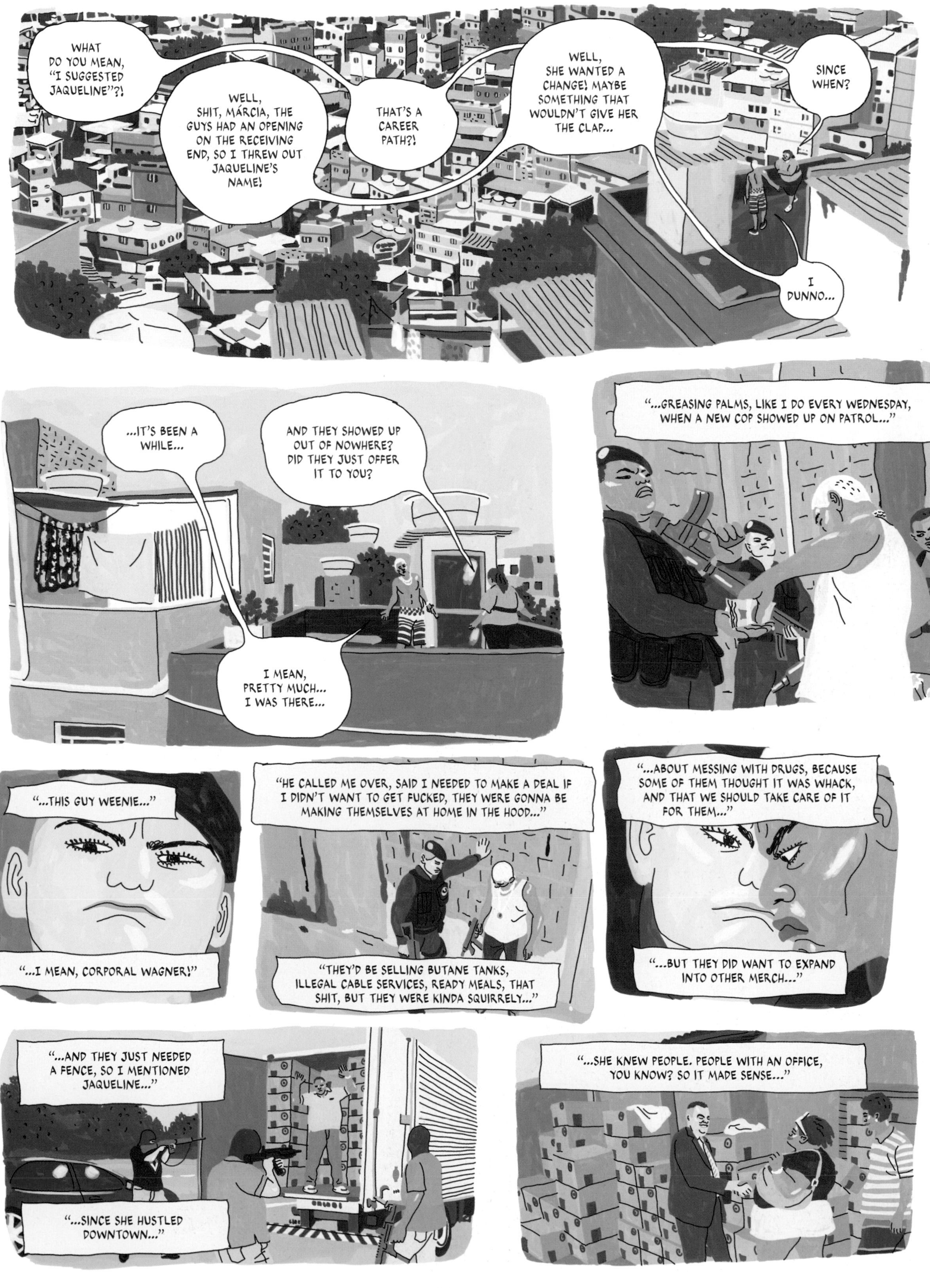
WHAT DO YOU MEAN, "I SUGGESTED JAQUELINE"?!
WELL, SHIT, MÁRCIA, THE GUYS HAD AN OPENING ON THE RECEIVING END, SO I THREW OUT JAQUELINE'S NAME!
THAT'S A CAREER PATH?!
WELL, SHE WANTED A CHANGE! MAYBE SOMETHING THAT WOULDN'T GIVE HER THE CLAP...
SINCE WHEN?
I DUNNO...
...IT'S BEEN A WHILE...
AND THEY SHOWED UP OUT OF NOWHERE? DID THEY JUST OFFER IT TO YOU?
I MEAN, PRETTY MUCH... I WAS THERE...
"...GREASING PALMS, LIKE I DO EVERY WEDNESDAY, WHEN A NEW COP SHOWED UP ON PATROL..."
"...THIS GUY WEENIE..."
"...I MEAN, CORPORAL WAGNER!"
"HE CALLED ME OVER, SAID I NEEDED TO MAKE A DEAL IF I DIDN'T WANT TO GET FUCKED, THEY WERE GONNA BE MAKING THEMSELVES AT HOME IN THE HOOD..."
"THEY'D BE SELLING BUTANE TANKS, ILLEGAL CABLE SERVICES, READY MEALS, THAT SHIT, BUT THEY WERE KINDA SQUIRRELY..."
"...ABOUT MESSING WITH DRUGS, BECAUSE SOME OF THEM THOUGHT IT WAS WHACK, AND THAT WE SHOULD TAKE CARE OF IT FOR THEM..."
"...BUT THEY DID WANT TO EXPAND INTO OTHER MERCH..."
"...AND THEY JUST NEEDED A FENCE, SO I MENTIONED JAQUELINE..."
"...SINCE SHE HUSTLED DOWNTOWN..."
"...SHE KNEW PEOPLE. PEOPLE WITH AN OFFICE, YOU KNOW? SO IT MADE SENSE..."

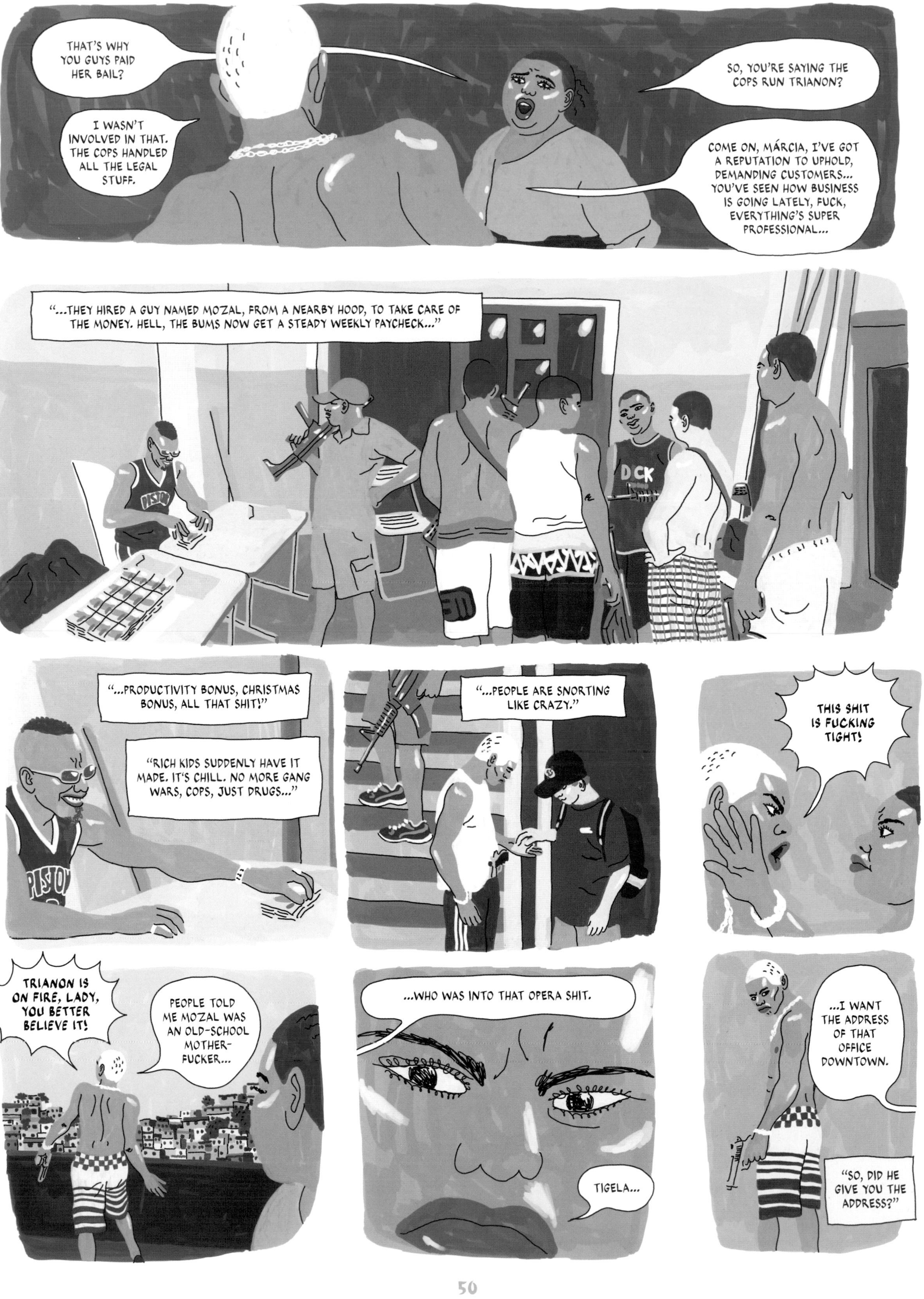
THAT'S WHY YOU GUYS PAID HER BAIL?
I WASN'T INVOLVED IN THAT. THE COPS HANDLED ALL THE LEGAL STUFF.
SO, YOU'RE SAYING THE COPS RUN TRIANON?
COME ON, MÁRCIA, I'VE GOT A REPUTATION TO UPHOLD, DEMANDING CUSTOMERS... YOU'VE SEEN HOW BUSINESS IS GOING LATELY, FUCK, EVERYTHING'S SUPER PROFESSIONAL...
"...THEY HIRED A GUY NAMED MOZAL, FROM A NEARBY HOOD, TO TAKE CARE OF THE MONEY. HELL, THE BUMS NOW GET A STEADY WEEKLY PAYCHECK..."
"...PRODUCTIVITY BONUS, CHRISTMAS BONUS, ALL THAT SHIT!"
"RICH KIDS SUDDENLY HAVE IT MADE. IT'S CHILL. NO MORE GANG WARS, COPS, JUST DRUGS..."
"...PEOPLE ARE SNORTING LIKE CRAZY."
THIS SHIT IS FUCKING TIGHT!
TRIANON IS ON FIRE, LADY, YOU BETTER BELIEVE IT!
PEOPLE TOLD ME MOZAL WAS AN OLD-SCHOOL MOTHER-FUCKER...
...WHO WAS INTO THAT OPERA SHIT.
TIGELA...
...I WANT THE ADDRESS OF THAT OFFICE DOWNTOWN.
"SO, DID HE GIVE YOU THE ADDRESS?"

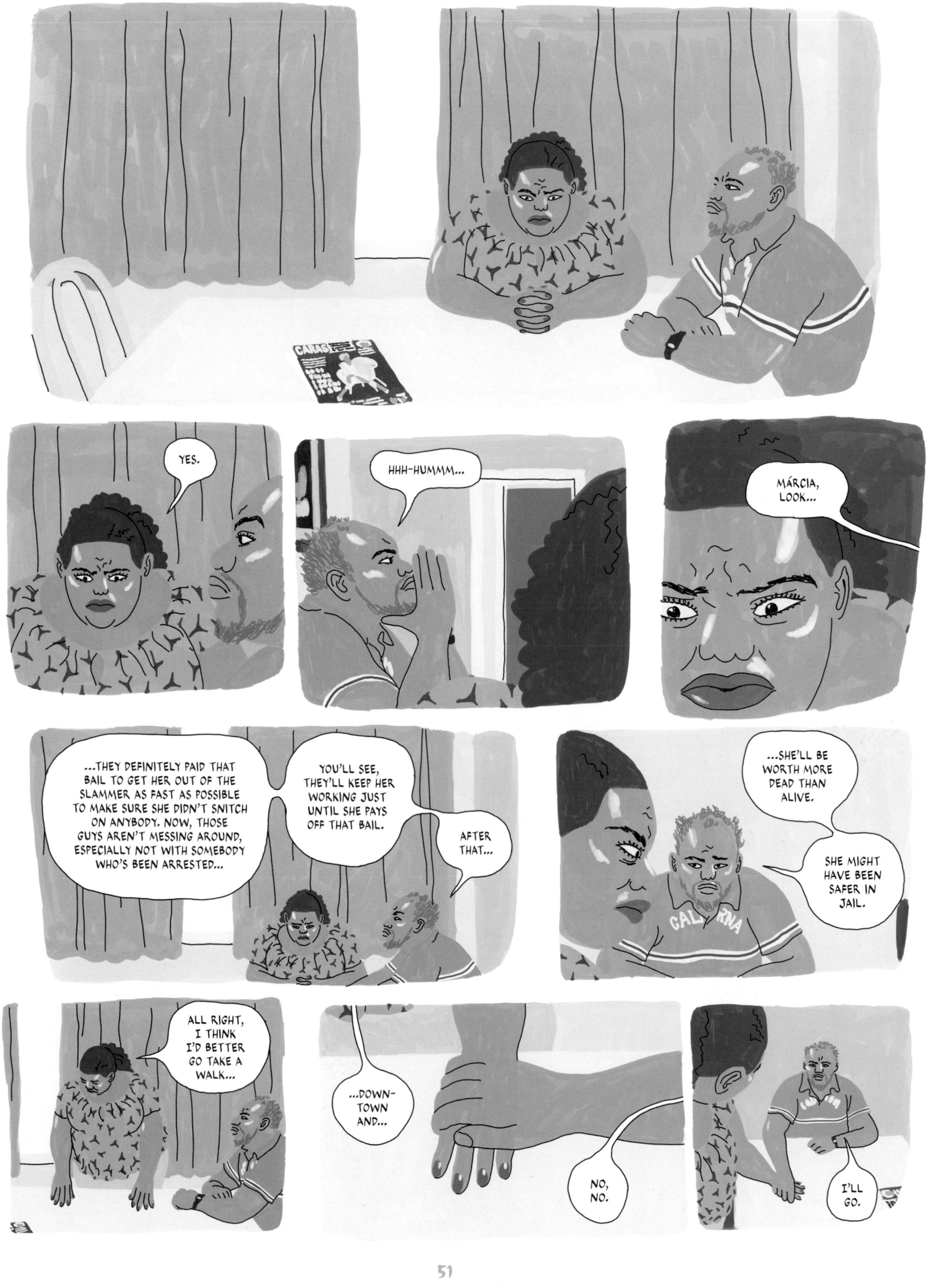
CARAS
YES.
HHH-HUMMM...
MÁRCIA, LOOK...
...THEY DEFINITELY PAID THAT BAIL TO GET HER OUT OF THE SLAMMER AS FAST AS POSSIBLE TO MAKE SURE SHE DIDN'T SNITCH ON ANYBODY. NOW, THOSE GUYS AREN'T MESSING AROUND, ESPECIALLY NOT WITH SOMEBODY WHO'S BEEN ARRESTED...
YOU'LL SEE, THEY'LL KEEP HER WORKING JUST UNTIL SHE PAYS OFF THAT BAIL.
AFTER THAT...
...SHE'LL BE WORTH MORE DEAD THAN ALIVE.
SHE MIGHT HAVE BEEN SAFER IN JAIL.
ALL RIGHT, I THINK I'D BETTER GO TAKE A WALK...
...DOWN-TOWN AND...
NO, NO.
I'LL GO.

YOU GAVE THE BOSS A GOOD SCARE, SUGAR, I'LL TELL YOU. FIRST THING I DID, I CALLED MARQUINHOS: "MARQUINHOS, HELP SUGAR!" RIGHT, MARQUINHOS?
YUP! I HEADED STRAIGHT FOR THE 27TH PRECINCT.
COME ON, GALVÃO, WHO DO YOU THINK I AM? DO YOU THINK I'D LET THOSE PIGS MAKE A FOOL OF ME? I'M NO FOOL!
THOSE PEOPLE AT THE 27TH ARE A PAIN IN THE ASS. THEY'VE...
EDIFICIO WALLACE GIMENEZ
...BEEN FUCKING WITH US FOREVER. IT'S LIKE THOSE FUCKERS DON'T LIKE MONEY!
MARQUINHOS REALLY HAS TO WORK FOR IT.
HEY, "WE DO WHAT WE CAN."
GOOD ONE, LAWYER-MAN!
BUT LOOK, DON'T GET USED TO IT, OKAY, SUGAR? IF THE BOSS GOES BANKRUPT, WHO WILL BAIL YOU OUT THEN, HUH? NOT EVEN YOUR MOTHER WILL BE ABLE TO IF THINGS GO SOUTH...
LUCKY YOU DIDN'T HAVE A CELL PHONE FOR THOSE GUYS TO GET INTO, OTHERWISE THAT WOULD HAVE BEEN A HUGE PAIN IN THE ASS.
THAT WASN'T LUCK, HONEY, THAT WAS ALL STRATEGY...

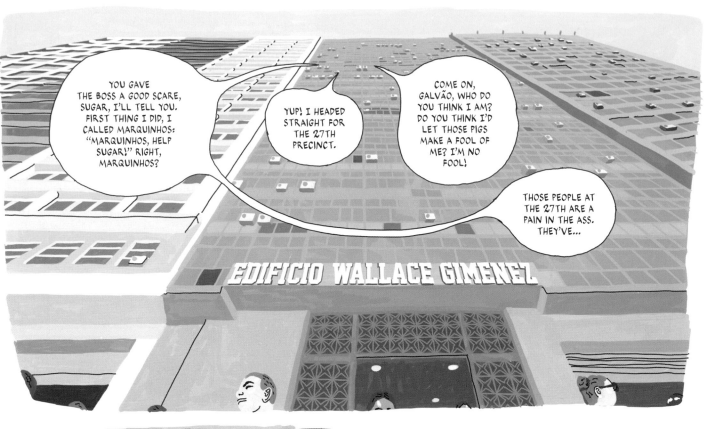

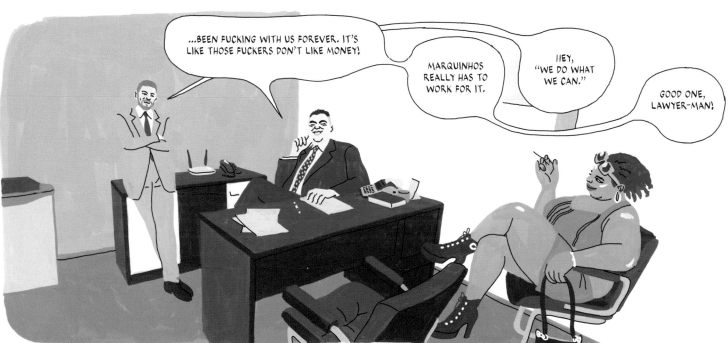

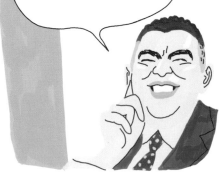

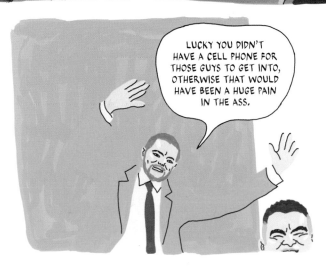

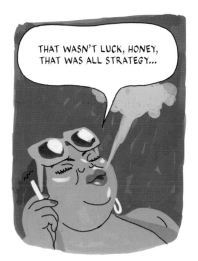

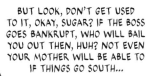

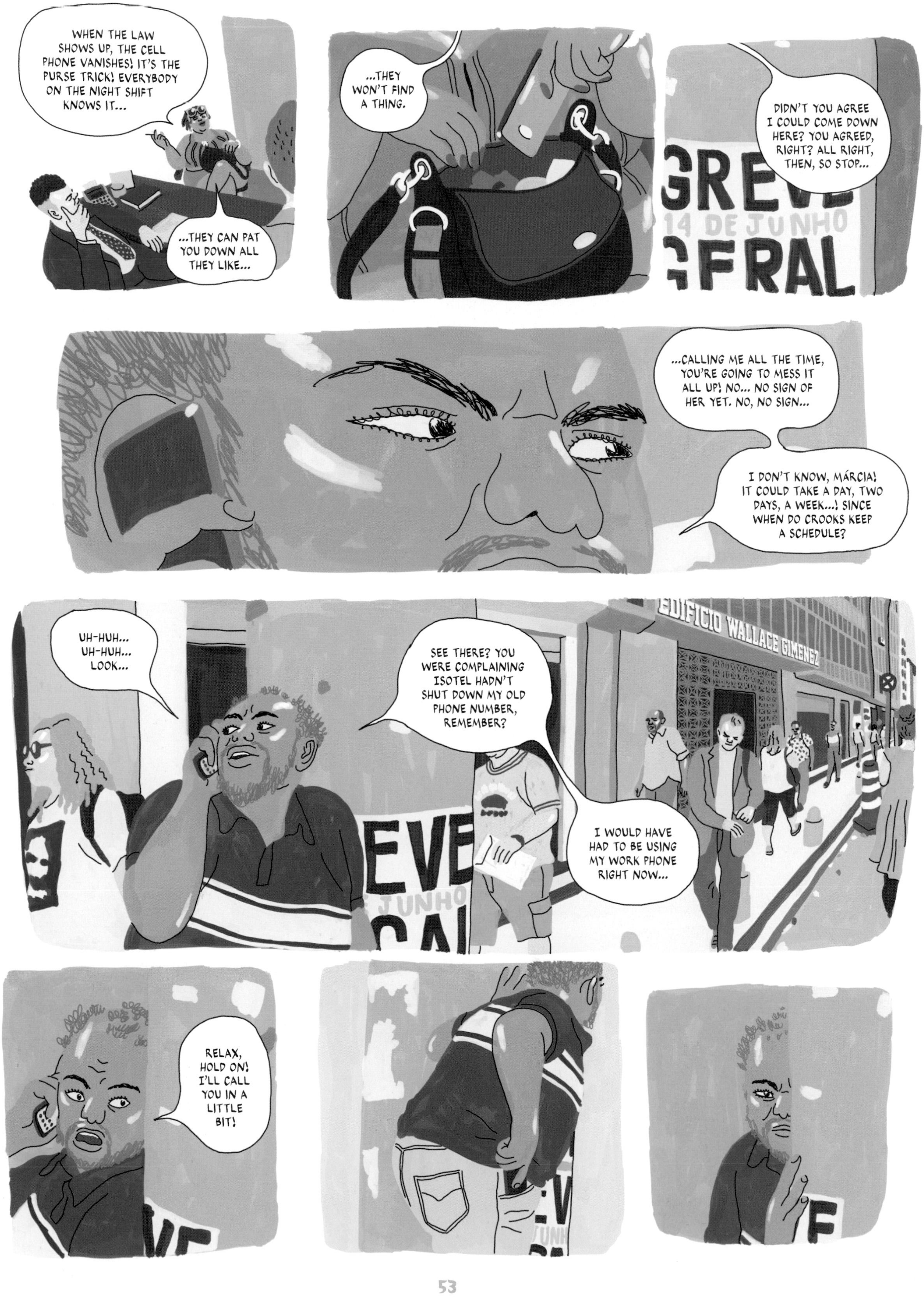
WHEN THE LAW SHOWS UP, THE CELL PHONE VANISHES! IT'S THE PURSE TRICK! EVERYBODY ON THE NIGHT SHIFT KNOWS IT...
...THEY CAN PAT YOU DOWN ALL THEY LIKE...
...THEY WON'T FIND A THING.
DIDN'T YOU AGREE I COULD COME DOWN HERE? YOU AGREED, RIGHT? ALL RIGHT, THEN, SO STOP...
GREVE
14 DE JUNHO
GERAL
...CALLING ME ALL THE TIME, YOU'RE GOING TO MESS IT ALL UP! NO... NO SIGN OF HER YET. NO, NO SIGN...
I DON'T KNOW, MÁRCIA! IT COULD TAKE A DAY, TWO DAYS, A WEEK...! SINCE WHEN DO CROOKS KEEP A SCHEDULE?
EDIFICIO WALLACE GIMENEZ
UH-HUH... UH-HUH... LOOK...
SEE THERE? YOU WERE COMPLAINING ISOTEL HADN'T SHUT DOWN MY OLD PHONE NUMBER, REMEMBER?
I WOULD HAVE HAD TO BE USING MY WORK PHONE RIGHT NOW...
RELAX, HOLD ON! I'LL CALL YOU IN A LITTLE BIT!

WALLACE GIMENEZ
vroom...
honk...
brrrrh...
ituá
PAGOS
HOLD IT RIGHT THERE, JAQUELINE! I WANT TO TALK TO YOU!

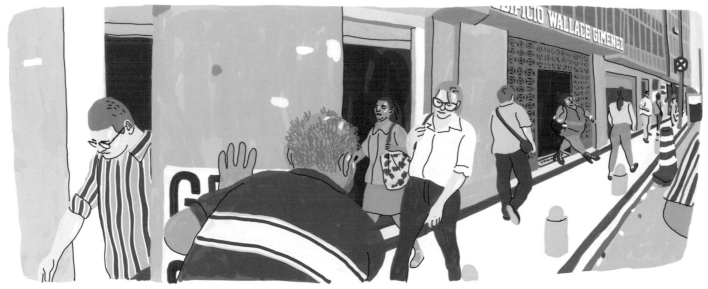

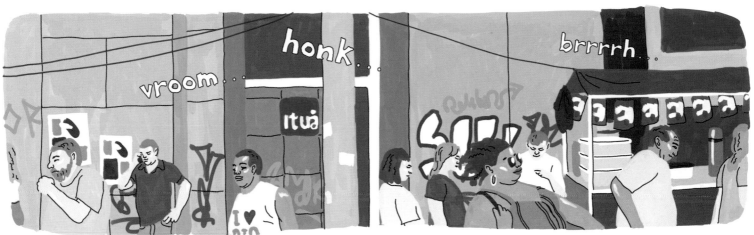

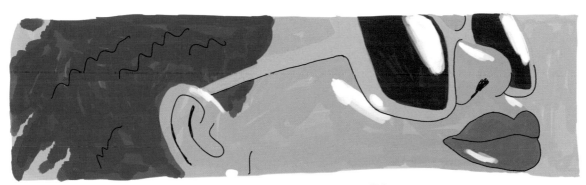

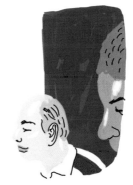

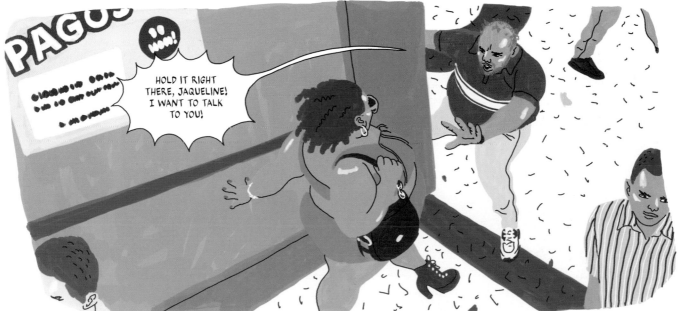

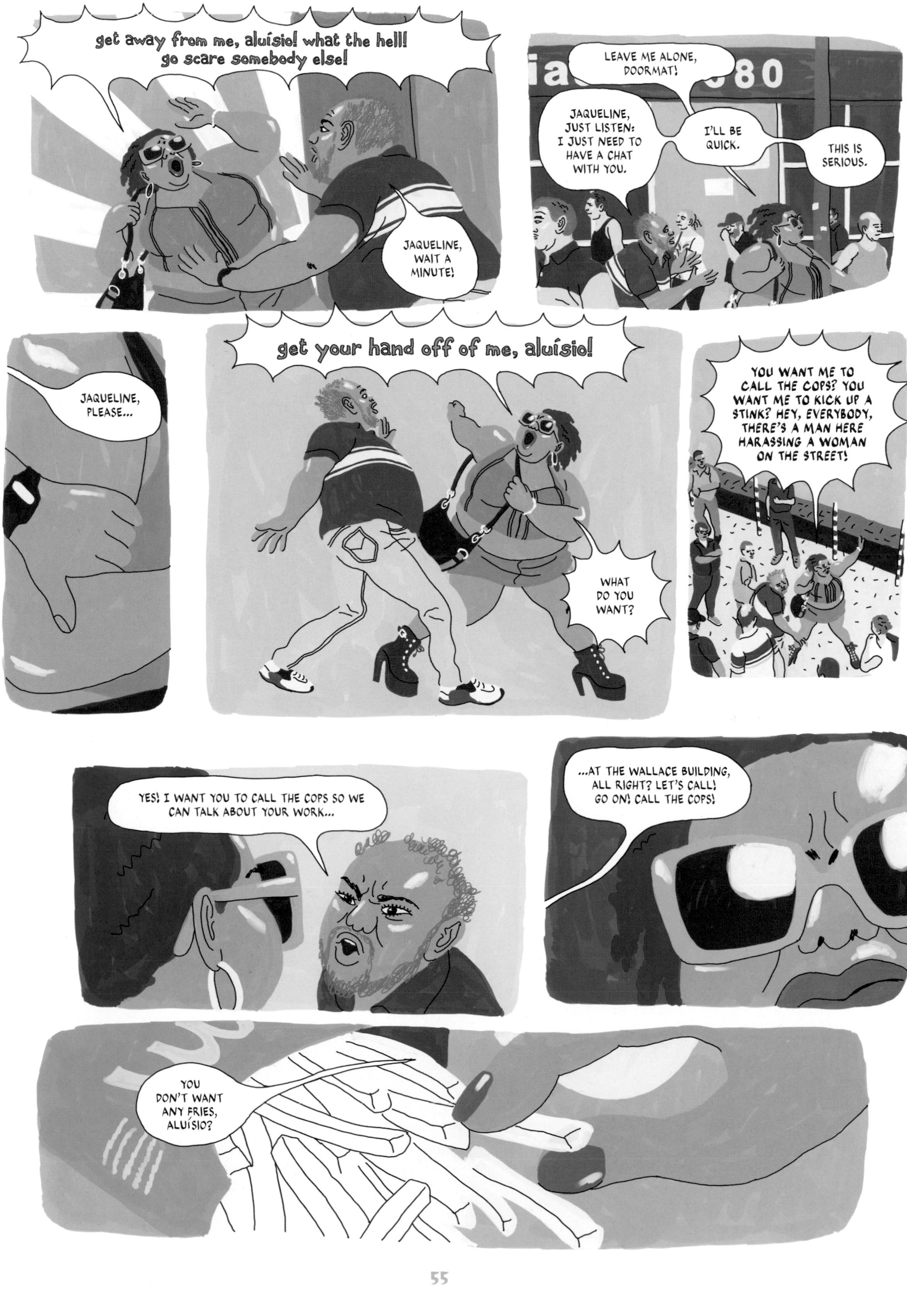
get away from me, aluísio! what the hell! go scare somebody else!
JAQUELINE, WAIT A MINUTE!
LEAVE ME ALONE, DOORMAT!
JAQUELINE, JUST LISTEN: I JUST NEED TO HAVE A CHAT WITH YOU.
I'LL BE QUICK.
THIS IS SERIOUS.
JAQUELINE, PLEASE...
get your hand off of me, aluísio!
WHAT DO YOU WANT?
YOU WANT ME TO CALL THE COPS? YOU WANT ME TO KICK UP A STINK? HEY, EVERYBODY, THERE'S A MAN HERE HARASSING A WOMAN ON THE STREET!
YES! I WANT YOU TO CALL THE COPS SO WE CAN TALK ABOUT YOUR WORK...
...AT THE WALLACE BUILDING, ALL RIGHT? LET'S CALL! GO ON! CALL THE COPS!
YOU DON'T WANT ANY FRIES, ALUÍSIO?

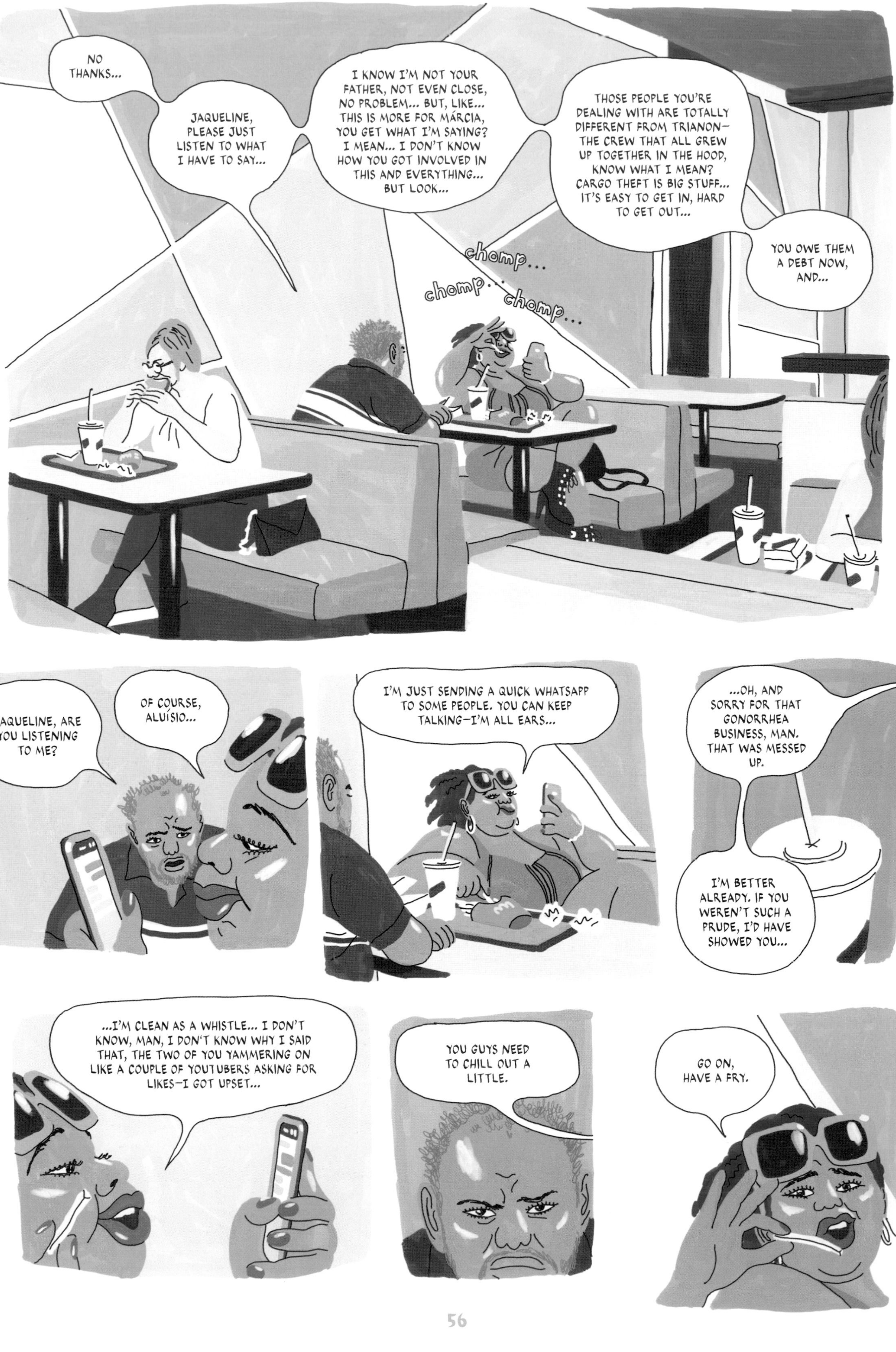
NO THANKS...
JAQUELINE, PLEASE JUST LISTEN TO WHAT I HAVE TO SAY...
I KNOW I'M NOT YOUR FATHER, NOT EVEN CLOSE, NO PROBLEM... BUT, LIKE... THIS IS MORE FOR MÁRCIA, YOU GET WHAT I'M SAYING? I MEAN... I DON'T KNOW HOW YOU GOT INVOLVED IN THIS AND EVERYTHING... BUT LOOK...
THOSE PEOPLE YOU'RE DEALING WITH ARE TOTALLY DIFFERENT FROM TRIANON—THE CREW THAT ALL GREW UP TOGETHER IN THE HOOD, KNOW WHAT I MEAN? CARGO THEFT IS BIG STUFF... IT'S EASY TO GET IN, HARD TO GET OUT...
YOU OWE THEM A DEBT NOW, AND...
chomp...
chomp...
chomp...
JAQUELINE, ARE YOU LISTENING TO ME?
OF COURSE, ALUÍSIO...
I'M JUST SENDING A QUICK WHATSAPP TO SOME PEOPLE. YOU CAN KEEP TALKING—I'M ALL EARS...
...OH, AND SORRY FOR THAT GONORRHEA BUSINESS, MAN. THAT WAS MESSED UP.
I'M BETTER ALREADY. IF YOU WEREN'T SUCH A PRUDE, I'D HAVE SHOWED YOU...
...I'M CLEAN AS A WHISTLE... I DON'T KNOW, MAN, I DON'T KNOW WHY I SAID THAT, THE TWO OF YOU YAMMERING ON LIKE A COUPLE OF YOUTUBERS ASKING FOR LIKES—I GOT UPSET...
YOU GUYS NEED TO CHILL OUT A LITTLE.
GO ON, HAVE A FRY.

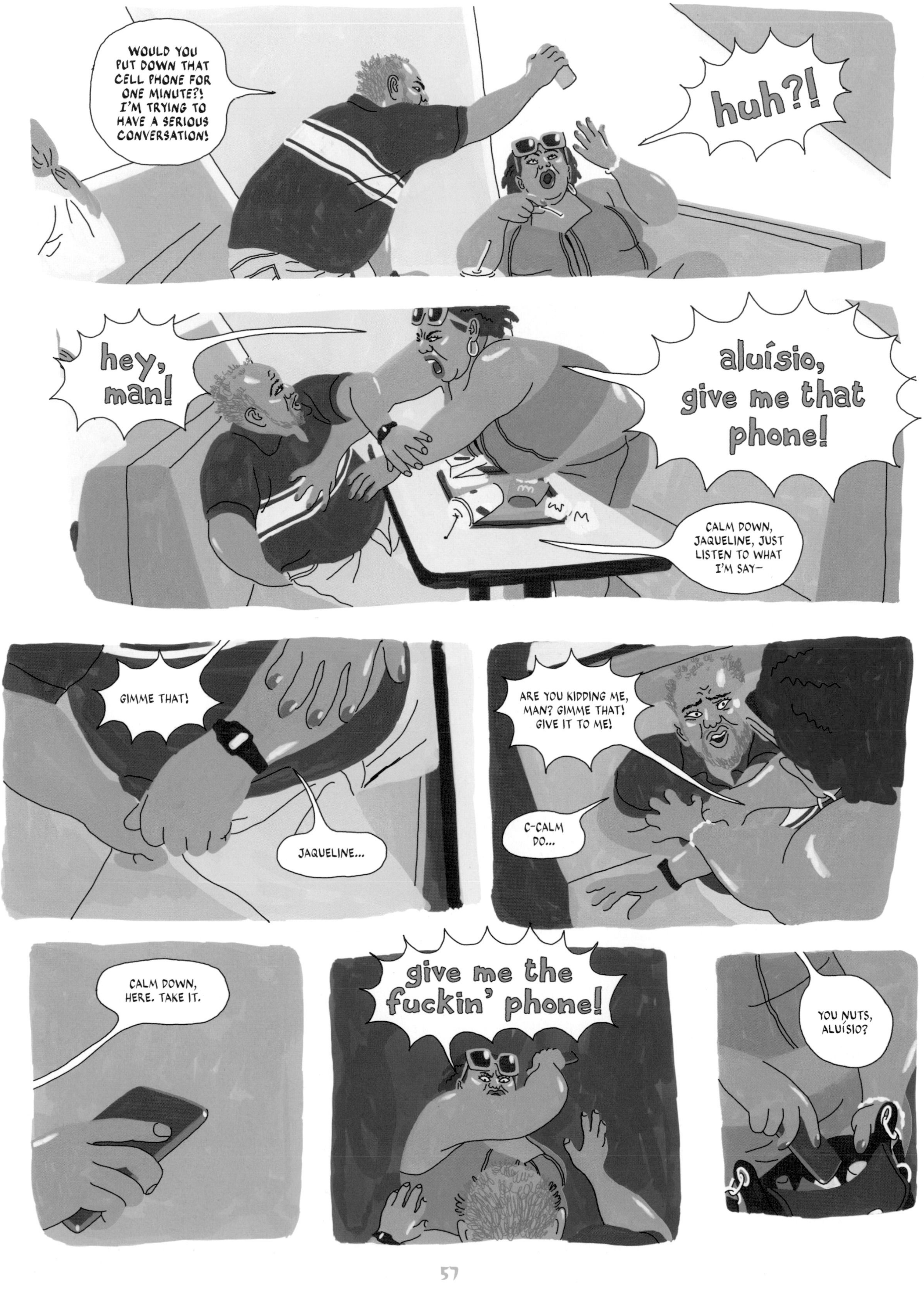
WOULD YOU PUT DOWN THAT CELL PHONE FOR ONE MINUTE?! I'M TRYING TO HAVE A SERIOUS CONVERSATION!
huh?!
hey, man!
aluísio, give me that phone!
CALM DOWN, JAQUELINE, JUST LISTEN TO WHAT I'M SAY–
GIMME THAT!
JAQUELINE...
ARE YOU KIDDING ME, MAN? GIMME THAT! GIVE IT TO ME!
C-CALM DO...
CALM DOWN, HERE. TAKE IT.
give me the fuckin' phone!
YOU NUTS, ALUÍSIO?

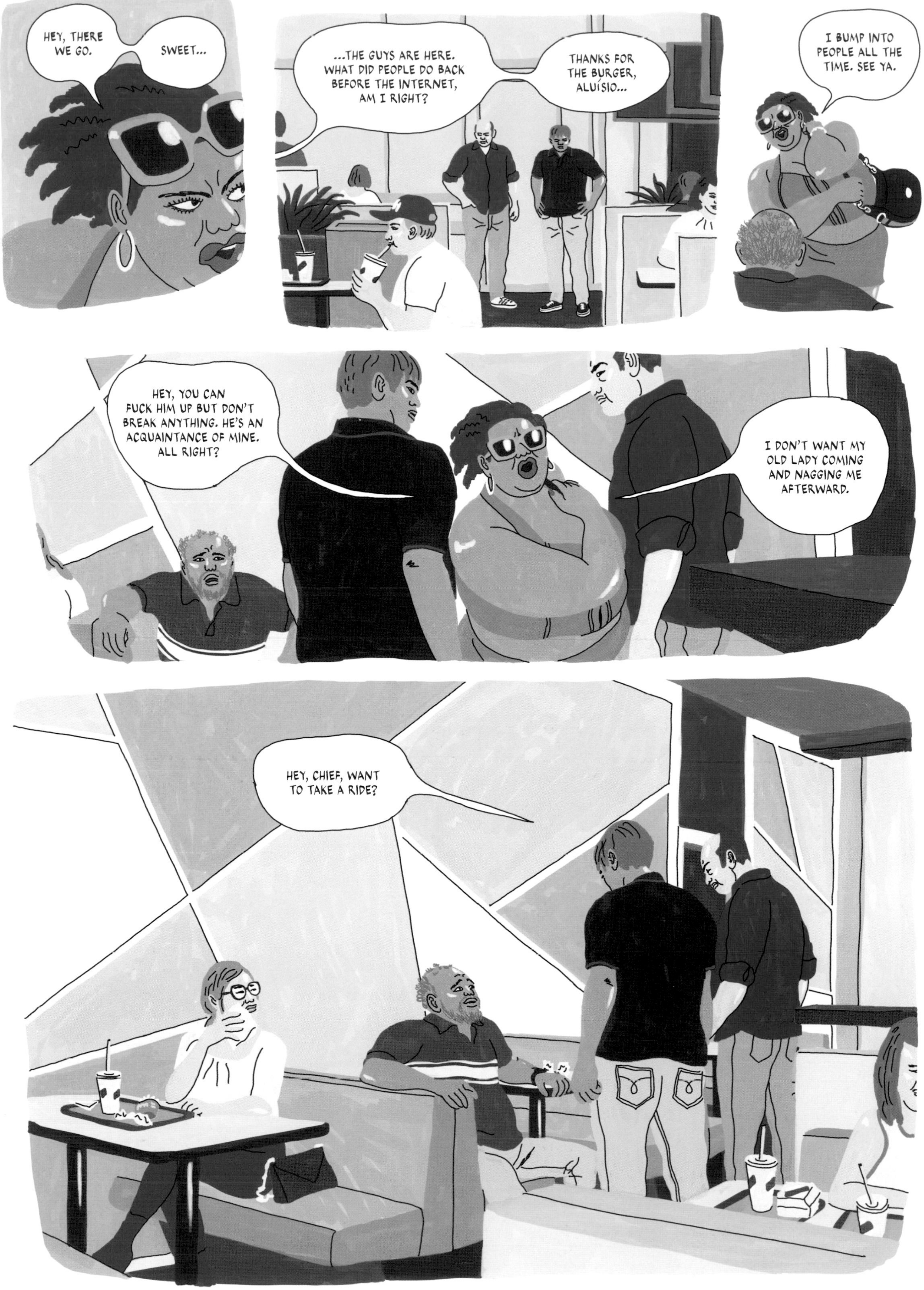
HEY, THERE WE GO.
SWEET...
...THE GUYS ARE HERE. WHAT DID PEOPLE DO BACK BEFORE THE INTERNET, AM I RIGHT?
THANKS FOR THE BURGER, ALUÍSIO...
I BUMP INTO PEOPLE ALL THE TIME. SEE YA.
HEY, YOU CAN FUCK HIM UP BUT DON'T BREAK ANYTHING. HE'S AN ACQUAINTANCE OF MINE. ALL RIGHT?
I DON'T WANT MY OLD LADY COMING AND NAGGING ME AFTERWARD.
HEY, CHIEF, WANT TO TAKE A RIDE?

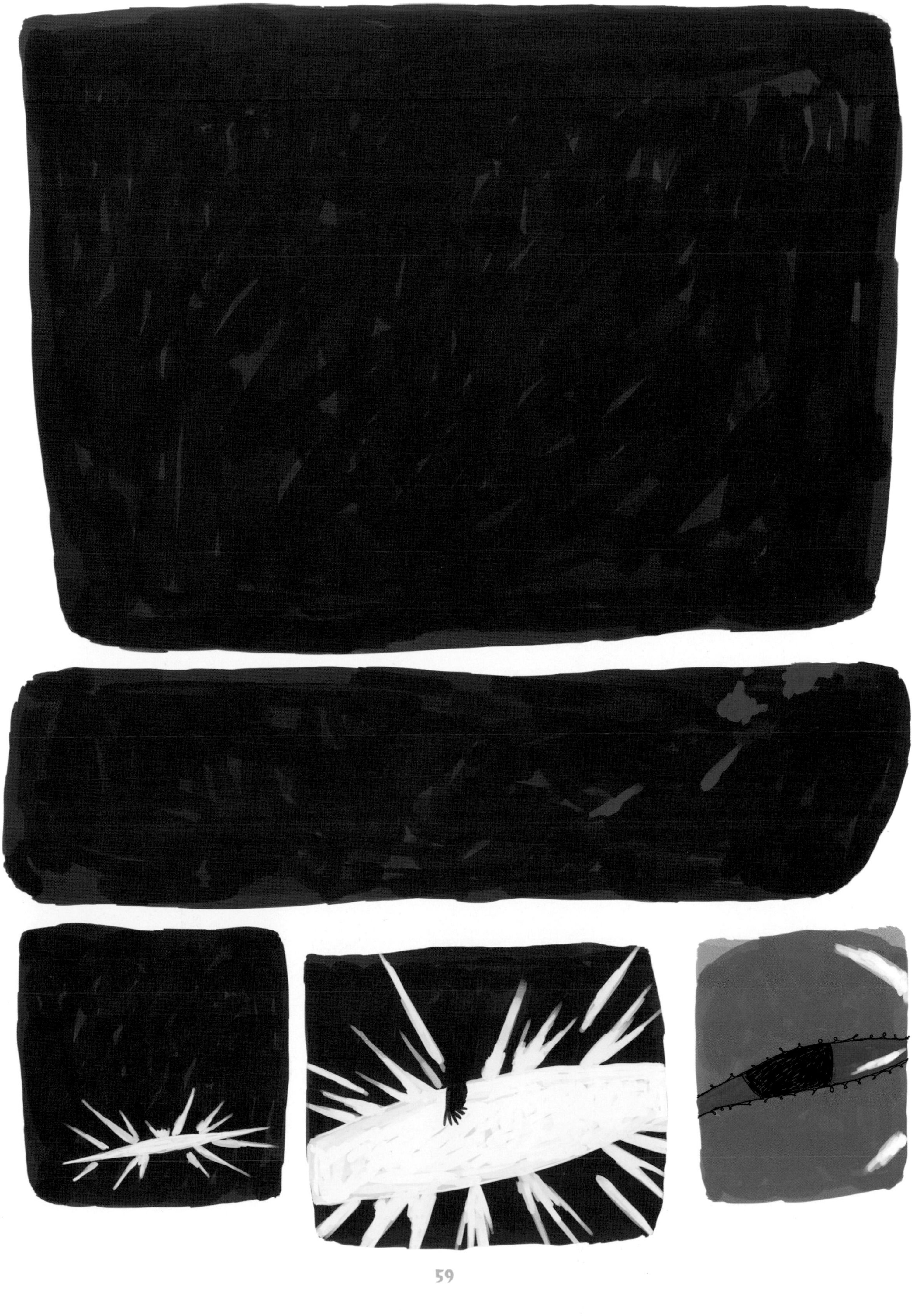

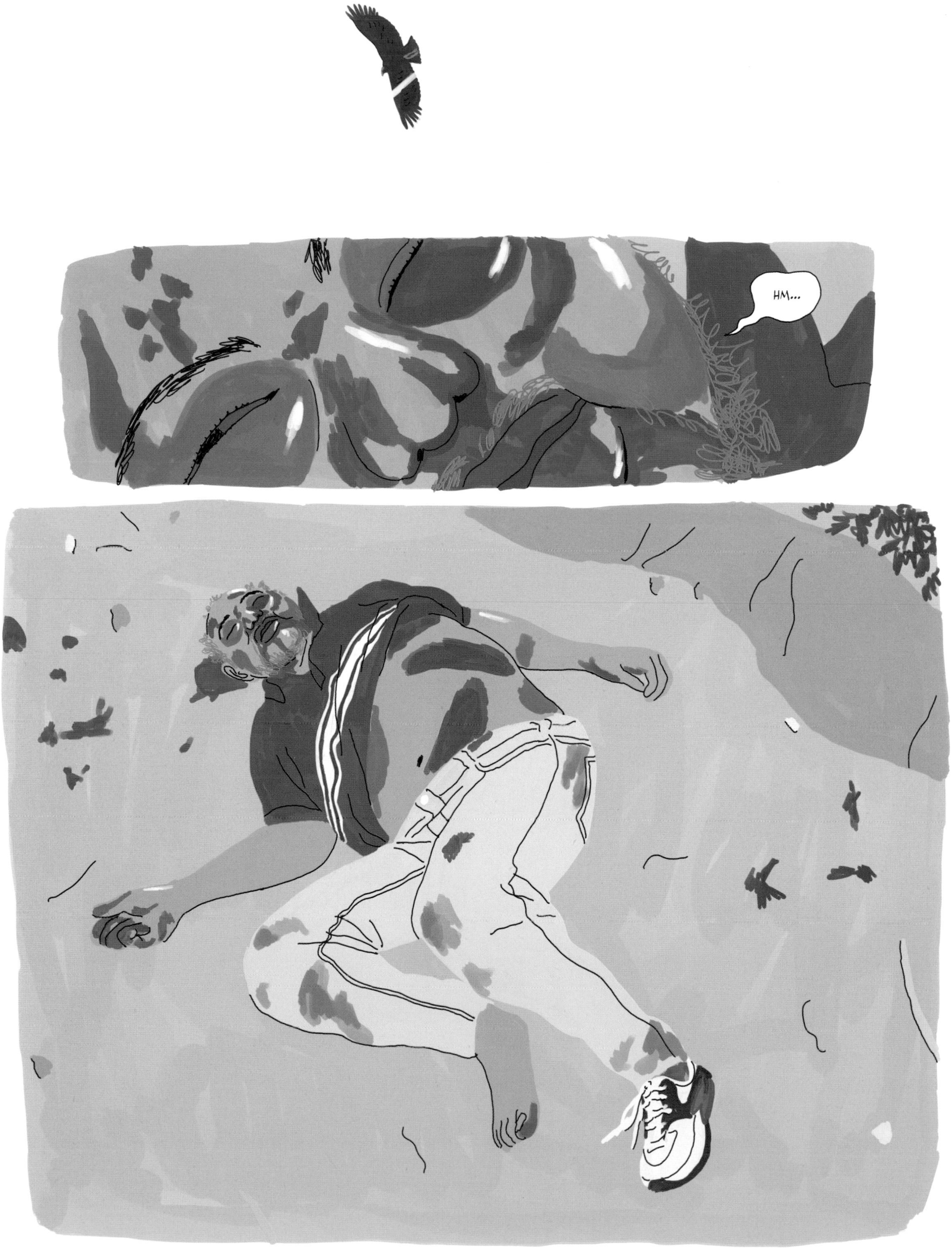
HM...

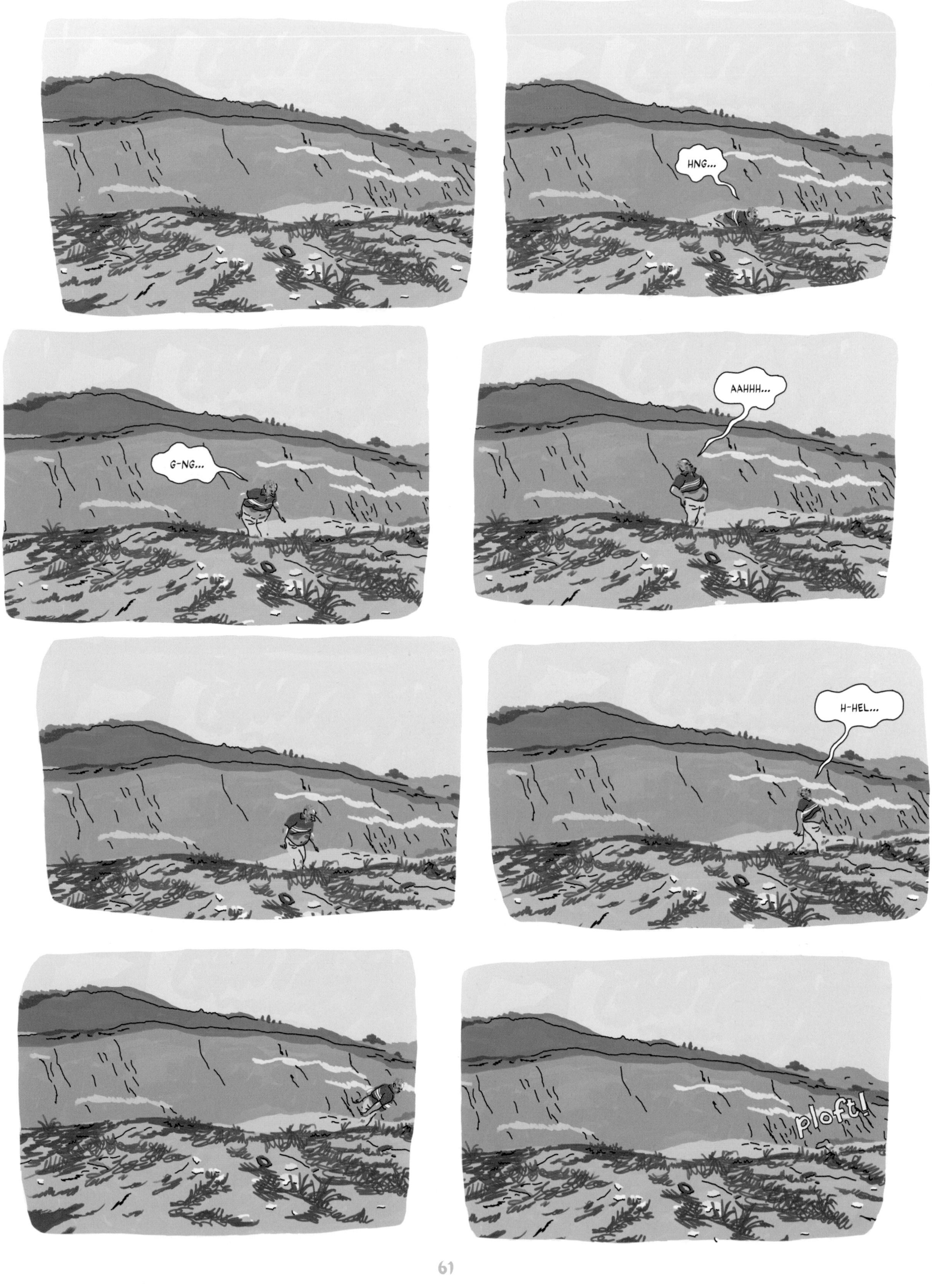
HNG...
G-NG...
AAHHH...
H-HEL...
ploft!

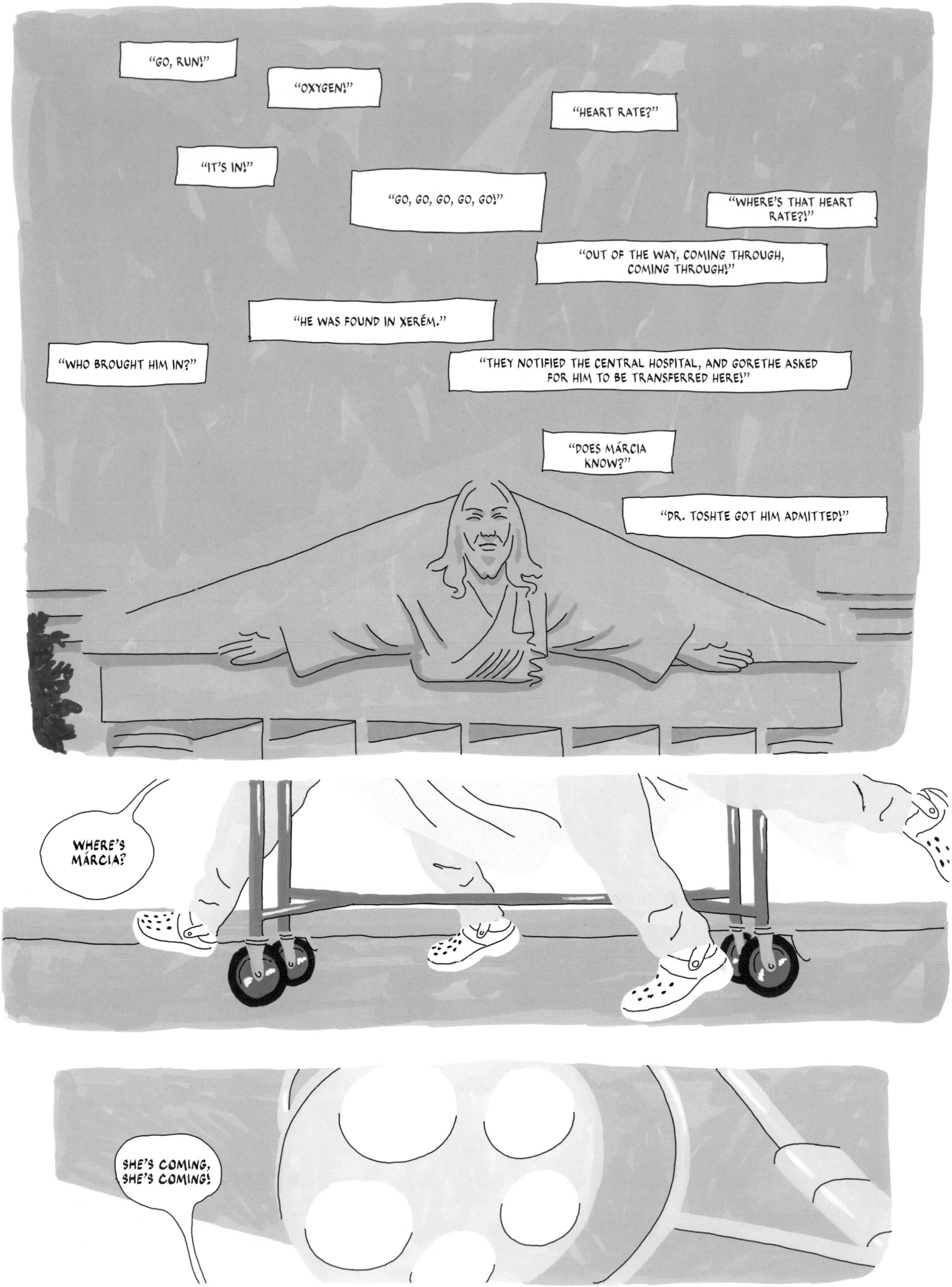
"GO, RUN!"
"OXYGEN!"
"HEART RATE?"
"IT'S IN!"
"GO, GO, GO, GO, GO!"
"WHERE'S THAT HEART RATE?!"
"OUT OF THE WAY, COMING THROUGH, COMING THROUGH!"
"HE WAS FOUND IN XERÉM."
"WHO BROUGHT HIM IN?"
"THEY NOTIFIED THE CENTRAL HOSPITAL, AND GORETHE ASKED FOR HIM TO BE TRANSFERRED HERE!"
"DOES MÁRCIA KNOW?"
"DR. TOSHTE GOT HIM ADMITTED!"
WHERE'S MÁRCIA?
SHE'S COMING, SHE'S COMING!

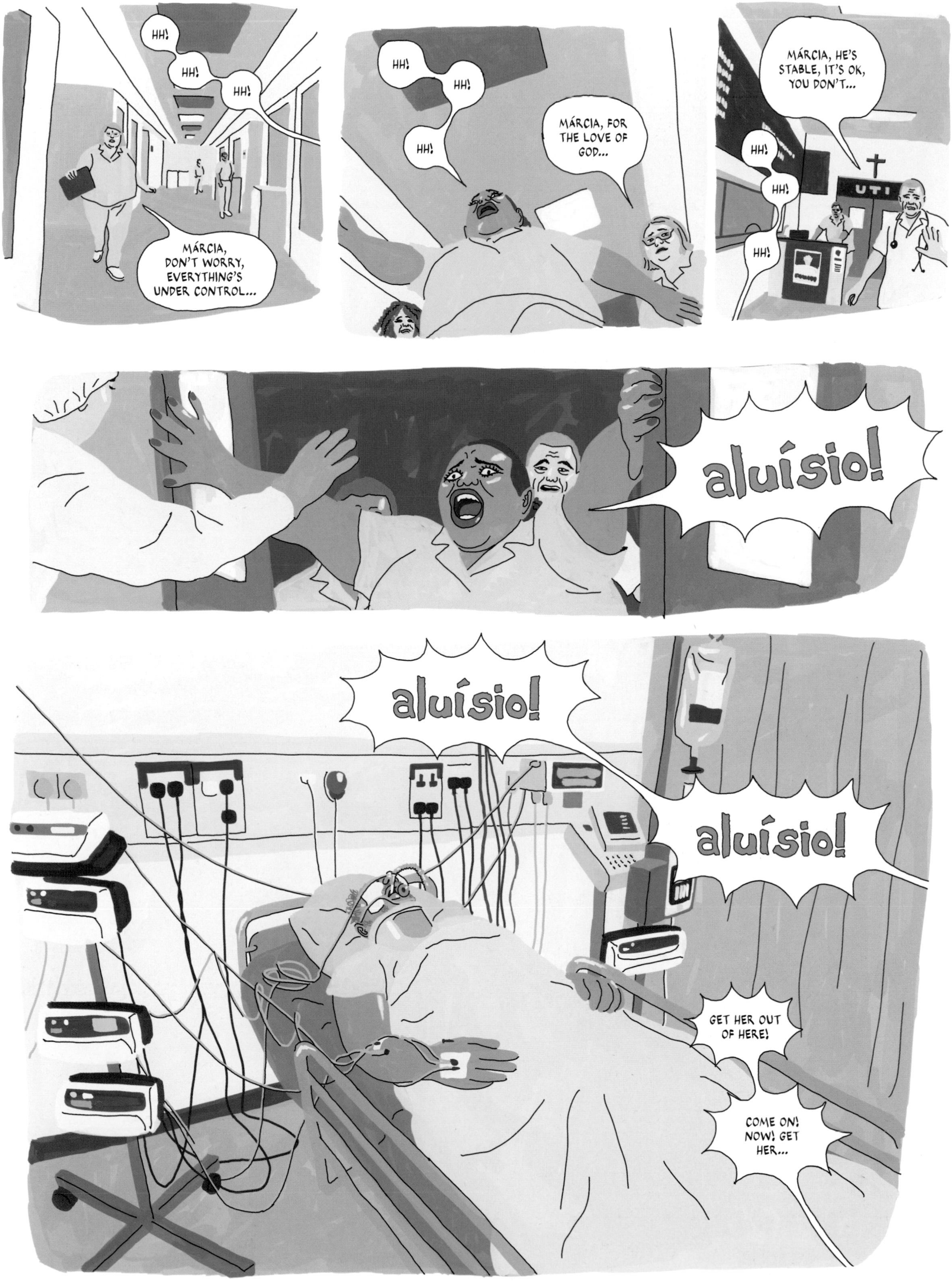
HH!
HH!
HH!
MÁRCIA, DON'T WORRY, EVERYTHING'S UNDER CONTROL...
HH!
HH!
HH!
MÁRCIA, FOR THE LOVE OF GOD...
MÁRCIA, HE'S STABLE, IT'S OK, YOU DON'T...
HH!
HH!
HH!
UTI
aluísio!
aluísio!
aluísio!
GET HER OUT OF HERE!
COME ON! NOW! GET HER...

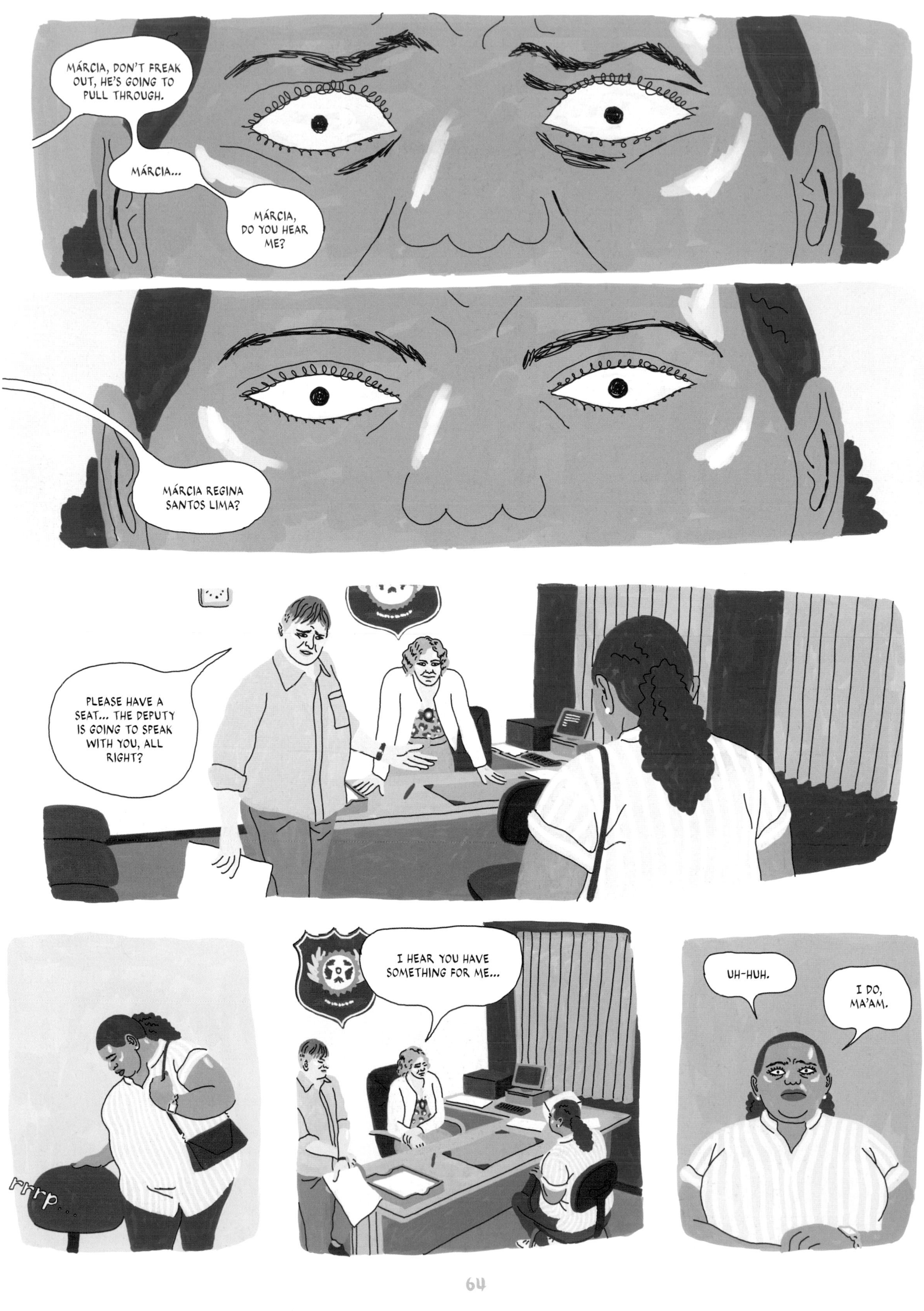
MÁRCIA, DON'T FREAK OUT, HE'S GOING TO PULL THROUGH.
MÁRCIA...
MÁRCIA, DO YOU HEAR ME?
MÁRCIA REGINA SANTOS LIMA?
PLEASE HAVE A SEAT... THE DEPUTY IS GOING TO SPEAK WITH YOU, ALL RIGHT?
rrrp...
I HEAR YOU HAVE SOMETHING FOR ME...
UH-HUH.
I DO, MA'AM.

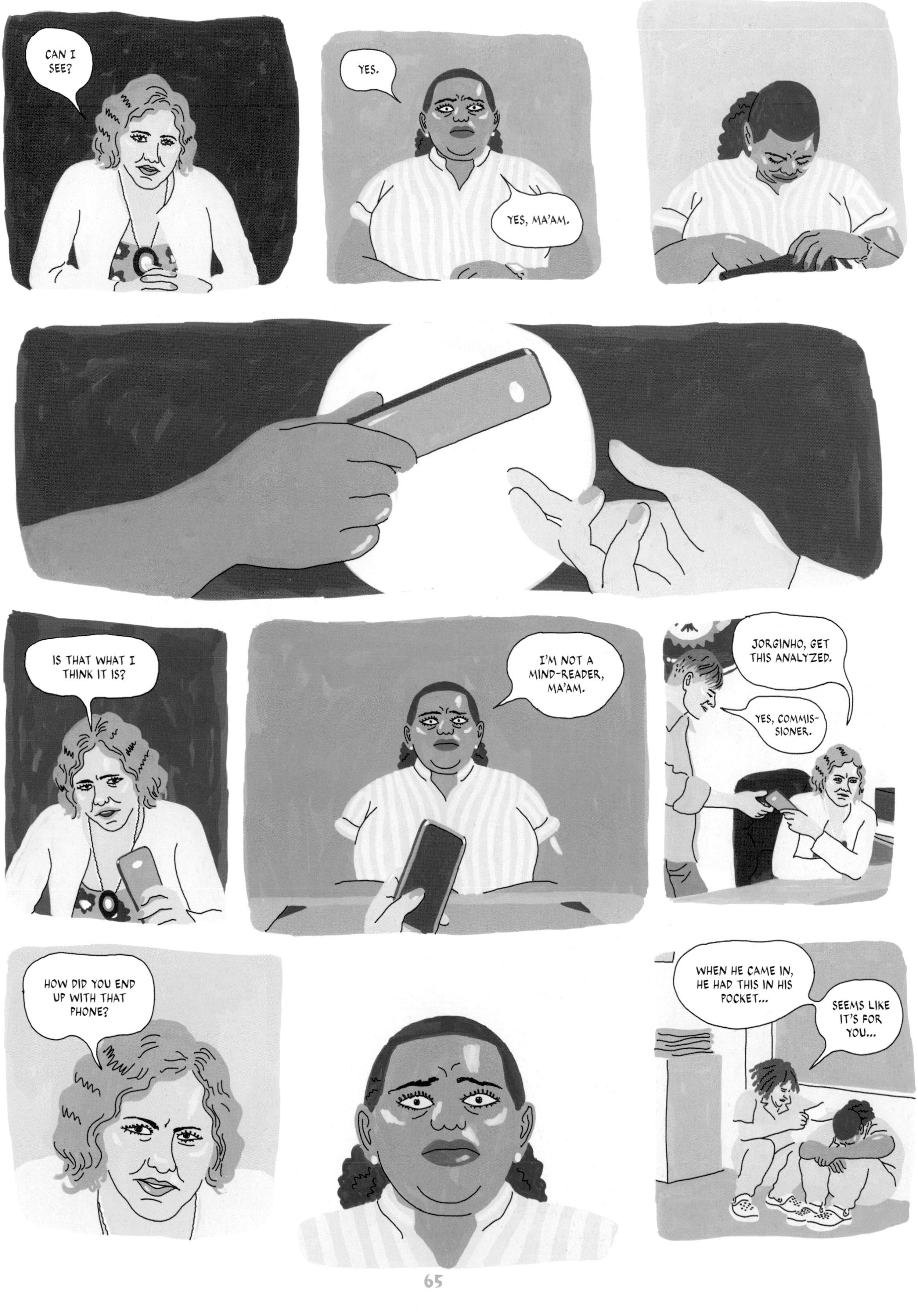
CAN I SEE?
YES.
YES, MA'AM.
IS THAT WHAT I THINK IT IS?
I'M NOT A MIND-READER, MA'AM.
JORGINHO, GET THIS ANALYZED.
YES, COMMIS-SIONER.
HOW DID YOU END UP WITH THAT PHONE?
WHEN HE CAME IN, HE HAD THIS IN HIS POCKET...
SEEMS LIKE IT'S FOR YOU...

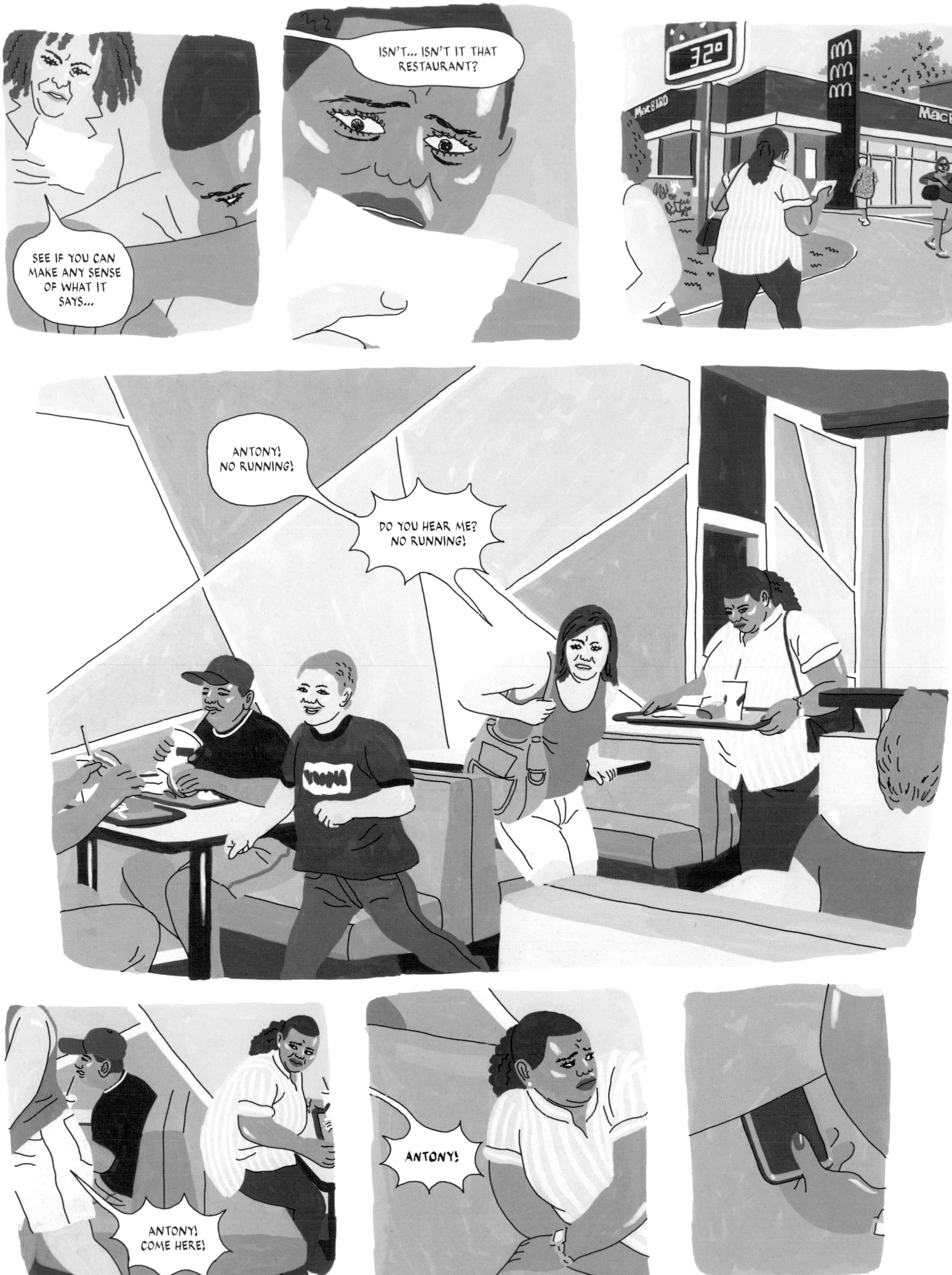
SEE IF YOU CAN MAKE ANY SENSE OF WHAT IT SAYS...
ISN'T... ISN'T IT THAT RESTAURANT?
32°
MacBIRD
MacBIRD
ANTONY! NO RUNNING!
DO YOU HEAR ME? NO RUNNING!
ANTONY! COME HERE!
ANTONY!

I DON'T KNOW.

I FORGET.

DID YOU TELL ANYBODY ELSE ABOUT THIS?

WHAT DO YOU MEAN, MÁRCIA? MAKE MYSELF "DISAPPEAR"?!

OMOLU, DON'T LET MONEY BLIND YOUR SON!

MAKE HIM SETTLE DOWN...

NO.

NO, MA'AM.

O-OF COURSE NOT...

I DIDN'T SAY ANYTHING TO ANYBODY.

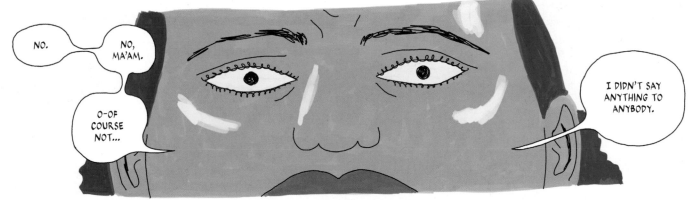
"DONA MÁRCIA, PLEASE BE AWARE THAT IF THE CELL PHONE CONTAINS INFORMATION USEFUL TO OUR INVESTIGATION..."

"...THINGS ARE GOING TO GET HOT."

WEEEOOOOWEEEOOOO!

"I MEAN, WHEN WE GO IN WITH SEARCH AND ARREST WARRANTS..."

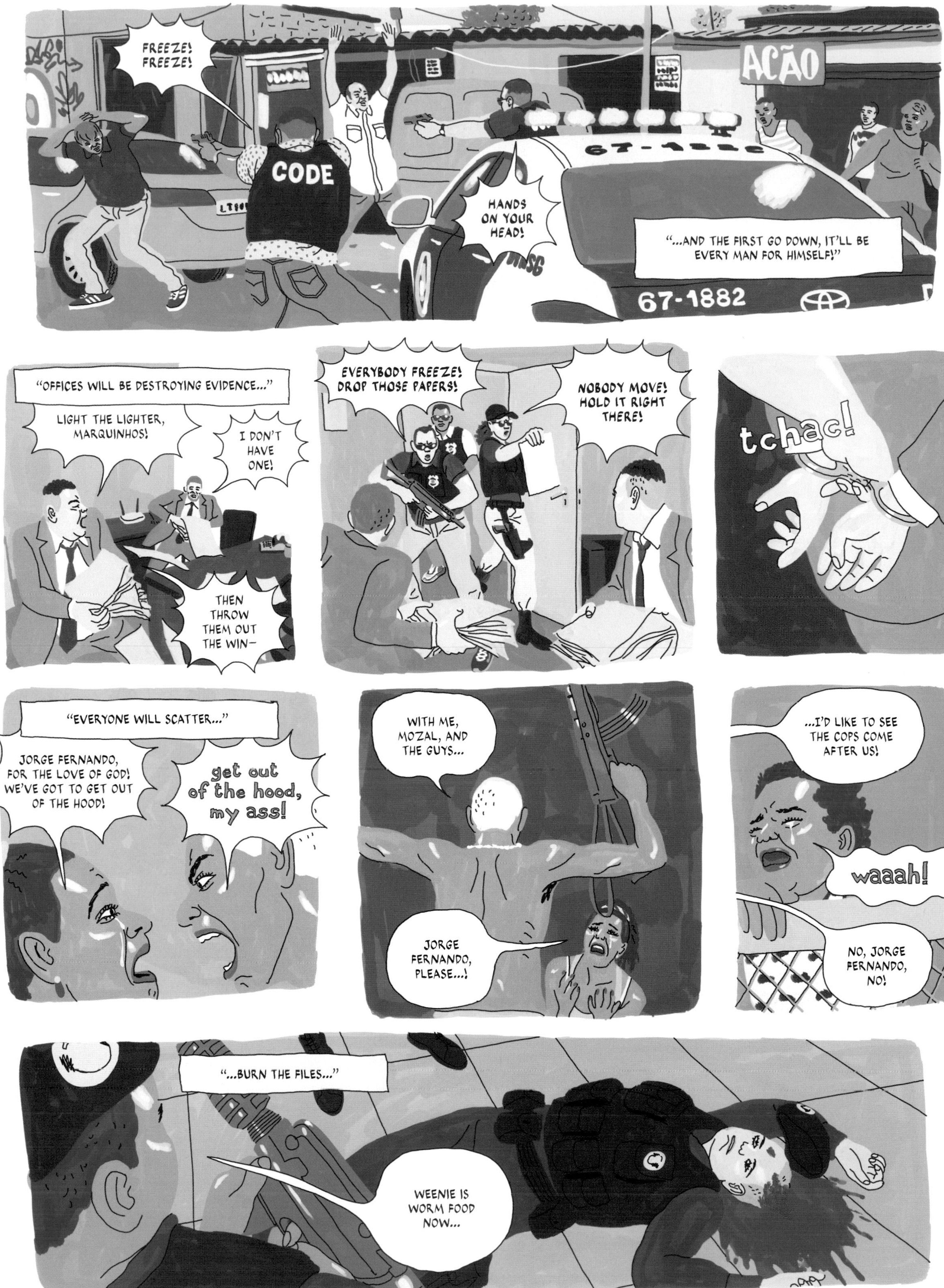

AÇÃO
FREEZE! FREEZE!
CODE
HANDS ON YOUR HEAD!
"...AND THE FIRST GO DOWN, IT'LL BE EVERY MAN FOR HIMSELF!"
67-1882
"OFFICES WILL BE DESTROYING EVIDENCE..."
LIGHT THE LIGHTER, MARQUINHOS!
I DON'T HAVE ONE!
THEN THROW THEM OUT THE WIN–
EVERYBODY FREEZE! DROP THOSE PAPERS!
NOBODY MOVE! HOLD IT RIGHT THERE!
tchac!
"EVERYONE WILL SCATTER..."
JORGE FERNANDO, FOR THE LOVE OF GOD! WE'VE GOT TO GET OUT OF THE HOOD!
get out of the hood, my ass!
WITH ME, MOZAL, AND THE GUYS...
JORGE FERNANDO, PLEASE...!
...I'D LIKE TO SEE THE COPS COME AFTER US!
waaah!
NO, JORGE FERNANDO, NO!
"...BURN THE FILES..."
WEENIE IS WORM FOOD NOW...

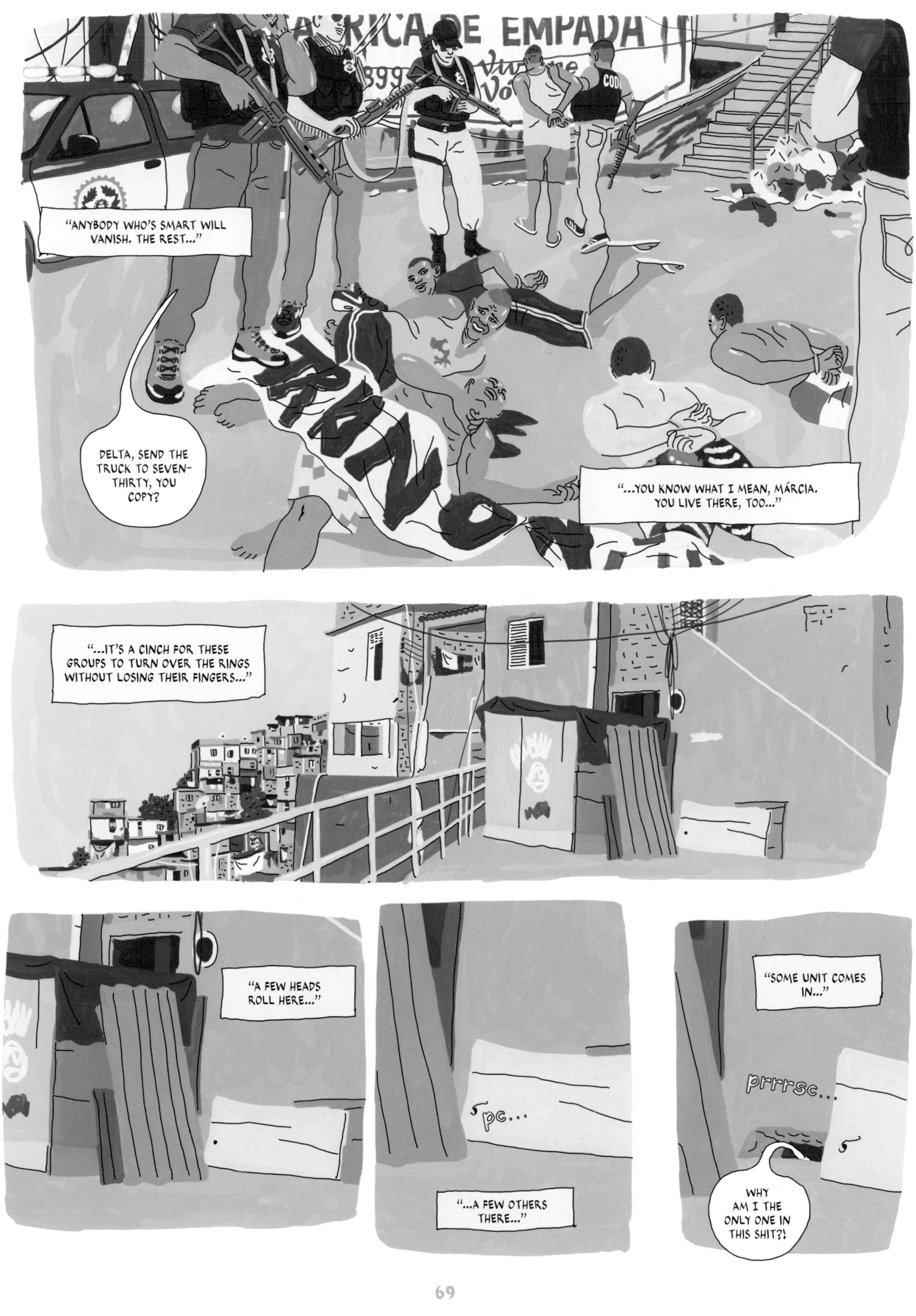
"ANYBODY WHO'S SMART WILL VANISH. THE REST..."
DELTA, SEND THE TRUCK TO SEVEN-THIRTY, YOU COPY?
"...YOU KNOW WHAT I MEAN, MÁRCIA. YOU LIVE THERE, TOO..."
"...IT'S A CINCH FOR THESE GROUPS TO TURN OVER THE RINGS WITHOUT LOSING THEIR FINGERS..."
"A FEW HEADS ROLL HERE..."
pc...
"...A FEW OTHERS THERE..."
"SOME UNIT COMES IN..."
prrrsc...
WHY AM I THE ONLY ONE IN THIS SHIT?!

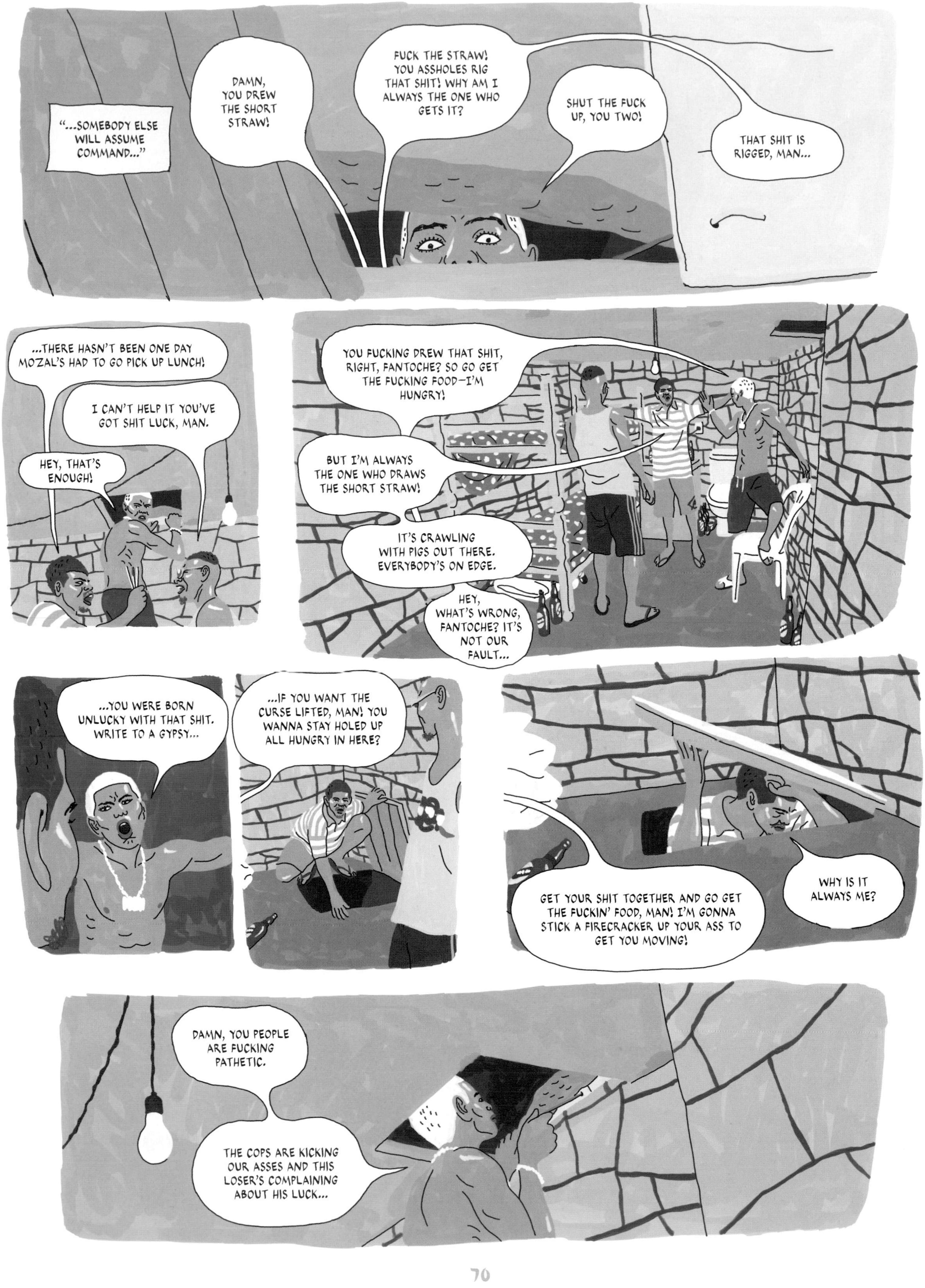
"...SOMEBODY ELSE WILL ASSUME COMMAND..."
DAMN, YOU DREW THE SHORT STRAW!
FUCK THE STRAW! YOU ASSHOLES RIG THAT SHIT! WHY AM I ALWAYS THE ONE WHO GETS IT?
SHUT THE FUCK UP, YOU TWO!
THAT SHIT IS RIGGED, MAN...
...THERE HASN'T BEEN ONE DAY MO'ZAL'S HAD TO GO PICK UP LUNCH!
I CAN'T HELP IT YOU'VE GOT SHIT LUCK, MAN.
HEY, THAT'S ENOUGH!
YOU FUCKING DREW THAT SHIT, RIGHT, FANTOCHE? SO GO GET THE FUCKING FOOD—I'M HUNGRY!
BUT I'M ALWAYS THE ONE WHO DRAWS THE SHORT STRAW!
IT'S CRAWLING WITH PIGS OUT THERE. EVERYBODY'S ON EDGE.
HEY, WHAT'S WRONG, FANTOCHE? IT'S NOT OUR FAULT...
...YOU WERE BORN UNLUCKY WITH THAT SHIT. WRITE TO A GYPSY...
...IF YOU WANT THE CURSE LIFTED, MAN! YOU WANNA STAY HOLED UP ALL HUNGRY IN HERE?
GET YOUR SHIT TOGETHER AND GO GET THE FUCKIN' FOOD, MAN! I'M GONNA STICK A FIRECRACKER UP YOUR ASS TO GET YOU MOVING!
WHY IS IT ALWAYS ME?
DAMN, YOU PEOPLE ARE FUCKING PATHETIC.
THE COPS ARE KICKING OUR ASSES AND THIS LOSER'S COMPLAINING ABOUT HIS LUCK...

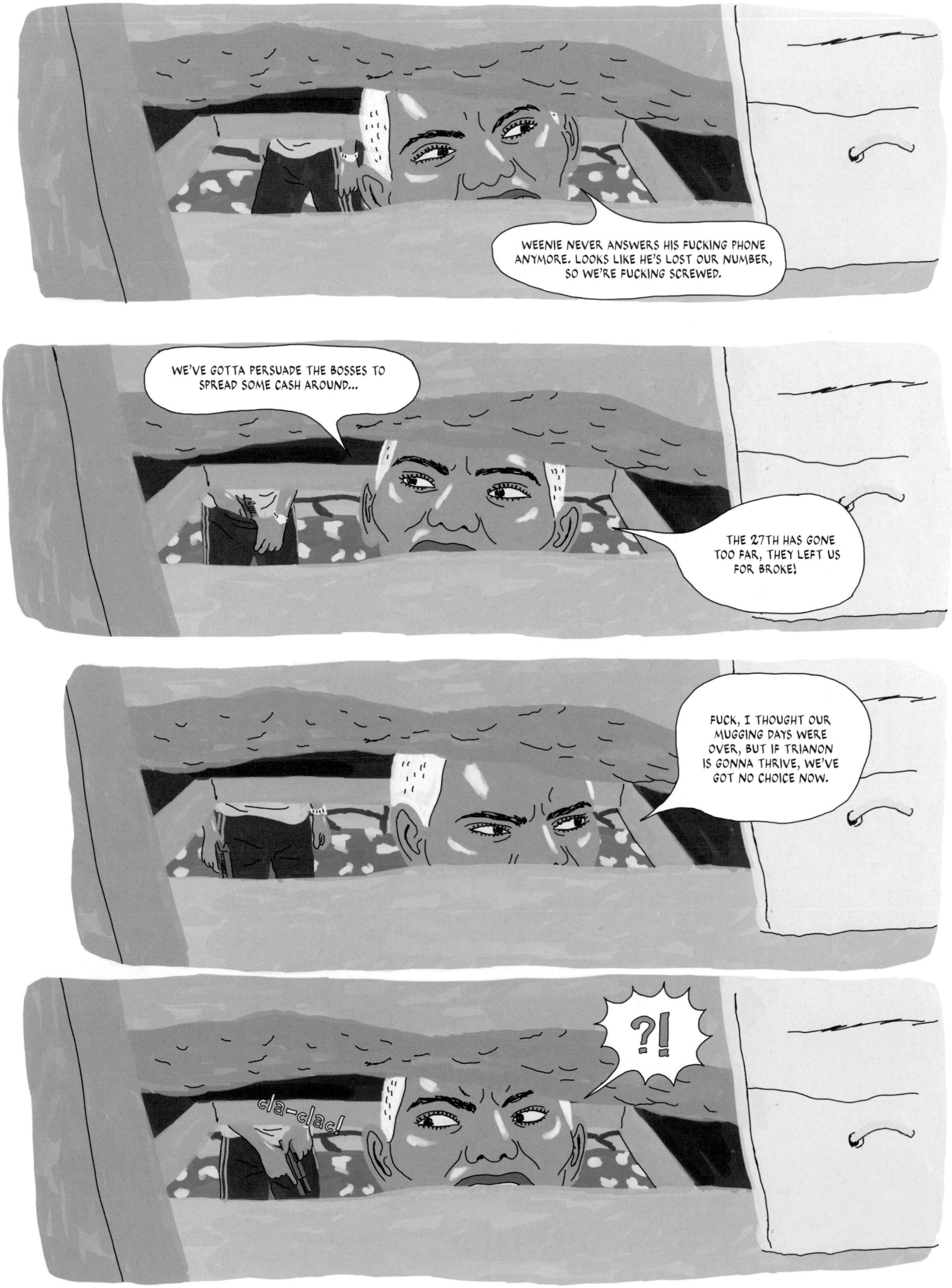
WEENIE NEVER ANSWERS HIS FUCKING PHONE ANYMORE. LOOKS LIKE HE'S LOST OUR NUMBER, SO WE'RE FUCKING SCREWED.
WE'VE GOTTA PERSUADE THE BOSSES TO SPREAD SOME CASH AROUND...
THE 27TH HAS GONE TOO FAR, THEY LEFT US FOR BROKE!
FUCK, I THOUGHT OUR MUGGING DAYS WERE OVER, BUT IF TRIANON IS GONNA THRIVE, WE'VE GOT NO CHOICE NOW.
cla-clac!
?!

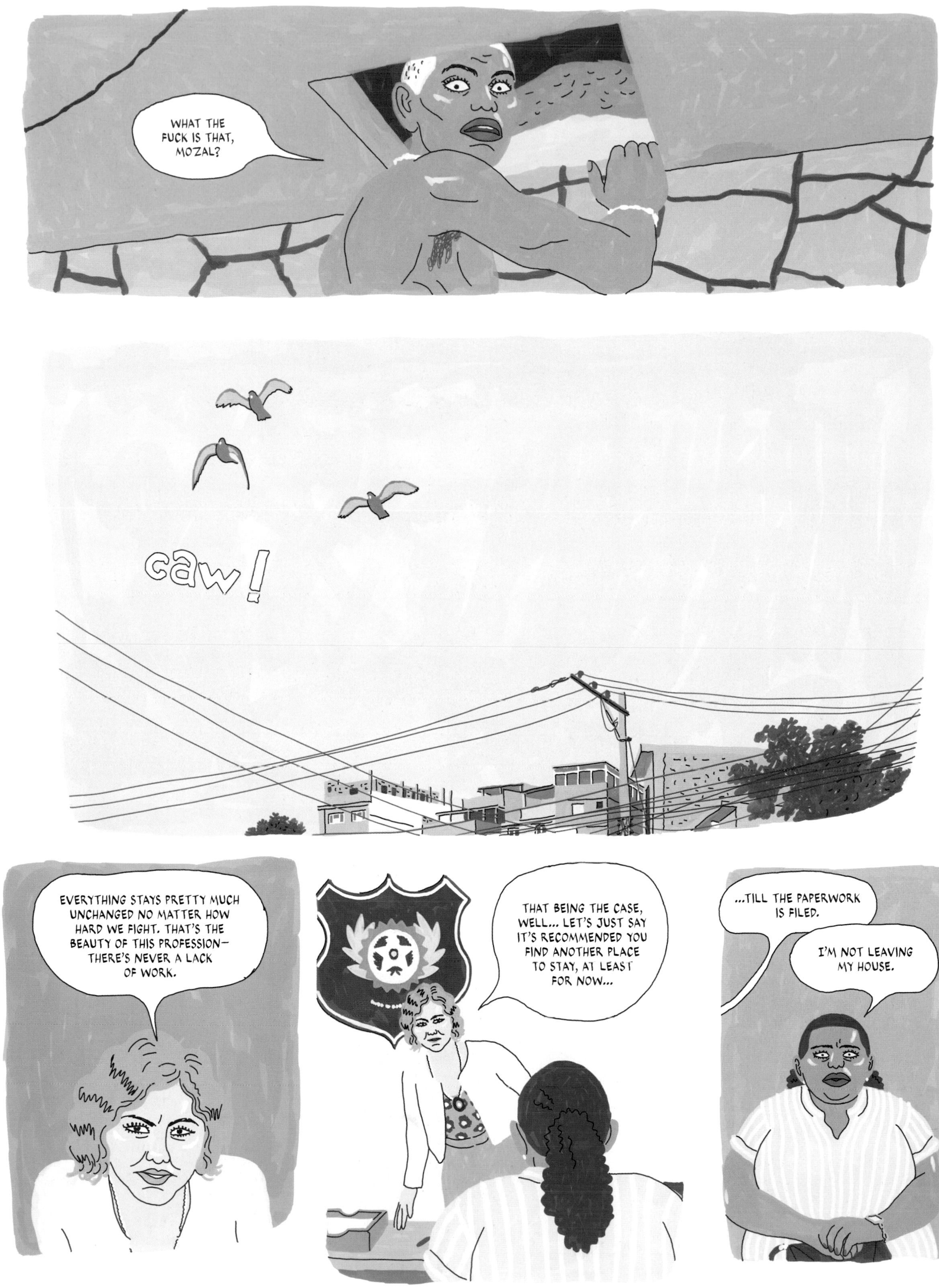
WHAT THE FUCK IS THAT, MOZAL?
caw!
EVERYTHING STAYS PRETTY MUCH UNCHANGED NO MATTER HOW HARD WE FIGHT. THAT'S THE BEAUTY OF THIS PROFESSION— THERE'S NEVER A LACK OF WORK.
THAT BEING THE CASE, WELL... LET'S JUST SAY IT'S RECOMMENDED YOU FIND ANOTHER PLACE TO STAY, AT LEAST FOR NOW...
...TILL THE PAPERWORK IS FILED.
I'M NOT LEAVING MY HOUSE.

DONA MÁRCIA, THE WITNESS PROTECTION PROGRAM ALREADY OFFERED TO FIND YOU SOMEWHERE SAFE TO GO.

IF I MAKE A BIG FUSS...

...I COULD ARRANGE FOR YOU TO RECEIVE A SMALL PENSION.

BUT IF YOU DON'T TAKE IT, WE HAVE NOTHING ELSE TO OFFER.

YES, YOU DO.

OH, DO I?

WHAT IS IT?

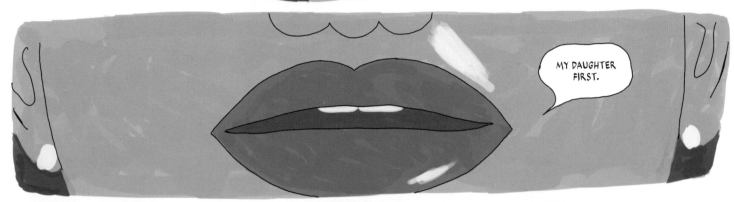

MY DAUGHTER FIRST.

THERE, STOP, STOP, STOP!

"I... IMAGINE THIS CAN'T HAVE BEEN AN EASY DECISION FOR YOU, DONA MÁRCIA..."

HEY, HANDS UP, HANDS UP!

"...SO..."

"...DON'T WORRY..."

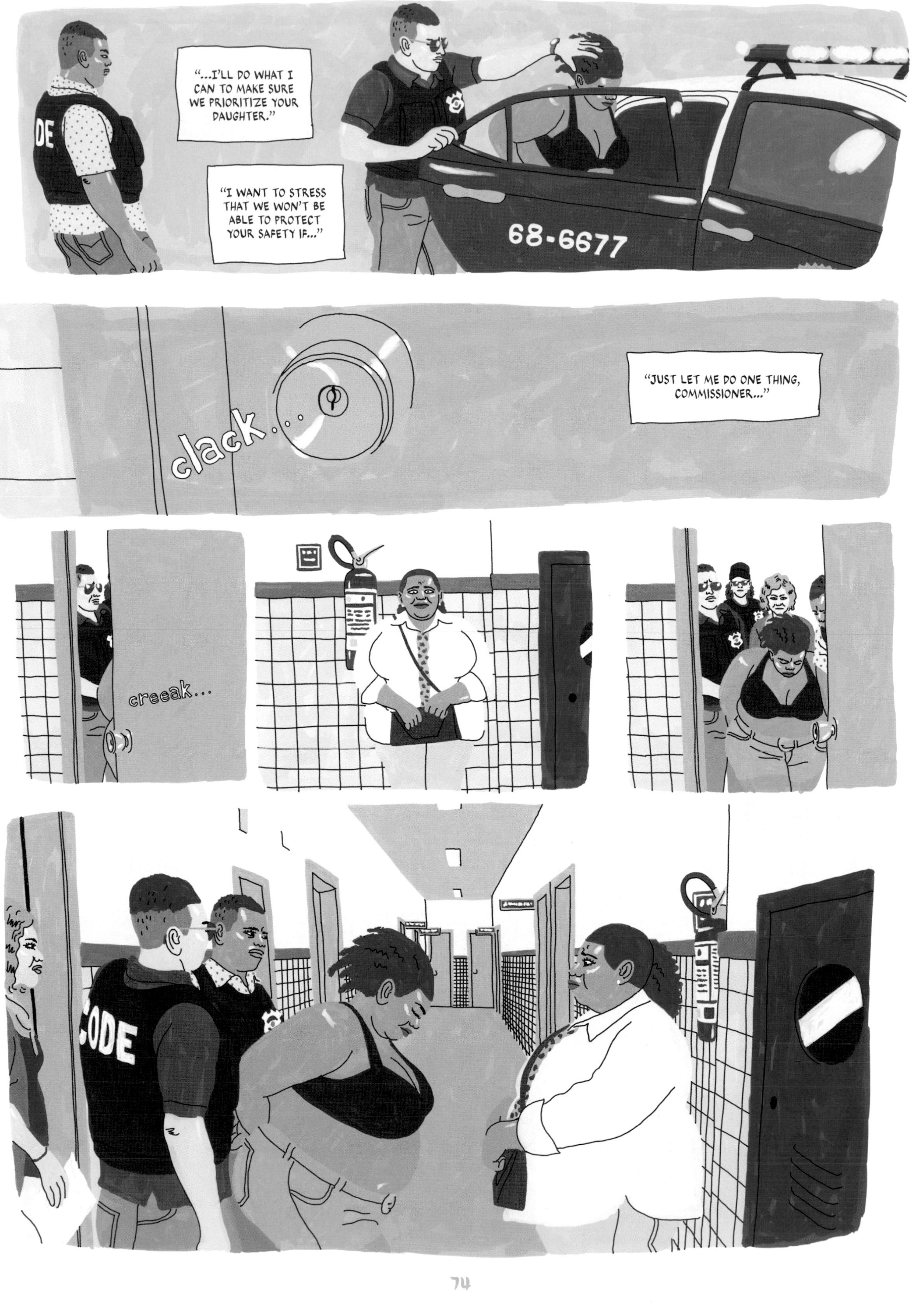

"...I'LL DO WHAT I CAN TO MAKE SURE WE PRIORITIZE YOUR DAUGHTER."
"I WANT TO STRESS THAT WE WON'T BE ABLE TO PROTECT YOUR SAFETY IF..."
DE
68-6677
clack...
"JUST LET ME DO ONE THING, COMMISSIONER..."
creeak...
CODE

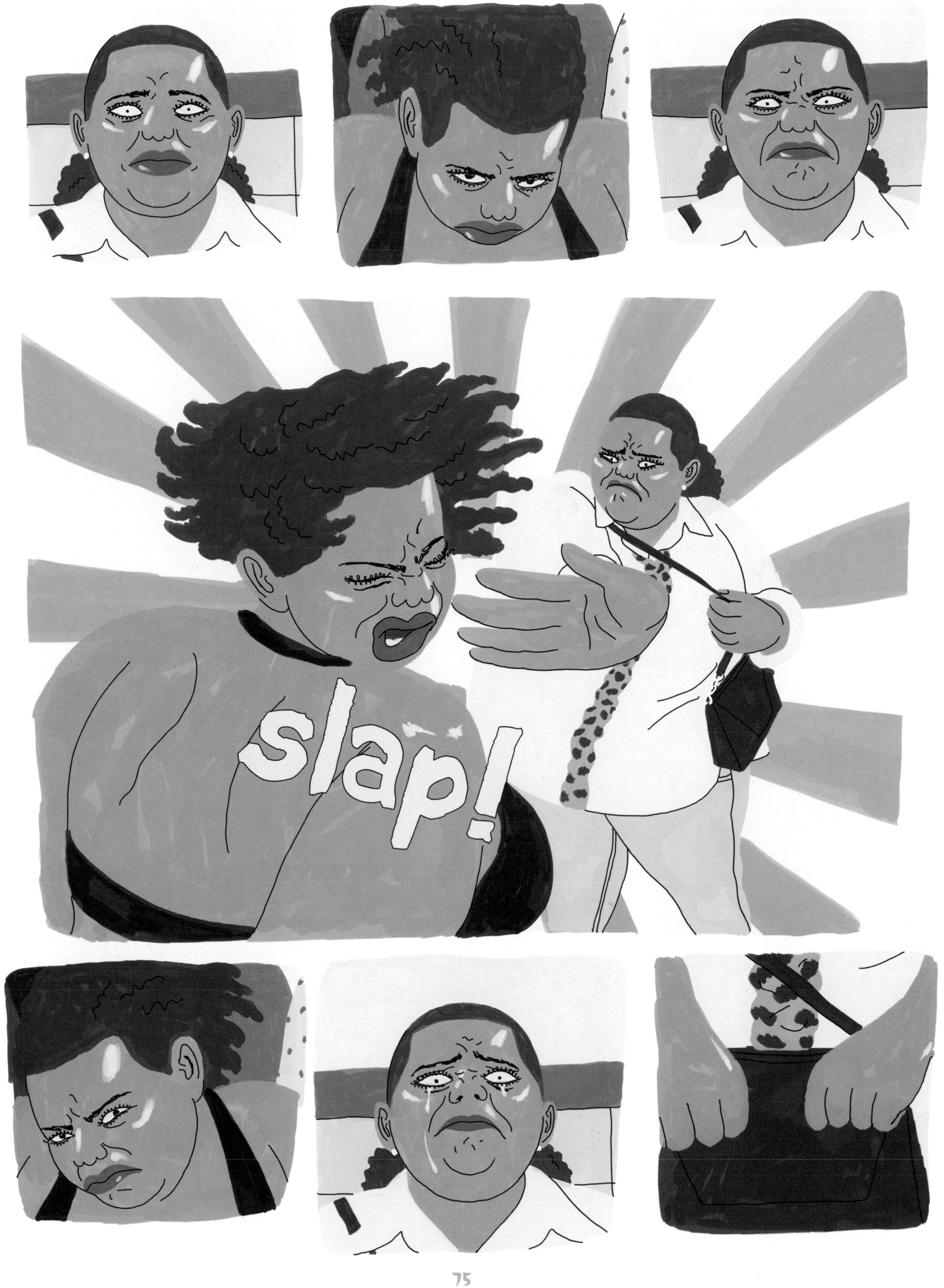
slap!

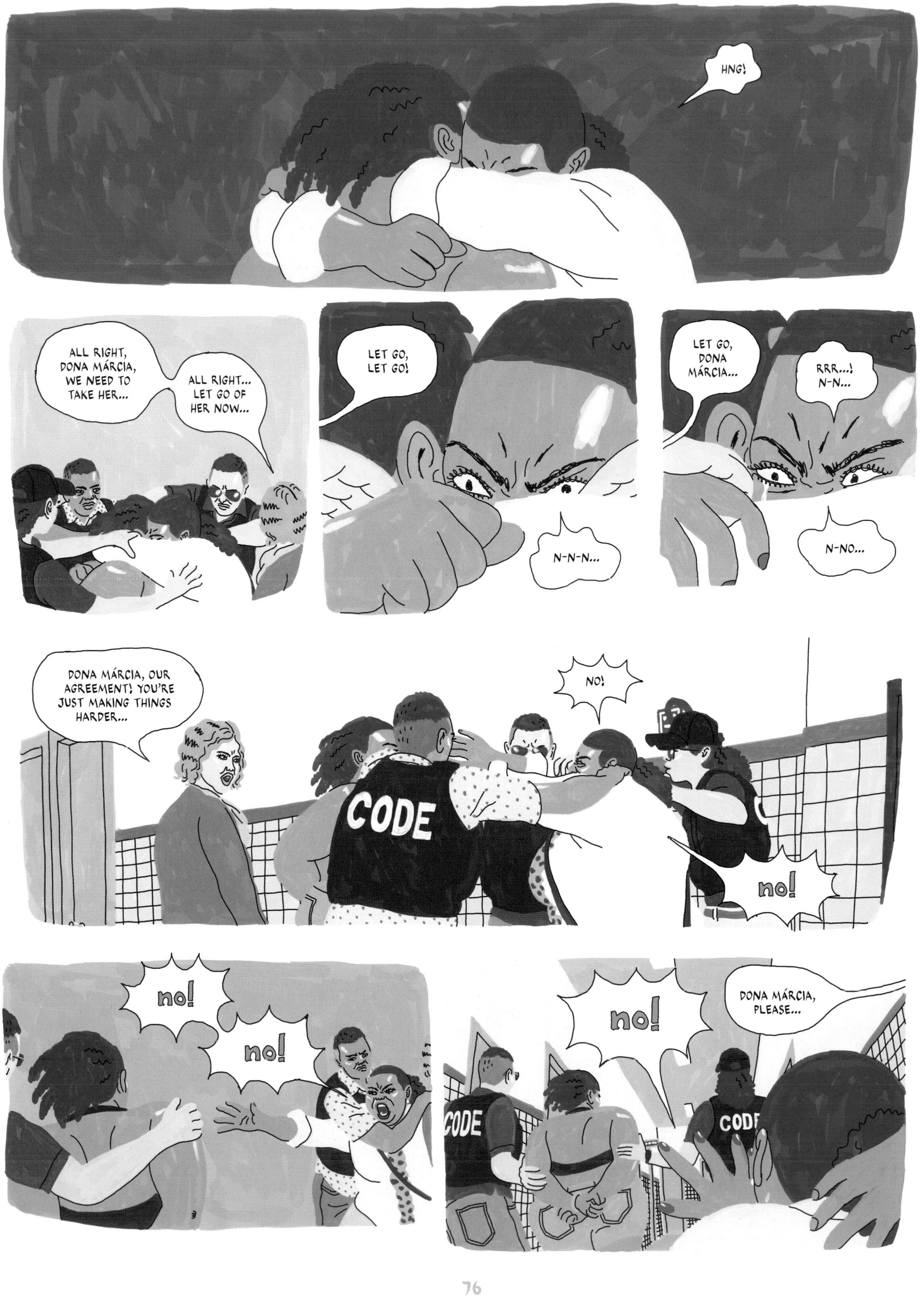
HNG!
ALL RIGHT, DONA MÁRCIA, WE NEED TO TAKE HER...
ALL RIGHT... LET GO OF HER NOW...
LET GO, LET GO!
N-N-N...
LET GO, DONA MÁRCIA...
RRR...! N-N...
N-NO...
DONA MÁRCIA, OUR AGREEMENT! YOU'RE JUST MAKING THINGS HARDER...
NO!
CODE
no!
no!
no!
no!
DONA MÁRCIA, PLEASE...
CODE
CODE

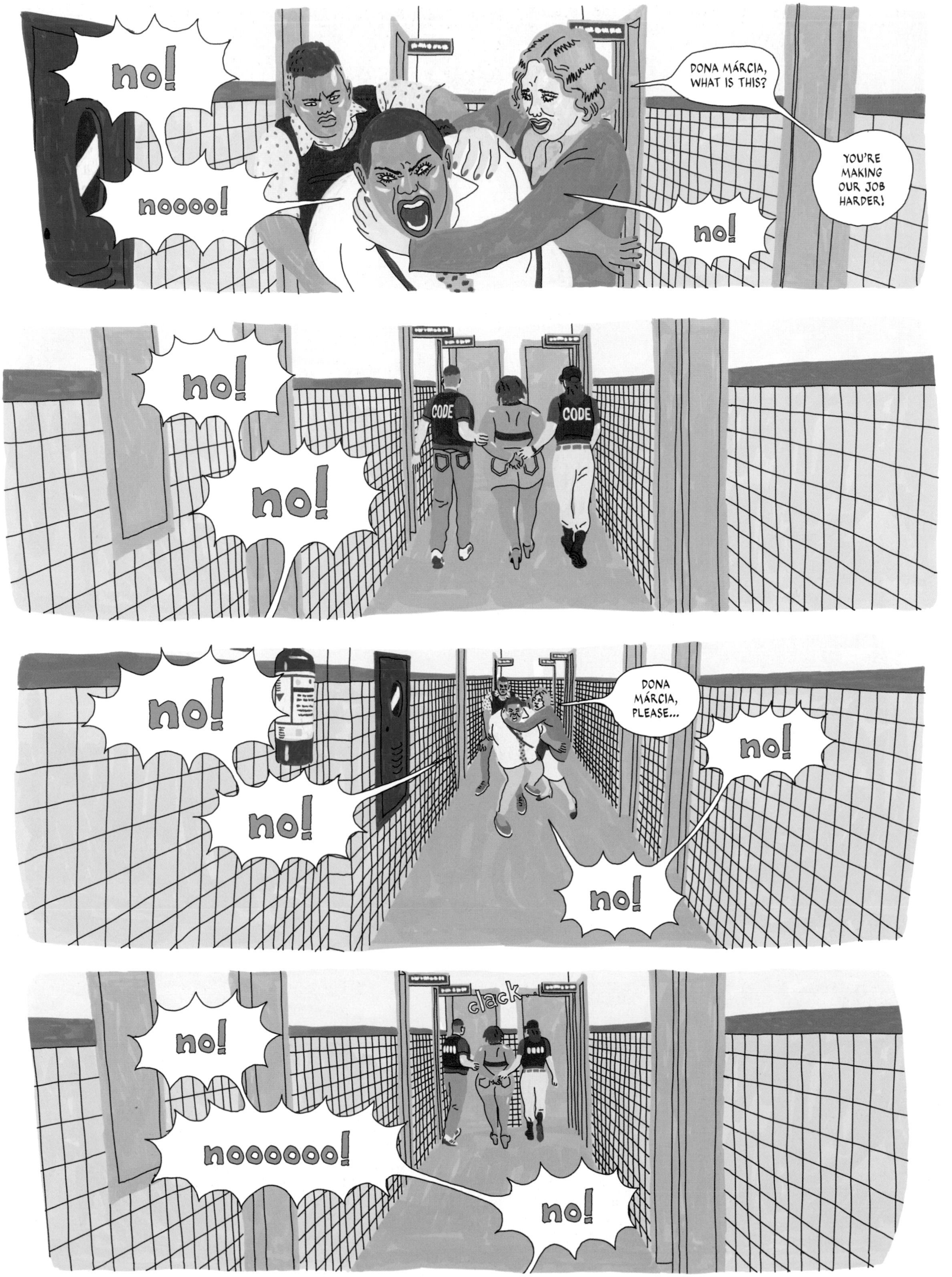
no!
noooo!
DONA MÁRCIA, WHAT IS THIS?
YOU'RE MAKING OUR JOB HARDER!
no!
no!
no!
CODE
CODE
no!
no!
DONA MÁRCIA, PLEASE...
no!
no!
no!
clack
noooooo!
no!

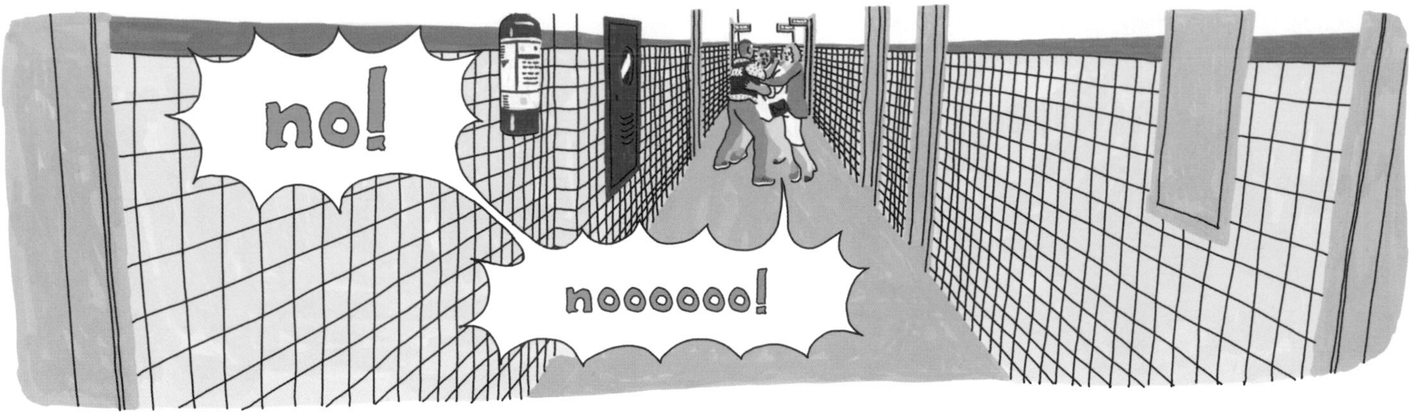
no!
noooooo!

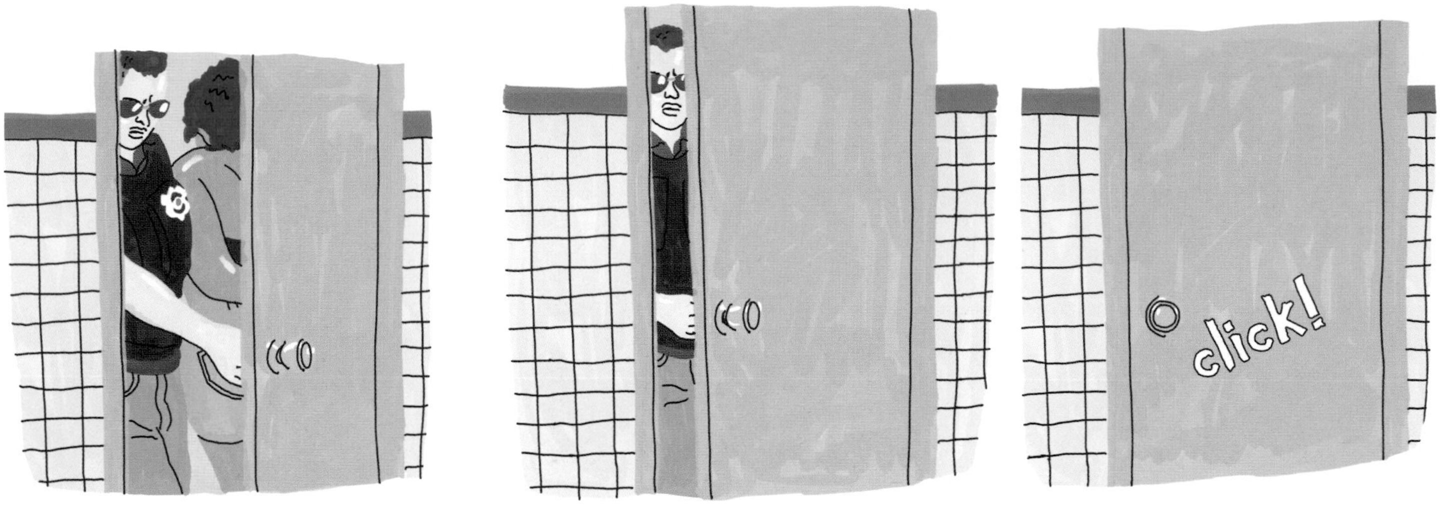
click!

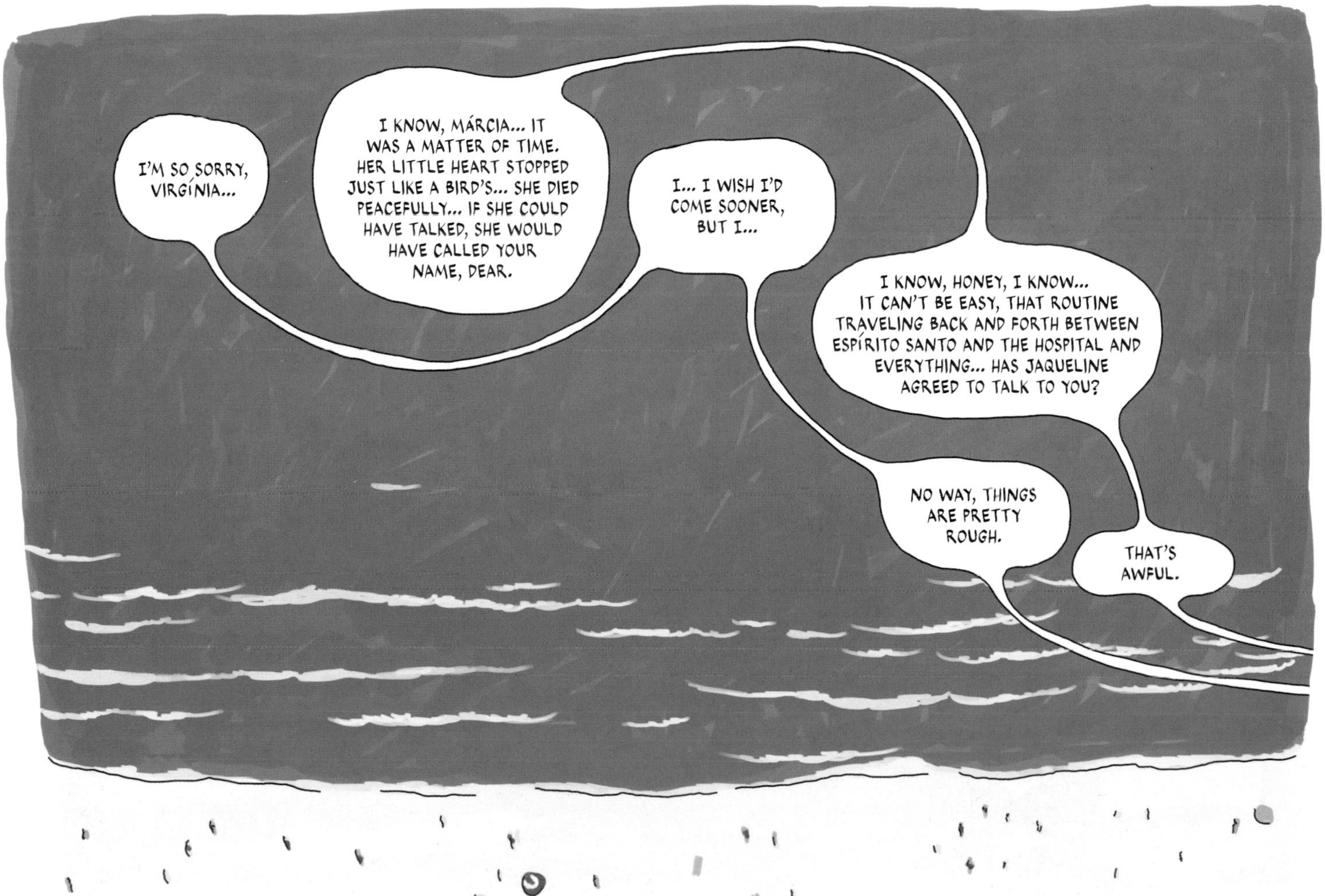
I'M SO SORRY, VIRGÍNIA...
I KNOW, MÁRCIA... IT WAS A MATTER OF TIME. HER LITTLE HEART STOPPED JUST LIKE A BIRD'S... SHE DIED PEACEFULLY... IF SHE COULD HAVE TALKED, SHE WOULD HAVE CALLED YOUR NAME, DEAR.
I... I WISH I'D COME SOONER, BUT I...
I KNOW, HONEY, I KNOW... IT CAN'T BE EASY, THAT ROUTINE TRAVELING BACK AND FORTH BETWEEN ESPÍRITO SANTO AND THE HOSPITAL AND EVERYTHING... HAS JAQUELINE AGREED TO TALK TO YOU?
NO WAY, THINGS ARE PRETTY ROUGH.
THAT'S AWFUL.

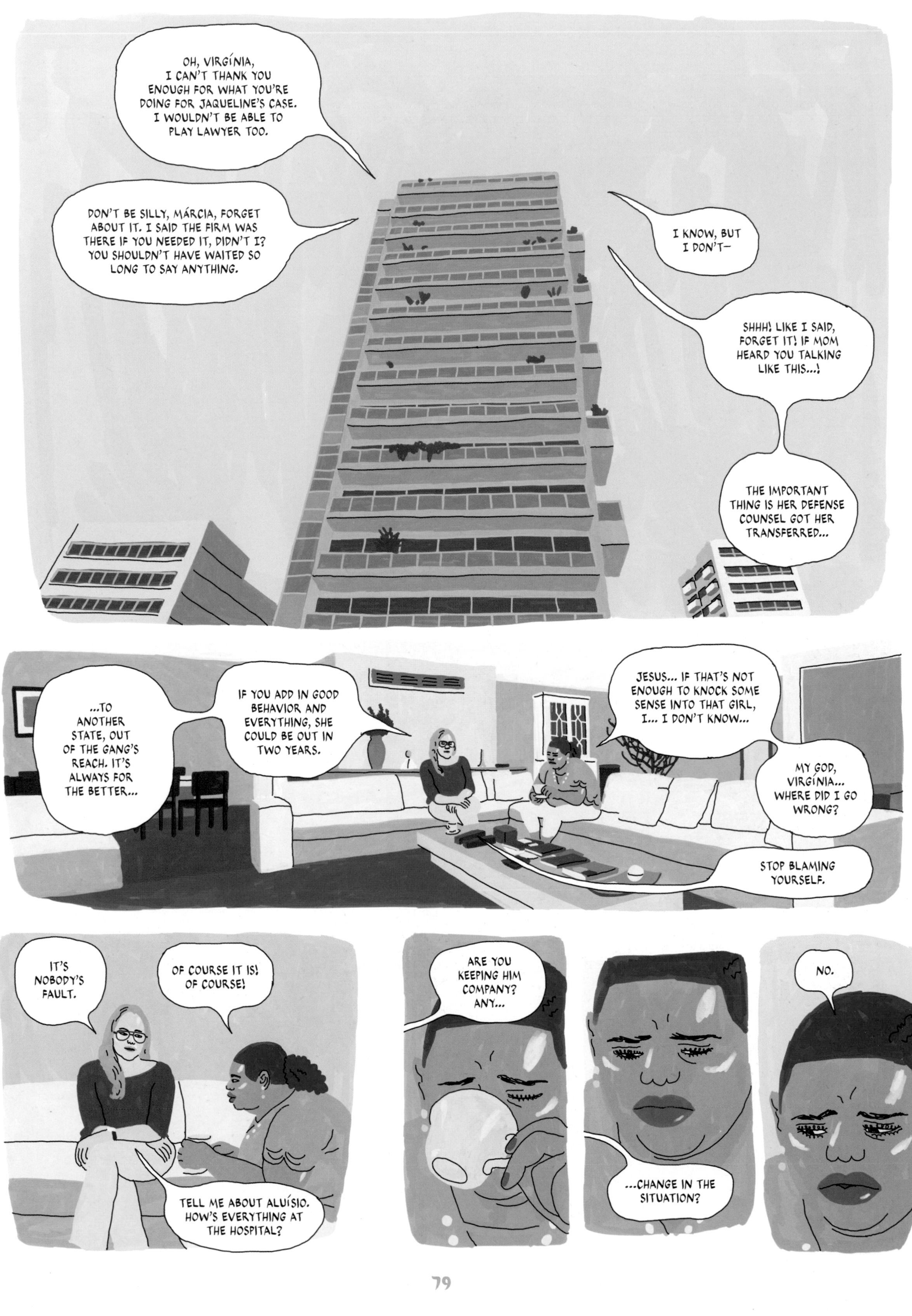
OH, VIRGÍNIA, I CAN'T THANK YOU ENOUGH FOR WHAT YOU'RE DOING FOR JAQUELINE'S CASE. I WOULDN'T BE ABLE TO PLAY LAWYER TOO.
DON'T BE SILLY, MÁRCIA, FORGET ABOUT IT. I SAID THE FIRM WAS THERE IF YOU NEEDED IT, DIDN'T I? YOU SHOULDN'T HAVE WAITED SO LONG TO SAY ANYTHING.
I KNOW, BUT I DON'T—
SHHH! LIKE I SAID, FORGET IT! IF MOM HEARD YOU TALKING LIKE THIS...!
THE IMPORTANT THING IS HER DEFENSE COUNSEL GOT HER TRANSFERRED...
...TO ANOTHER STATE, OUT OF THE GANG'S REACH. IT'S ALWAYS FOR THE BETTER...
IF YOU ADD IN GOOD BEHAVIOR AND EVERYTHING, SHE COULD BE OUT IN TWO YEARS.
JESUS... IF THAT'S NOT ENOUGH TO KNOCK SOME SENSE INTO THAT GIRL, I... I DON'T KNOW...
MY GOD, VIRGÍNIA... WHERE DID I GO WRONG?
STOP BLAMING YOURSELF.
IT'S NOBODY'S FAULT.
OF COURSE IT IS! OF COURSE!
TELL ME ABOUT ALUÍSIO. HOW'S EVERYTHING AT THE HOSPITAL?
ARE YOU KEEPING HIM COMPANY? ANY...
...CHANGE IN THE SITUATION?
NO.

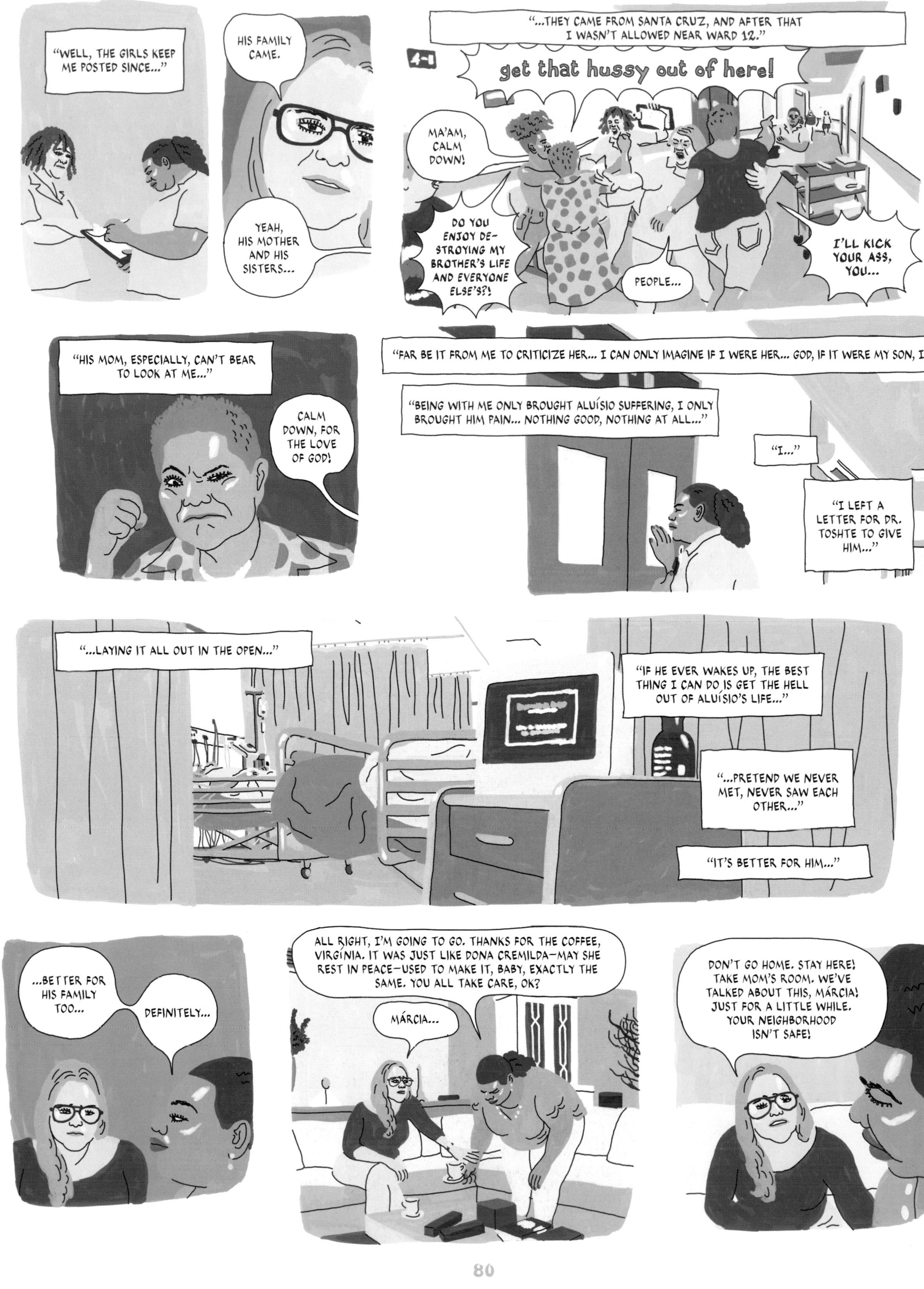
"WELL, THE GIRLS KEEP ME POSTED SINCE..."
HIS FAMILY CAME.
YEAH, HIS MOTHER AND HIS SISTERS...
"...THEY CAME FROM SANTA CRUZ, AND AFTER THAT I WASN'T ALLOWED NEAR WARD 12."
4-1
get that hussy out of here!
MA'AM, CALM DOWN!
DO YOU ENJOY DE-STROYING MY BROTHER'S LIFE AND EVERYONE ELSE'S?!
PEOPLE...
I'LL KICK YOUR ASS, YOU...
"HIS MOM, ESPECIALLY, CAN'T BEAR TO LOOK AT ME..."
CALM DOWN, FOR THE LOVE OF GOD!
"FAR BE IT FROM ME TO CRITICIZE HER... I CAN ONLY IMAGINE IF I WERE HER... GOD, IF IT WERE MY SON, I..."
"BEING WITH ME ONLY BROUGHT ALUÍSIO SUFFERING, I ONLY BROUGHT HIM PAIN... NOTHING GOOD, NOTHING AT ALL..."
"I..."
"I LEFT A LETTER FOR DR. TOSHTE TO GIVE HIM..."
"...LAYING IT ALL OUT IN THE OPEN..."
"IF HE EVER WAKES UP, THE BEST THING I CAN DO IS GET THE HELL OUT OF ALUÍSIO'S LIFE..."
"...PRETEND WE NEVER MET, NEVER SAW EACH OTHER..."
"IT'S BETTER FOR HIM..."
...BETTER FOR HIS FAMILY TOO...
DEFINITELY...
ALL RIGHT, I'M GOING TO GO. THANKS FOR THE COFFEE, VIRGÍNIA. IT WAS JUST LIKE DONA CREMILDA—MAY SHE REST IN PEACE—USED TO MAKE IT, BABY, EXACTLY THE SAME. YOU ALL TAKE CARE, OK?
MÁRCIA...
DON'T GO HOME. STAY HERE! TAKE MOM'S ROOM. WE'VE TALKED ABOUT THIS, MÁRCIA! JUST FOR A LITTLE WHILE. YOUR NEIGHBORHOOD ISN'T SAFE!

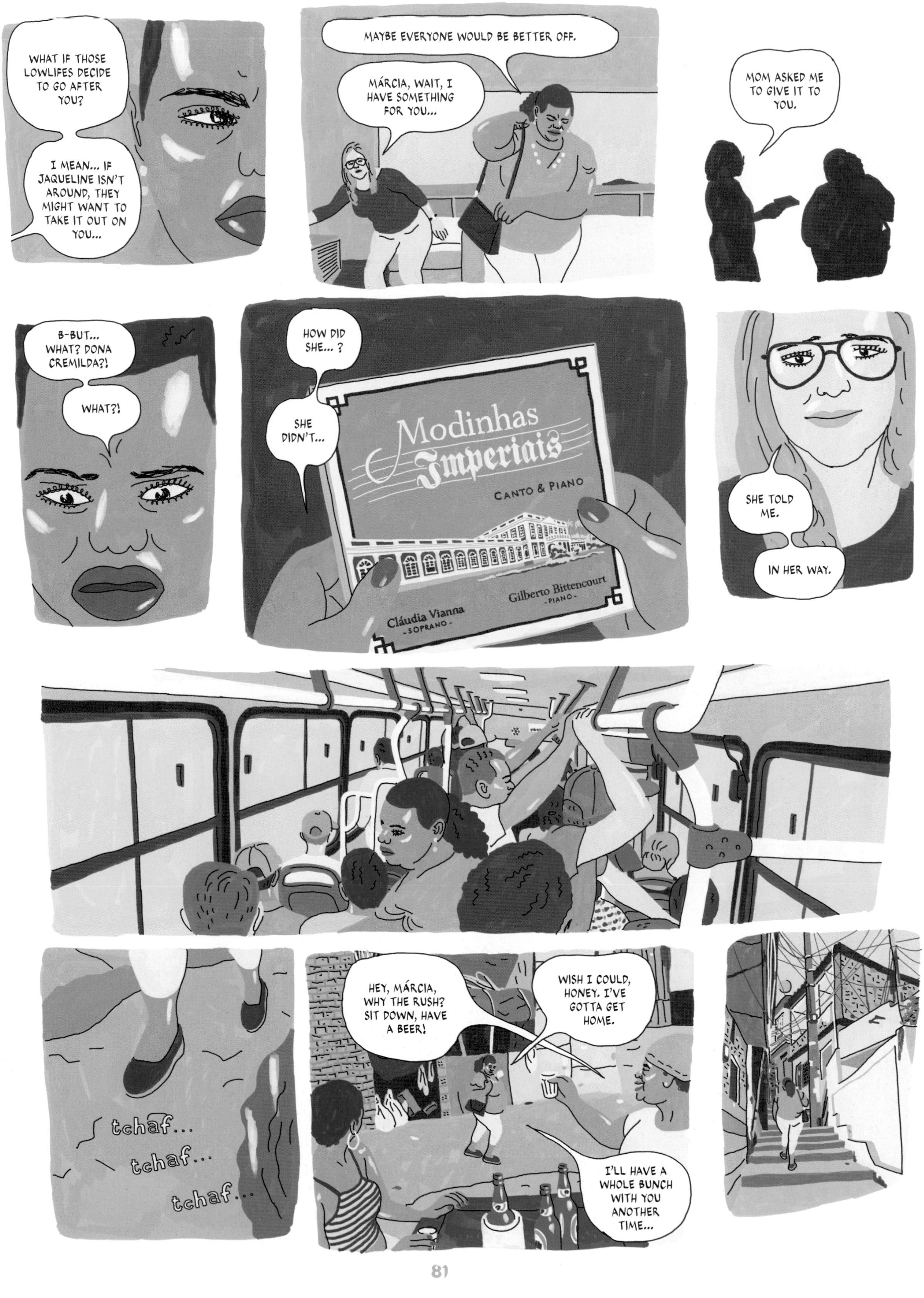
WHAT IF THOSE LOWLIFES DECIDE TO GO AFTER YOU?
I MEAN... IF JAQUELINE ISN'T AROUND, THEY MIGHT WANT TO TAKE IT OUT ON YOU...
MAYBE EVERYONE WOULD BE BETTER OFF.
MÁRCIA, WAIT, I HAVE SOMETHING FOR YOU...
MOM ASKED ME TO GIVE IT TO YOU.
B-BUT... WHAT? DONA CREMILDA?!
WHAT?!
HOW DID SHE... ?
SHE DIDN'T...
Modinhas Imperiais
CANTO & PIANO
Cláudia Vianna
-SOPRANO-
Gilberto Bittencourt
-PIANO-
SHE TOLD ME.
IN HER WAY.
tchaf...
tchaf...
tchaf...
HEY, MÁRCIA, WHY THE RUSH? SIT DOWN, HAVE A BEER!
WISH I COULD, HONEY. I'VE GOTTA GET HOME.
I'LL HAVE A WHOLE BUNCH WITH YOU ANOTHER TIME...

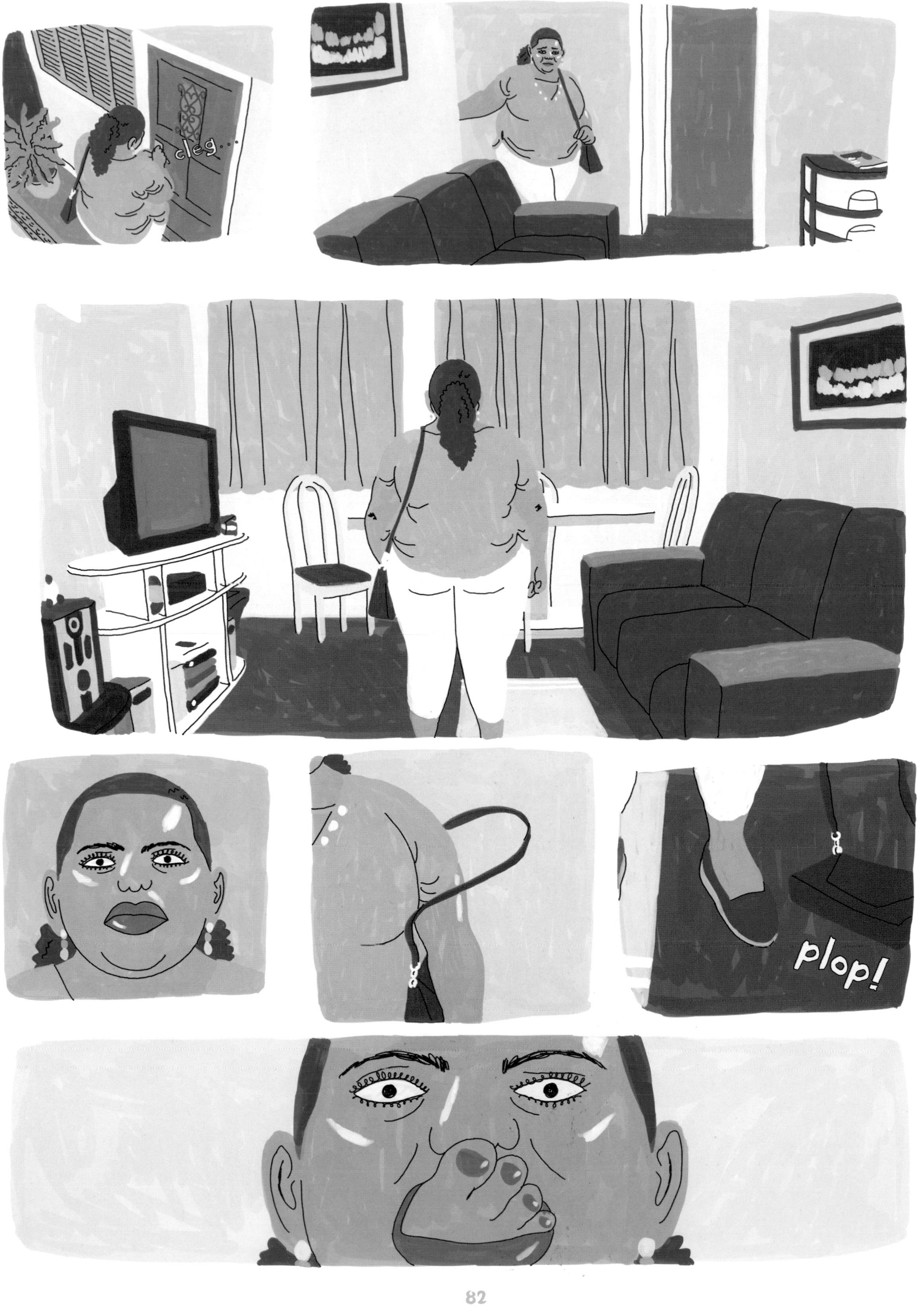
cleg...
plop!

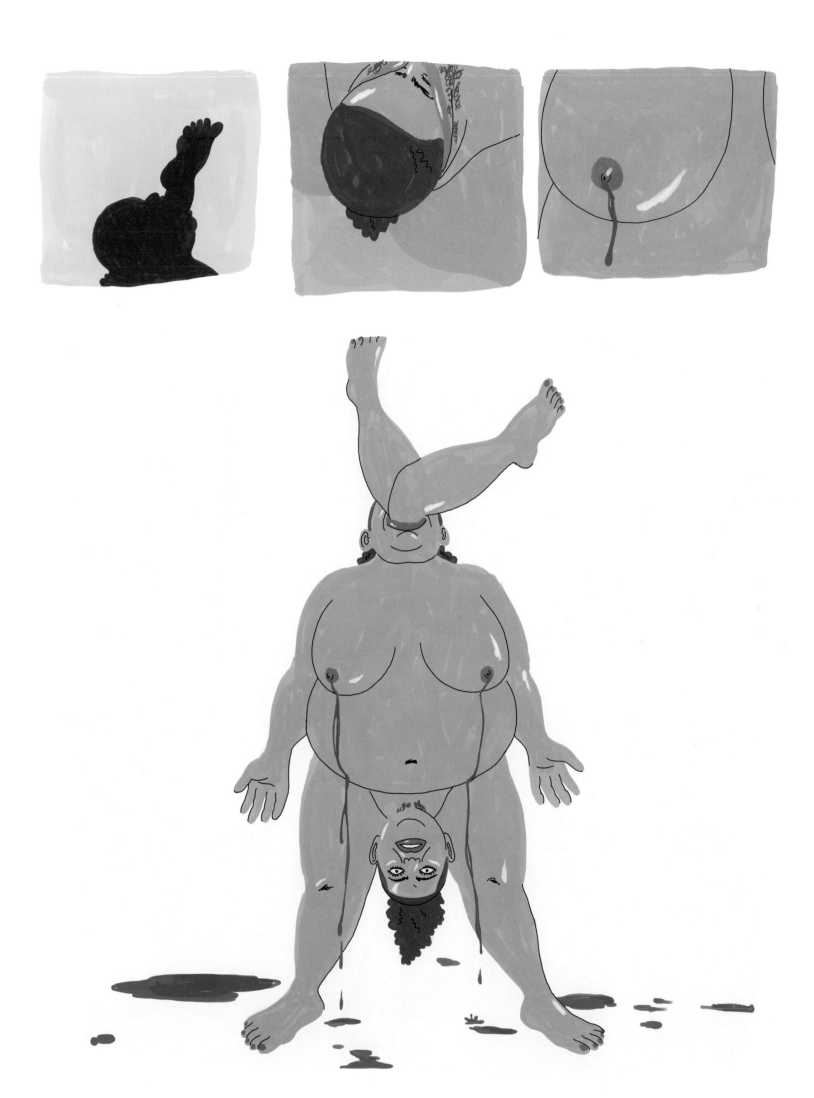

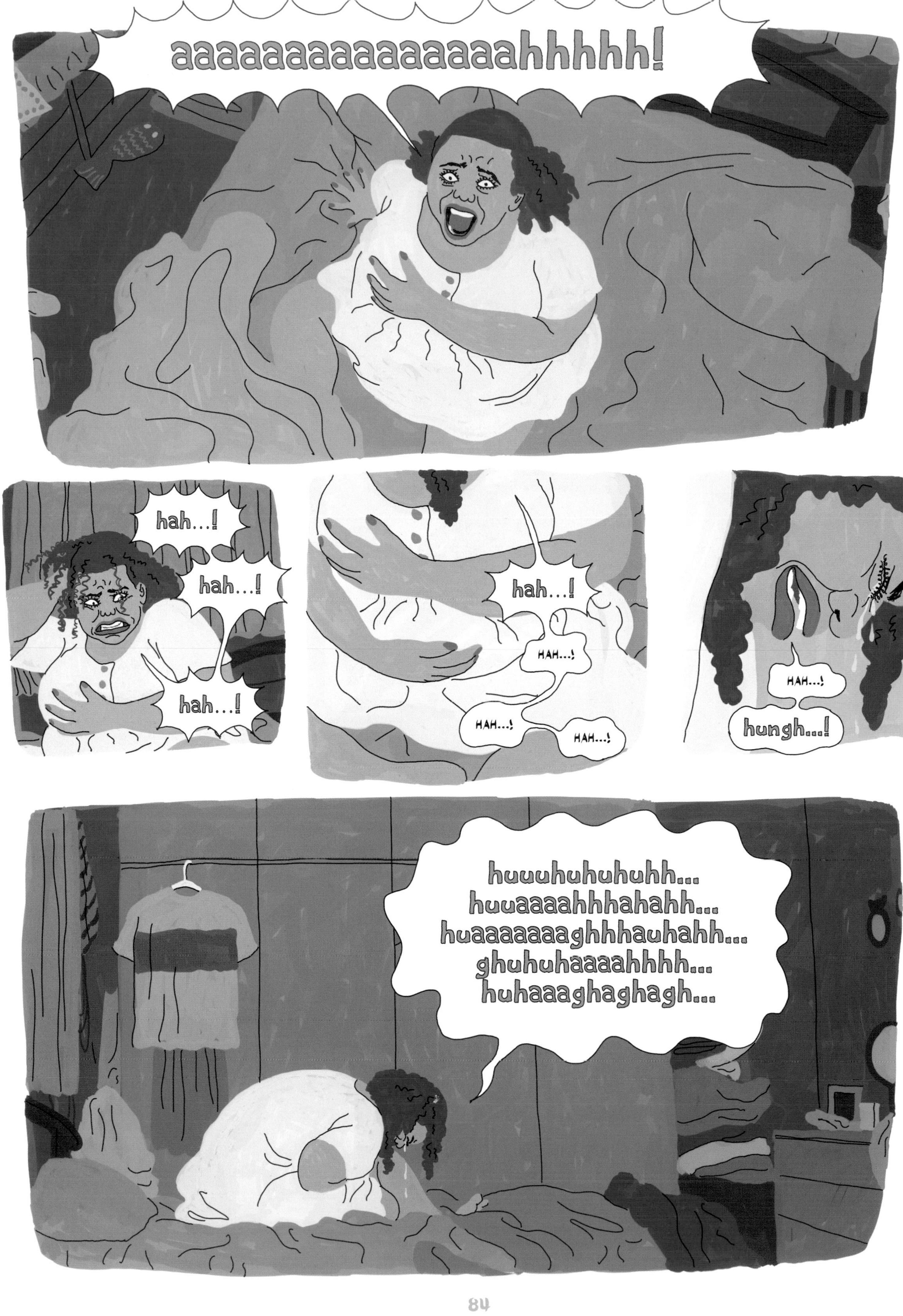
aaaaaaaaaaaaaaaahhhhh!
hah...!
hah...!
hah...!
hah...!
HAH...!
HAH...!
HAH...!
HAH...!
hungh...!
huuuhuhuhuhh...
huuaaaahhhahahh...
huaaaaaaaghhhauhahh...
ghuhuhaaaahhhh...
huhaaaghaghagh...

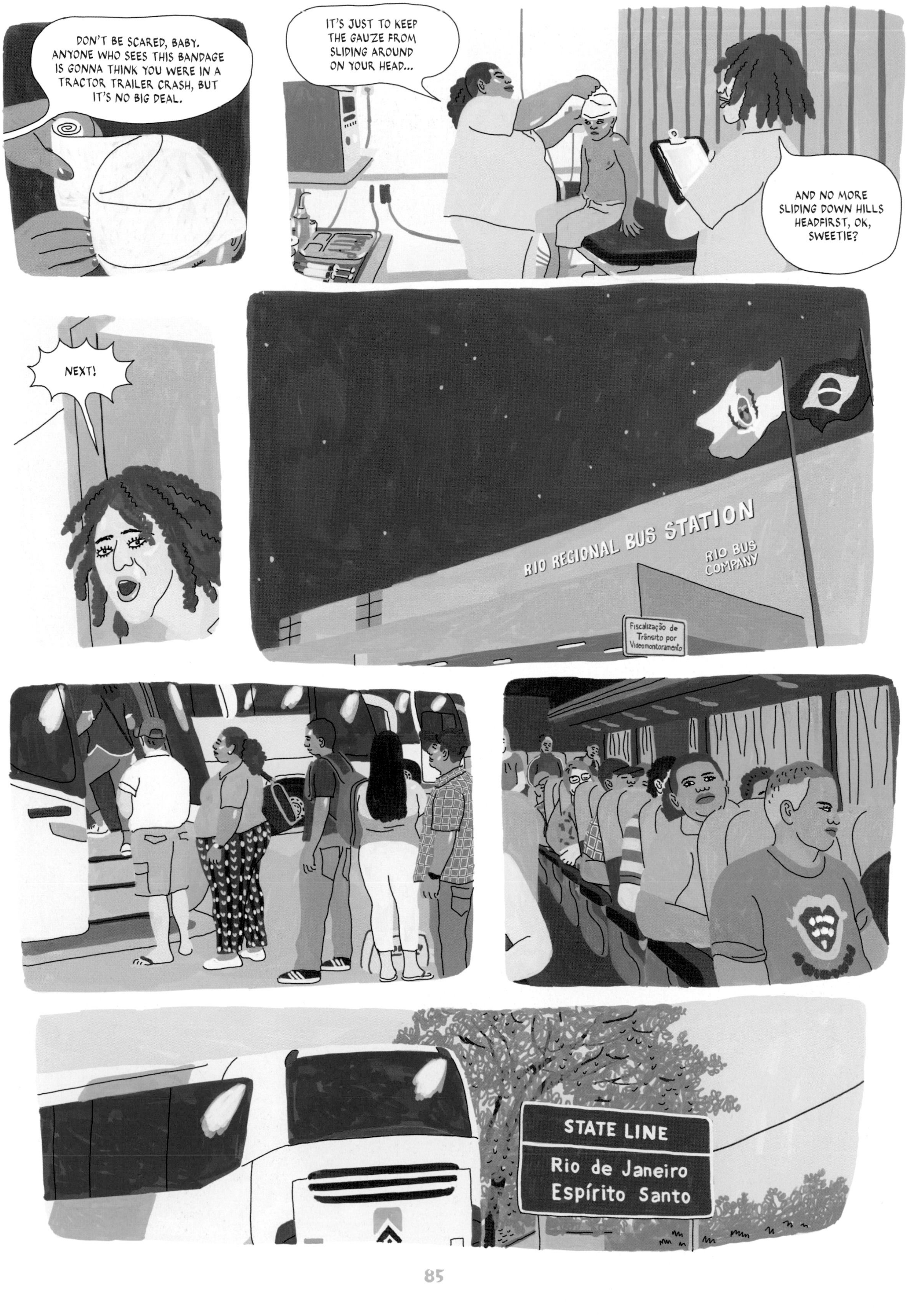
DON'T BE SCARED, BABY. ANYONE WHO SEES THIS BANDAGE IS GONNA THINK YOU WERE IN A TRACTOR TRAILER CRASH, BUT IT'S NO BIG DEAL.
IT'S JUST TO KEEP THE GAUZE FROM SLIDING AROUND ON YOUR HEAD...
AND NO MORE SLIDING DOWN HILLS HEADFIRST, OK, SWEETIE?
NEXT!
RIO REGIONAL BUS STATION
RIO BUS COMPANY
Fiscalização de Trânsito por Videomontoramento
STATE LINE
Rio de Janeiro
Espírito Santo

ANDERSON, WHERE'S THE...
rrrooom...
ZZZZZZ...
MA'AM...!
HEY, MA'AM!
ahh!
WE'RE HERE...
...END OF THE LINE.

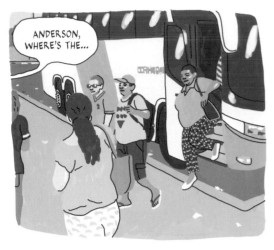

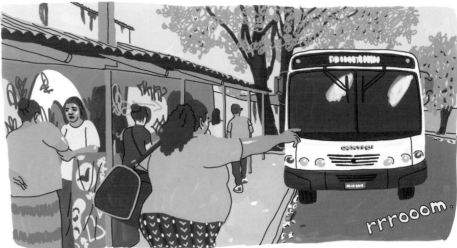

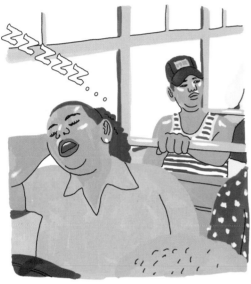

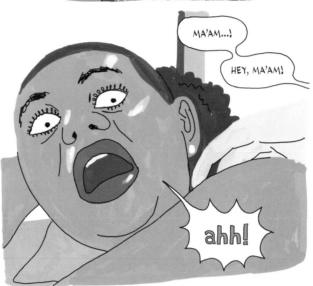

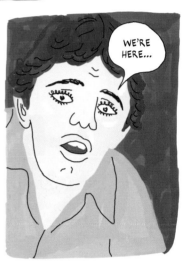

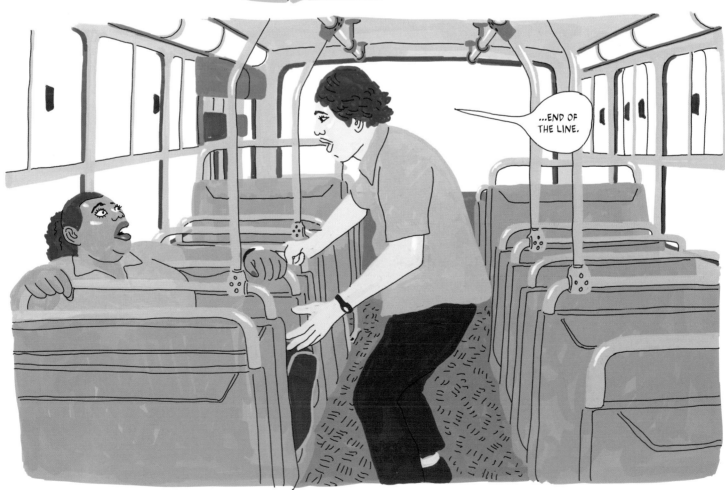

vroommm...
rra-claclah...
rroommm...
squelch...
squelch...
squelch...
squelch...
ALDO DINIZ PENITENTIARY COMPLEX

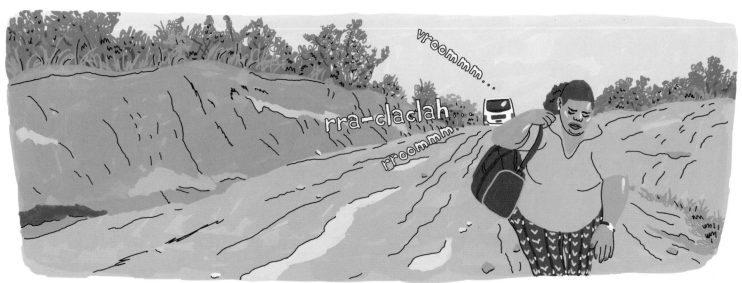

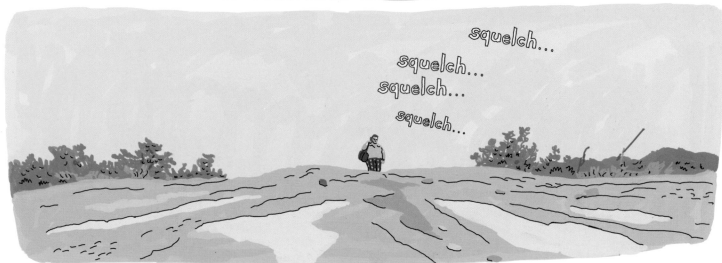

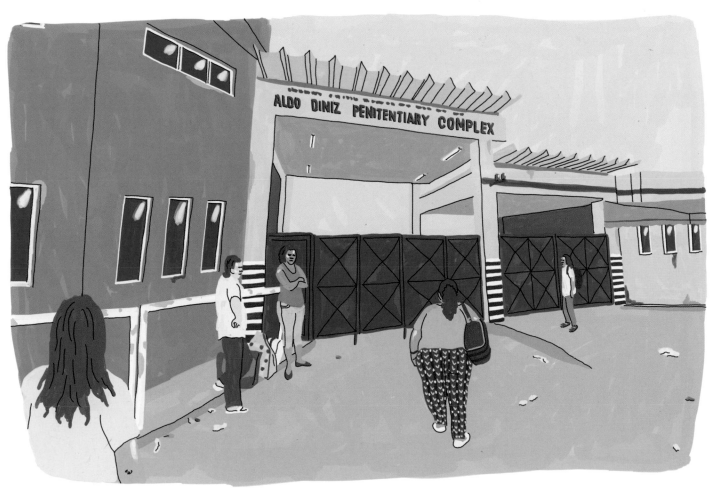

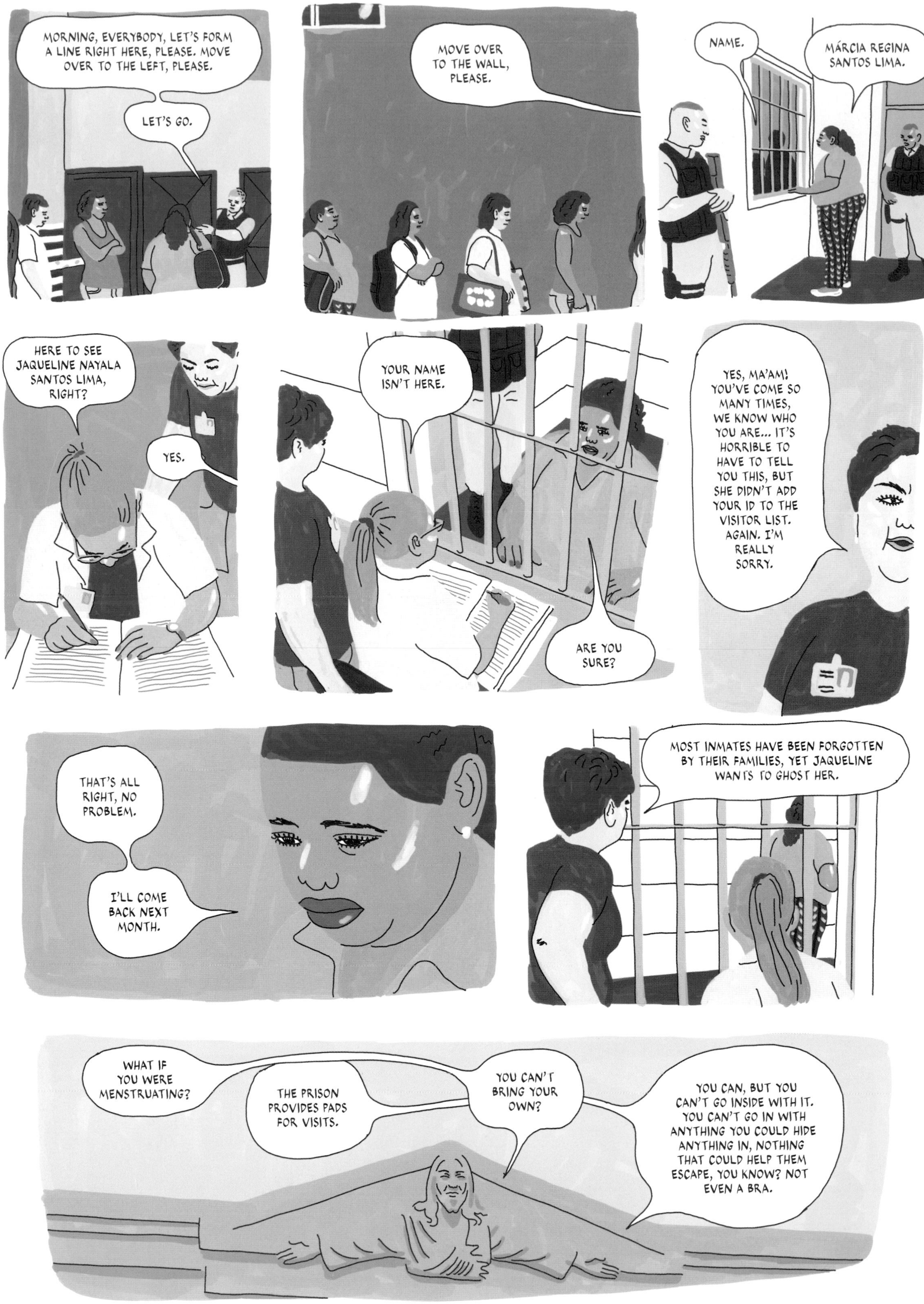

MORNING, EVERYBODY, LET'S FORM A LINE RIGHT HERE, PLEASE. MOVE OVER TO THE LEFT, PLEASE.
LET'S GO.
MOVE OVER TO THE WALL, PLEASE.
NAME.
MÁRCIA REGINA SANTOS LIMA.
HERE TO SEE JAQUELINE NAYALA SANTOS LIMA, RIGHT?
YES.
YOUR NAME ISN'T HERE.
ARE YOU SURE?
YES, MA'AM! YOU'VE COME SO MANY TIMES, WE KNOW WHO YOU ARE... IT'S HORRIBLE TO HAVE TO TELL YOU THIS, BUT SHE DIDN'T ADD YOUR ID TO THE VISITOR LIST. AGAIN. I'M REALLY SORRY.
THAT'S ALL RIGHT, NO PROBLEM.
I'LL COME BACK NEXT MONTH.
MOST INMATES HAVE BEEN FORGOTTEN BY THEIR FAMILIES, YET JAQUELINE WANTS TO GHOST HER.
WHAT IF YOU WERE MENSTRUATING?
THE PRISON PROVIDES PADS FOR VISITS.
YOU CAN'T BRING YOUR OWN?
YOU CAN, BUT YOU CAN'T GO INSIDE WITH IT. YOU CAN'T GO IN WITH ANYTHING YOU COULD HIDE ANYTHING IN, NOTHING THAT COULD HELP THEM ESCAPE, YOU KNOW? NOT EVEN A BRA.

...YOU HAVE TO GO IN BRALESS.
I DON'T KNOW IF I COULD TAKE IT, MÁRCIA. GOING UP THERE EVERY MONTH, TEN HOURS THERE AND TEN HOURS BACK... YOU KNOW?
ALL THAT EFFORT TO GET THERE JUST TO HAVE THEM SLAM THE DOOR IN YOUR FACE.
WELL, THERE'S NO GOOD THAT LASTS FOREVER...
...NOR EVIL THAT NEVER EN—
ACK, IT VIBRATED!
bzzzzng!
HANG ON, I JUST GOT A TEXT.
DR. TOSHTE.
HE'S SAYING THAT—
plang!
WHAT'S GOING ON, HONEY?
MÁRCIA, IS EVERYTHING OK?
YOU'RE PALE...

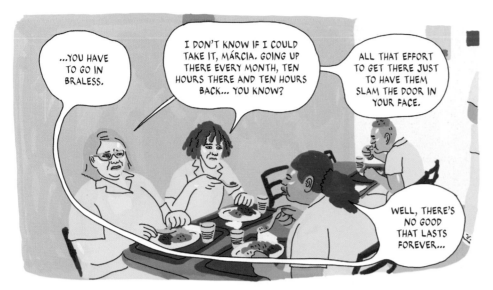

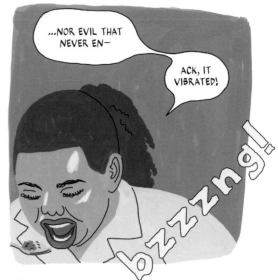

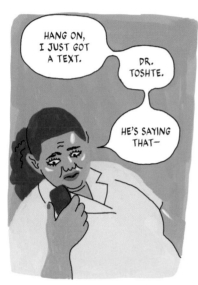

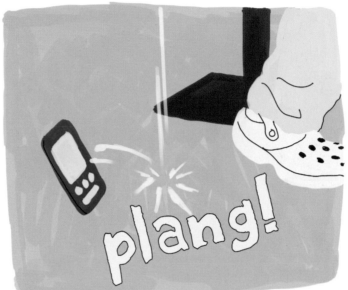

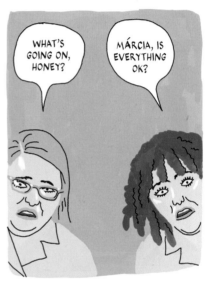

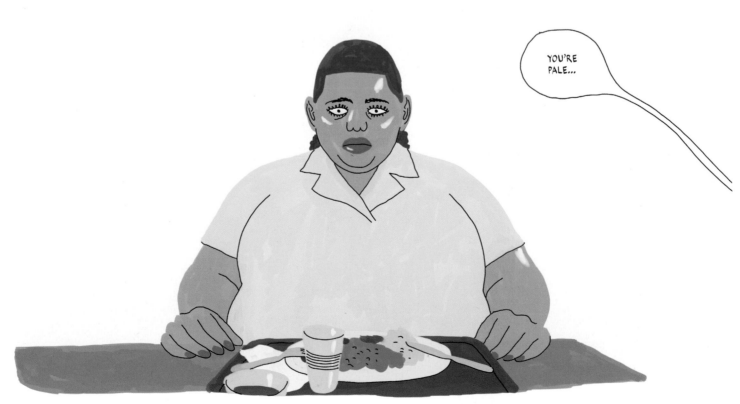

ALUÍSIO WOKE UP.

OH MY GOD, HONEY, THAT'S WONDERFUL!

LET'S HURRY DOWN TO WARD 12!

MÁRCIA, COME ON!

NO, SWEETIES, I'M NOT GOING ANYWHERE. I ALREADY SETTLED EVERYTHING I HAD TO SETTLE WITH ALUÍSIO.

I'M NOT POURING ANY MORE BROTH INTO THAT STEW.

WHAT? WHAT'S WITH THE FACES?

HE'S FINE, I'M FINE, HE'S THERE WITH HIS MOM, HIS SISTERS...

LEAVE THE GUY ALONE!

EAT UP, IT'S GETTING COLD! I STILL NEED TO CHANGE THE IV IN 407.

IT'S NOT HERE.

I'M REALLY SORRY.

I'M SURE.

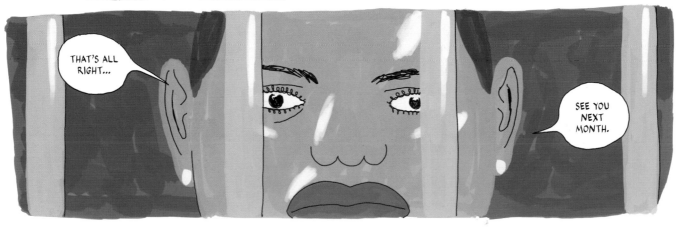

THAT'S ALL RIGHT...

SEE YOU NEXT MONTH.

90

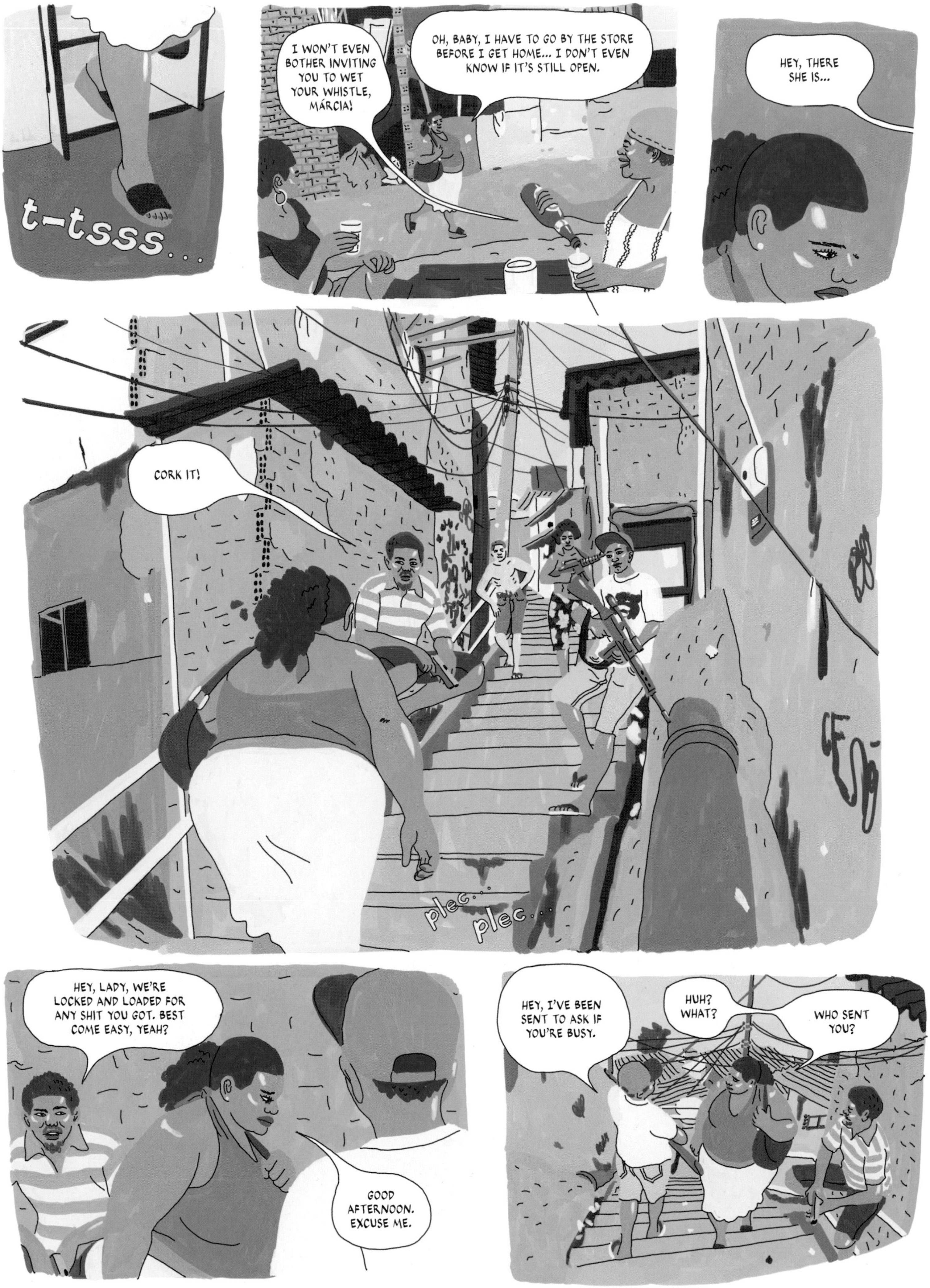
t-tsss...
I WON'T EVEN BOTHER INVITING YOU TO WET YOUR WHISTLE, MÁRCIA!
OH, BABY, I HAVE TO GO BY THE STORE BEFORE I GET HOME... I DON'T EVEN KNOW IF IT'S STILL OPEN.
HEY, THERE SHE IS...
CORK IT!
plec...
plec...
HEY, LADY, WE'RE LOCKED AND LOADED FOR ANY SHIT YOU GOT. BEST COME EASY, YEAH?
GOOD AFTERNOON. EXCUSE ME.
HEY, I'VE BEEN SENT TO ASK IF YOU'RE BUSY.
HUH? WHAT?
WHO SENT YOU?

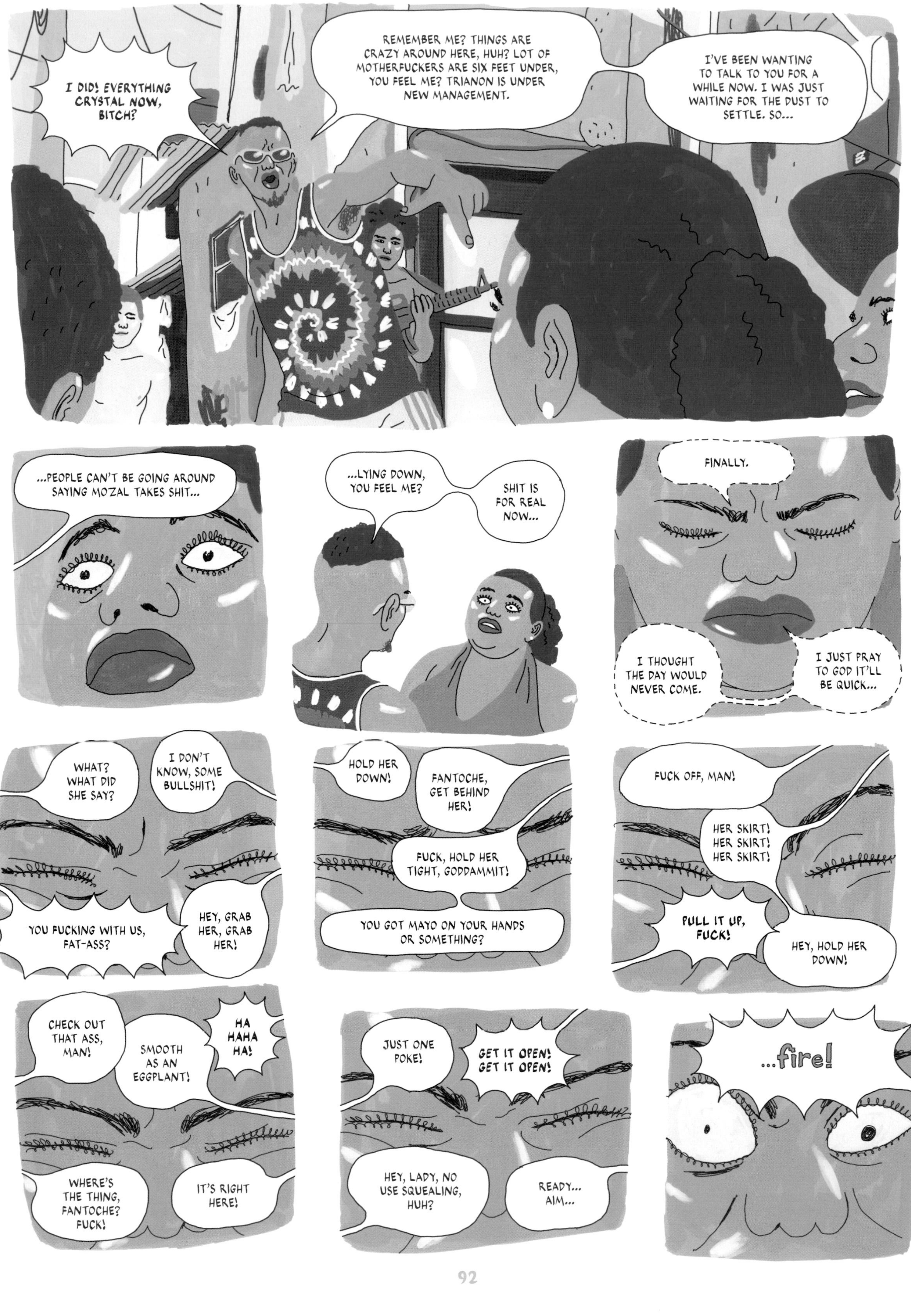
I DID! EVERYTHING CRYSTAL NOW, BITCH?
REMEMBER ME? THINGS ARE CRAZY AROUND HERE, HUH? LOT OF MOTHERFUCKERS ARE SIX FEET UNDER, YOU FEEL ME? TRIANON IS UNDER NEW MANAGEMENT.
I'VE BEEN WANTING TO TALK TO YOU FOR A WHILE NOW. I WAS JUST WAITING FOR THE DUST TO SETTLE. SO...
...PEOPLE CAN'T BE GOING AROUND SAYING MOZAL TAKES SHIT...
...LYING DOWN, YOU FEEL ME?
SHIT IS FOR REAL NOW...
FINALLY.
I THOUGHT THE DAY WOULD NEVER COME.
I JUST PRAY TO GOD IT'LL BE QUICK...
WHAT? WHAT DID SHE SAY?
I DON'T KNOW, SOME BULLSHIT!
YOU FUCKING WITH US, FAT-ASS?
HEY, GRAB HER, GRAB HER!
HOLD HER DOWN!
FANTOCHE, GET BEHIND HER!
FUCK, HOLD HER TIGHT, GODDAMMIT!
YOU GOT MAYO ON YOUR HANDS OR SOMETHING?
FUCK OFF, MAN!
HER SKIRT! HER SKIRT! HER SKIRT!
PULL IT UP, FUCK!
HEY, HOLD HER DOWN!
CHECK OUT THAT ASS, MAN!
SMOOTH AS AN EGGPLANT!
HA HAHA HA!
WHERE'S THE THING, FANTOCHE? FUCK!
IT'S RIGHT HERE!
JUST ONE POKE!
GET IT OPEN! GET IT OPEN!
HEY, LADY, NO USE SQUEALING, HUH?
READY... AIM...
...fire!

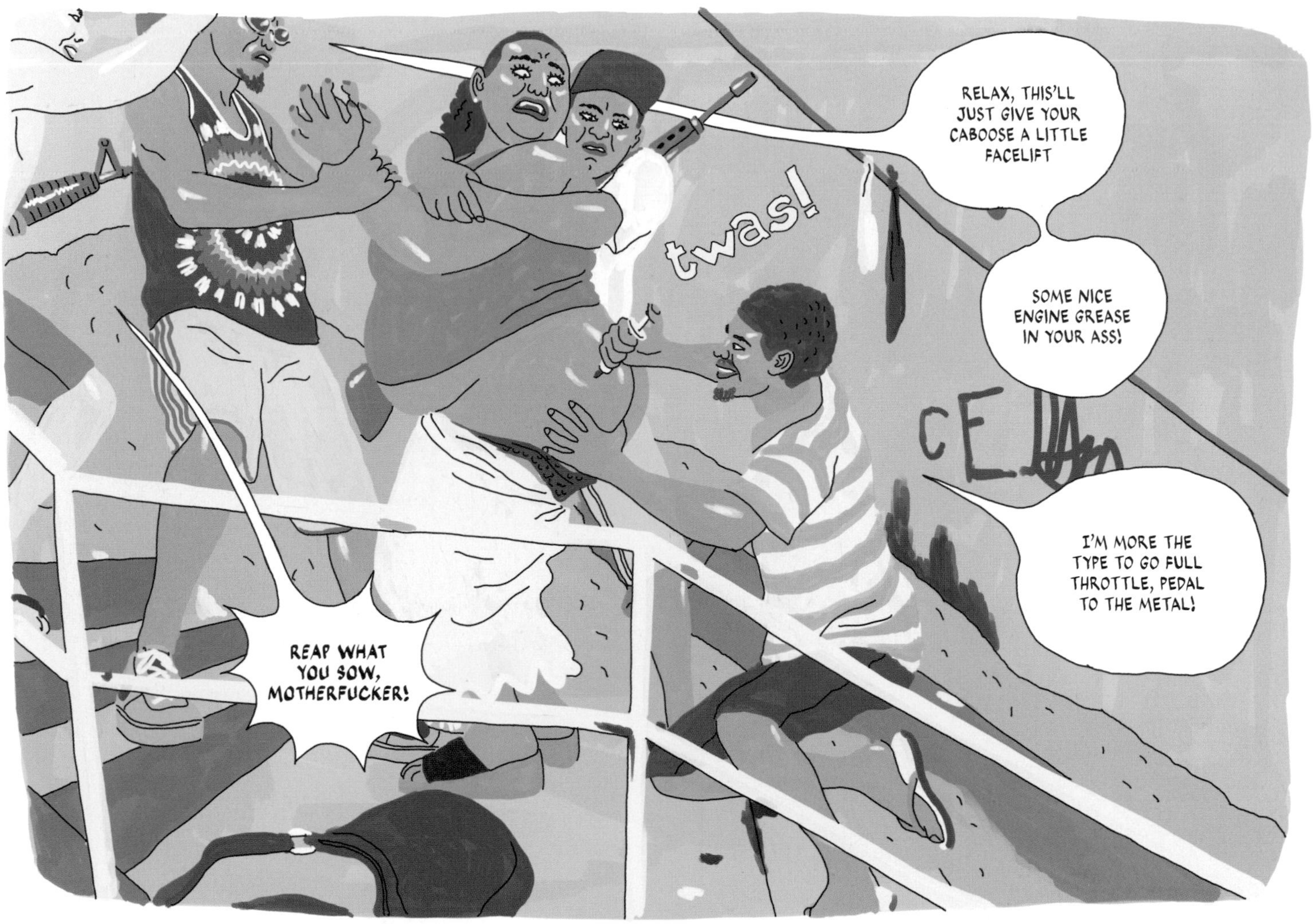
RELAX, THIS'LL JUST GIVE YOUR CABOOSE A LITTLE FACELIFT
SOME NICE ENGINE GREASE IN YOUR ASS!
twas!
CE
I'M MORE THE TYPE TO GO FULL THROTTLE, PEDAL TO THE METAL!
REAP WHAT YOU SOW, MOTHERFUCKER!

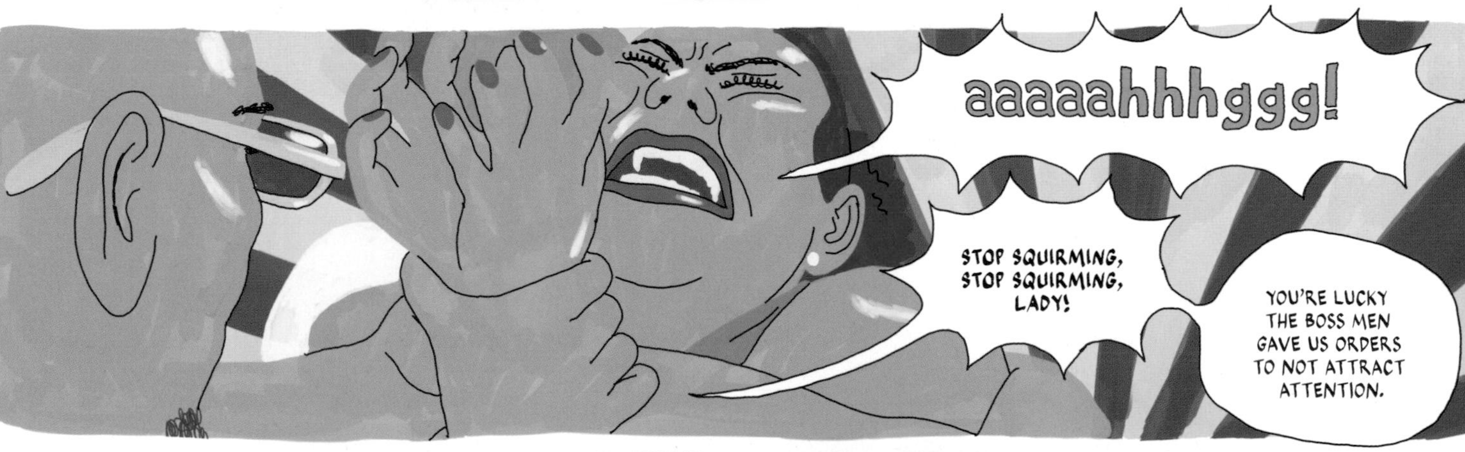
aaaaahhhggg!
STOP SQUIRMING, STOP SQUIRMING, LADY!
YOU'RE LUCKY THE BOSS MEN GAVE US ORDERS TO NOT ATTRACT ATTENTION.

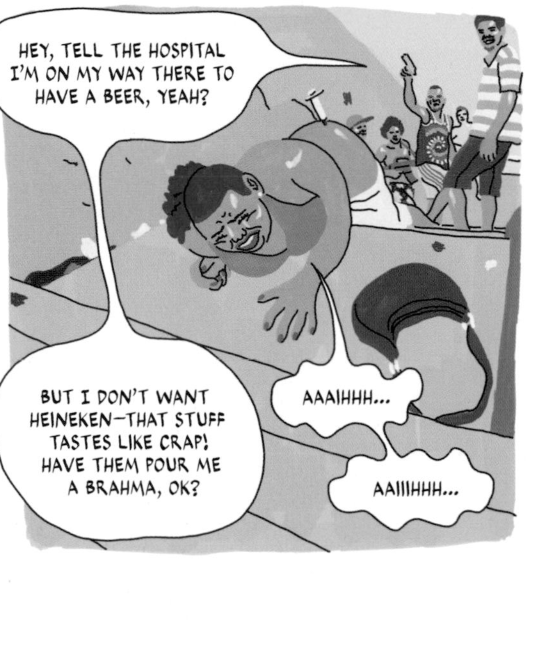
HEY, TELL THE HOSPITAL I'M ON MY WAY THERE TO HAVE A BEER, YEAH?
BUT I DON'T WANT HEINEKEN—THAT STUFF TASTES LIKE CRAP! HAVE THEM POUR ME A BRAHMA, OK?
AAAIHHH...
AAIIIHHH...

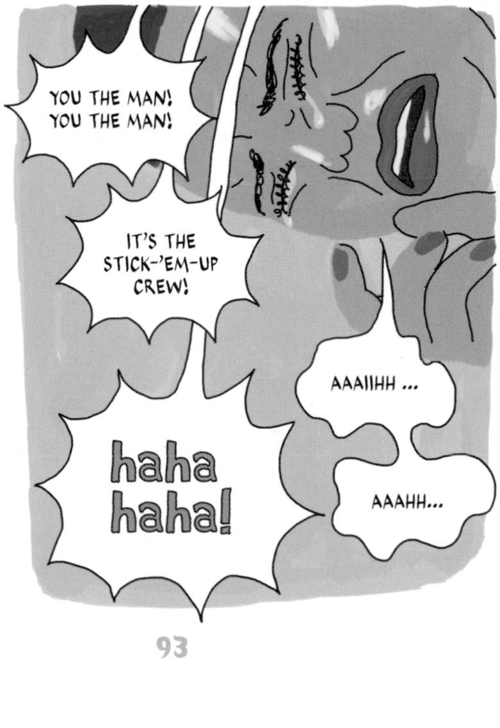
YOU THE MAN! YOU THE MAN!
IT'S THE STICK-'EM-UP CREW!
AAAIIHH ...
haha haha!
AAAHH...

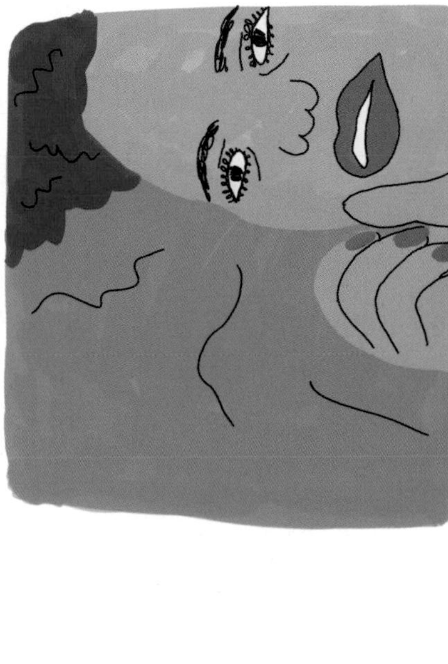

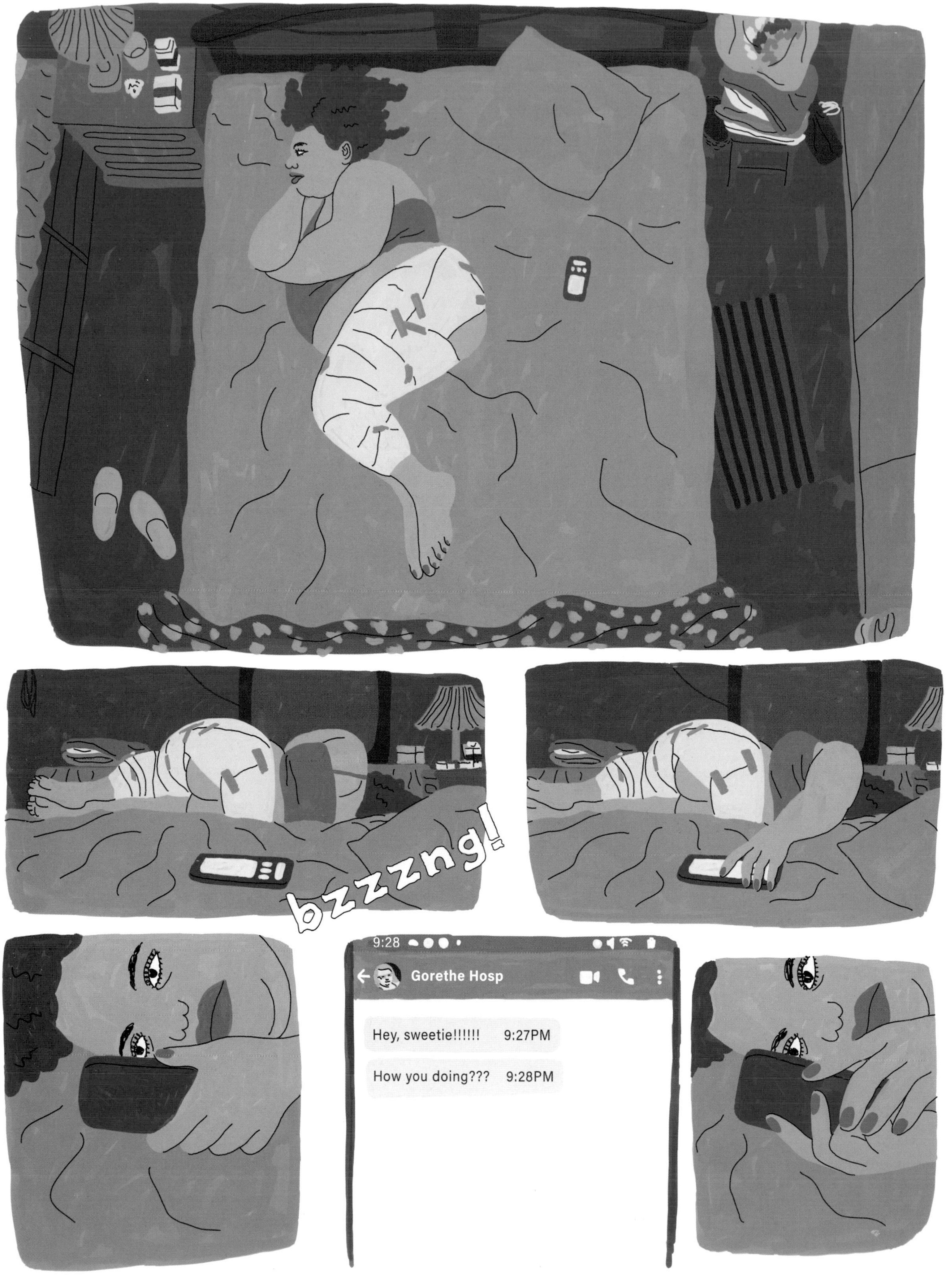
bzzzng!
9:28
Gorethe Hosp
Hey, sweetie!!!!!! 9:27PM
How you doing??? 9:28PM

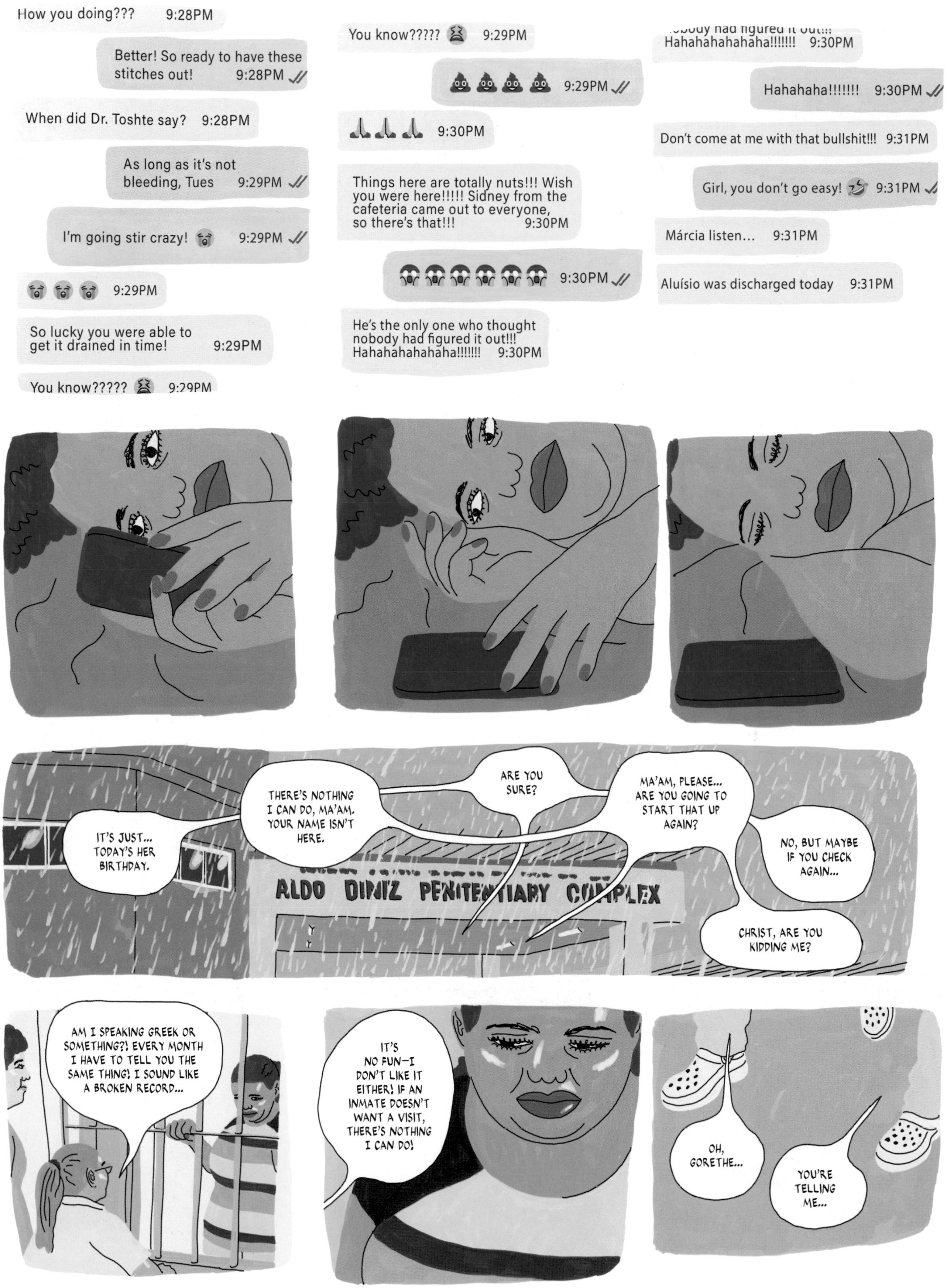
How you doing??? 9:28PM
Better! So ready to have these stitches out! 9:28PM
When did Dr. Toshte say? 9:28PM
As long as it's not bleeding, Tues 9:29PM
I'm going stir crazy! 9:29PM
9:29PM
So lucky you were able to get it drained in time! 9:29PM
You know????? 9:29PM
You know????? 9:29PM
9:29PM
9:30PM
Things here are totally nuts!!! Wish you were here!!!!! Sidney from the cafeteria came out to everyone, so there's that!!! 9:30PM
9:30PM
He's the only one who thought nobody had figured it out!!! Hahahahahahaha!!!!!!! 9:30PM
Hahahahahahaha!!!!!!! 9:30PM
Hahahaha!!!!!!! 9:30PM
Don't come at me with that bullshit!!! 9:31PM
Girl, you don't go easy! 9:31PM
Márcia listen… 9:31PM
Aluísio was discharged today 9:31PM
IT'S JUST… TODAY'S HER BIRTHDAY.
THERE'S NOTHING I CAN DO, MA'AM. YOUR NAME ISN'T HERE.
ARE YOU SURE?
MA'AM, PLEASE… ARE YOU GOING TO START THAT UP AGAIN?
NO, BUT MAYBE IF YOU CHECK AGAIN…
CHRIST, ARE YOU KIDDING ME?
ALDO DINIZ PENITENTIARY COMPLEX
AM I SPEAKING GREEK OR SOMETHING?! EVERY MONTH I HAVE TO TELL YOU THE SAME THING! I SOUND LIKE A BROKEN RECORD…
IT'S NO FUN—I DON'T LIKE IT EITHER! IF AN INMATE DOESN'T WANT A VISIT, THERE'S NOTHING I CAN DO!
OH, GORETHE…
YOU'RE TELLING ME…

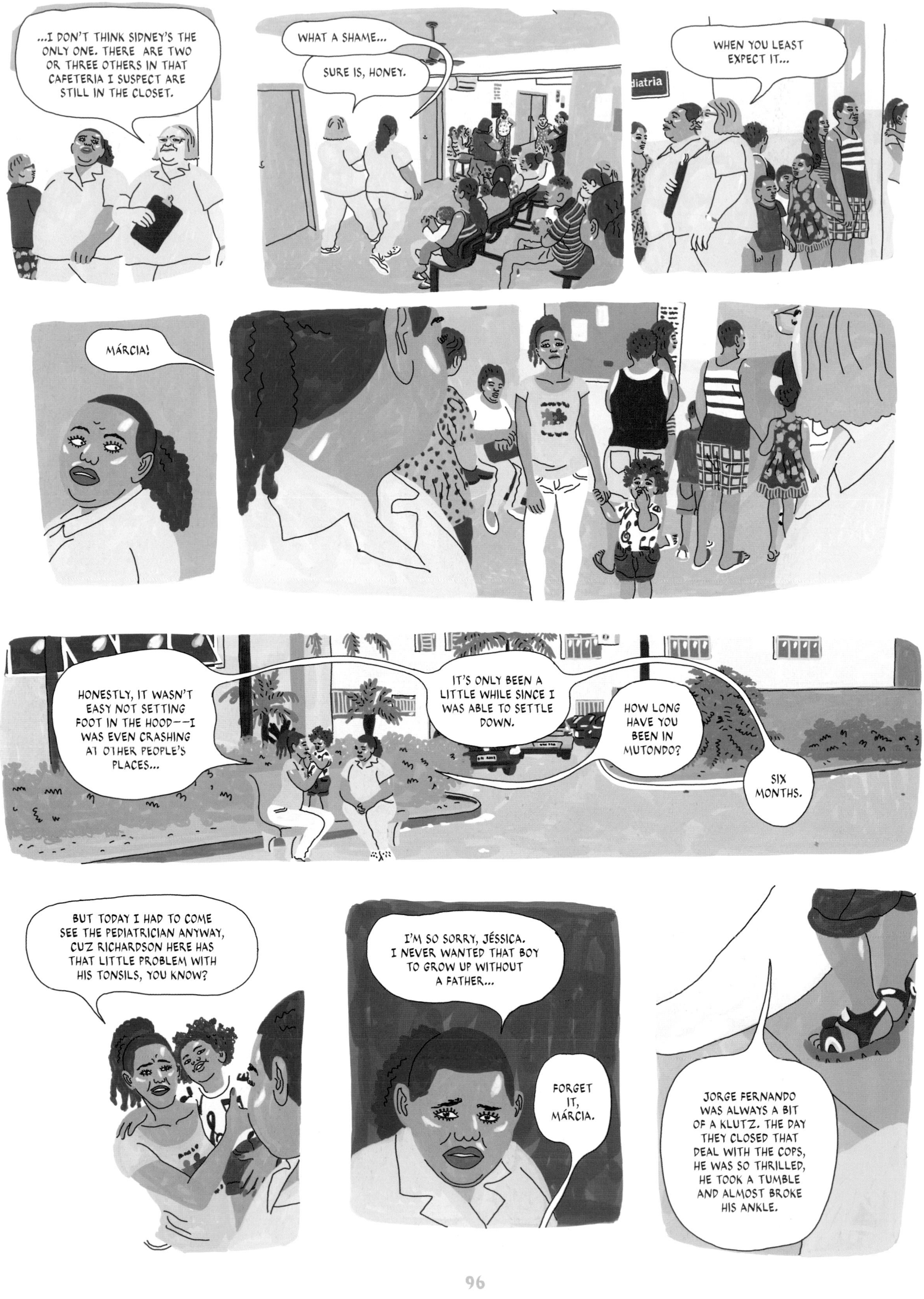
...I DON'T THINK SIDNEY'S THE ONLY ONE. THERE ARE TWO OR THREE OTHERS IN THAT CAFETERIA I SUSPECT ARE STILL IN THE CLOSET.
WHAT A SHAME...
SURE IS, HONEY.
diatria
WHEN YOU LEAST EXPECT IT...
MÁRCIA!
HONESTLY, IT WASN'T EASY NOT SETTING FOOT IN THE HOOD--I WAS EVEN CRASHING AT OTHER PEOPLE'S PLACES...
IT'S ONLY BEEN A LITTLE WHILE SINCE I WAS ABLE TO SETTLE DOWN.
HOW LONG HAVE YOU BEEN IN MUTONDO?
SIX MONTHS.
BUT TODAY I HAD TO COME SEE THE PEDIATRICIAN ANYWAY, CUZ RICHARDSON HERE HAS THAT LITTLE PROBLEM WITH HIS TONSILS, YOU KNOW?
I'M SO SORRY, JÉSSICA. I NEVER WANTED THAT BOY TO GROW UP WITHOUT A FATHER...
FORGET IT, MÁRCIA.
JORGE FERNANDO WAS ALWAYS A BIT OF A KLUTZ. THE DAY THEY CLOSED THAT DEAL WITH THE COPS, HE WAS SO THRILLED, HE TOOK A TUMBLE AND ALMOST BROKE HIS ANKLE.

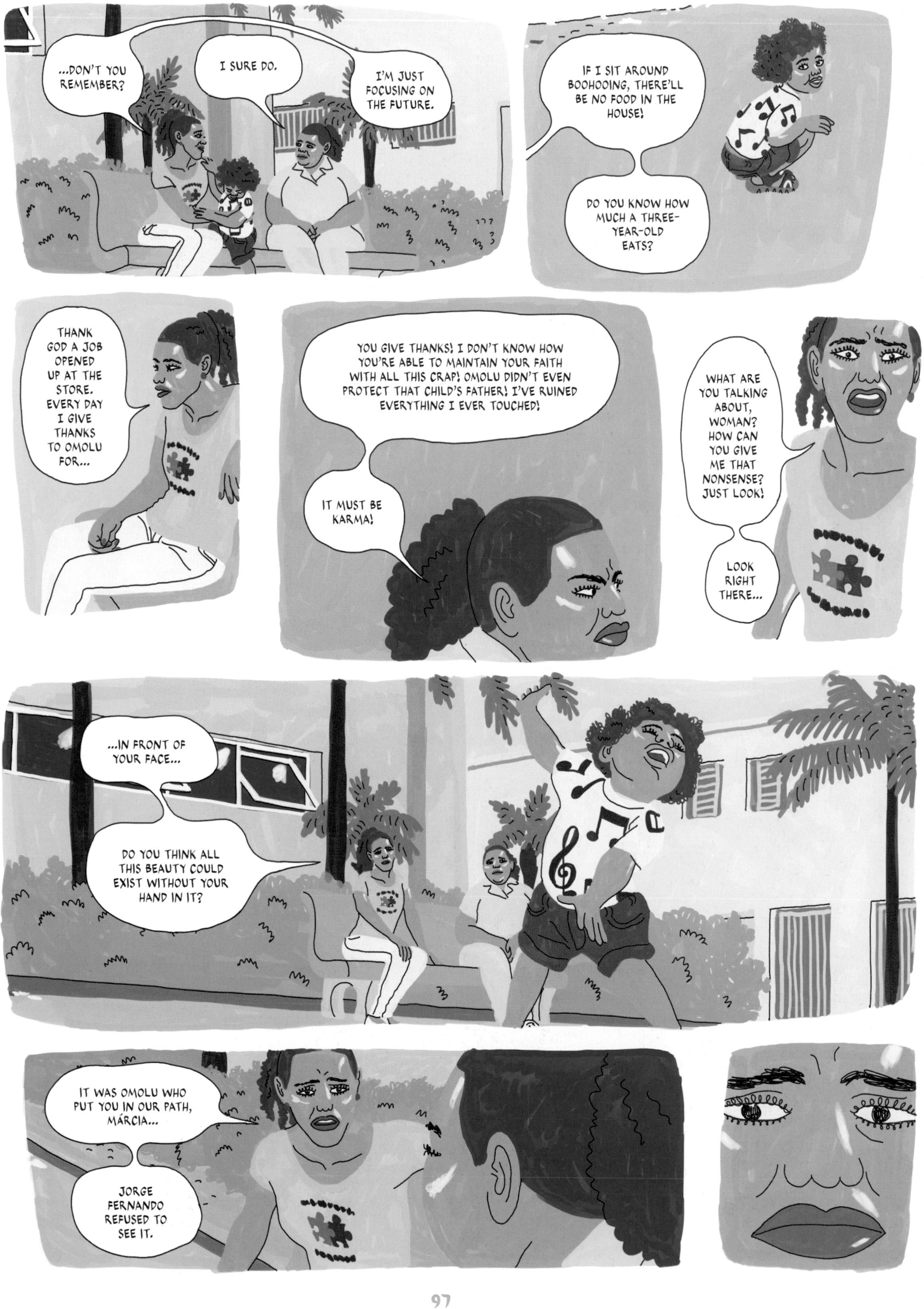
...DON'T YOU REMEMBER?
I SURE DO.
I'M JUST FOCUSING ON THE FUTURE.
IF I SIT AROUND BOOHOOING, THERE'LL BE NO FOOD IN THE HOUSE!
DO YOU KNOW HOW MUCH A THREE-YEAR-OLD EATS?
THANK GOD A JOB OPENED UP AT THE STORE. EVERY DAY I GIVE THANKS TO OMOLU FOR...
YOU GIVE THANKS! I DON'T KNOW HOW YOU'RE ABLE TO MAINTAIN YOUR FAITH WITH ALL THIS CRAP! OMOLU DIDN'T EVEN PROTECT THAT CHILD'S FATHER! I'VE RUINED EVERYTHING I EVER TOUCHED!
IT MUST BE KARMA!
WHAT ARE YOU TALKING ABOUT, WOMAN? HOW CAN YOU GIVE ME THAT NONSENSE? JUST LOOK!
LOOK RIGHT THERE...
...IN FRONT OF YOUR FACE...
DO YOU THINK ALL THIS BEAUTY COULD EXIST WITHOUT YOUR HAND IN IT?
IT WAS OMOLU WHO PUT YOU IN OUR PATH, MÁRCIA...
JORGE FERNANDO REFUSED TO SEE IT.

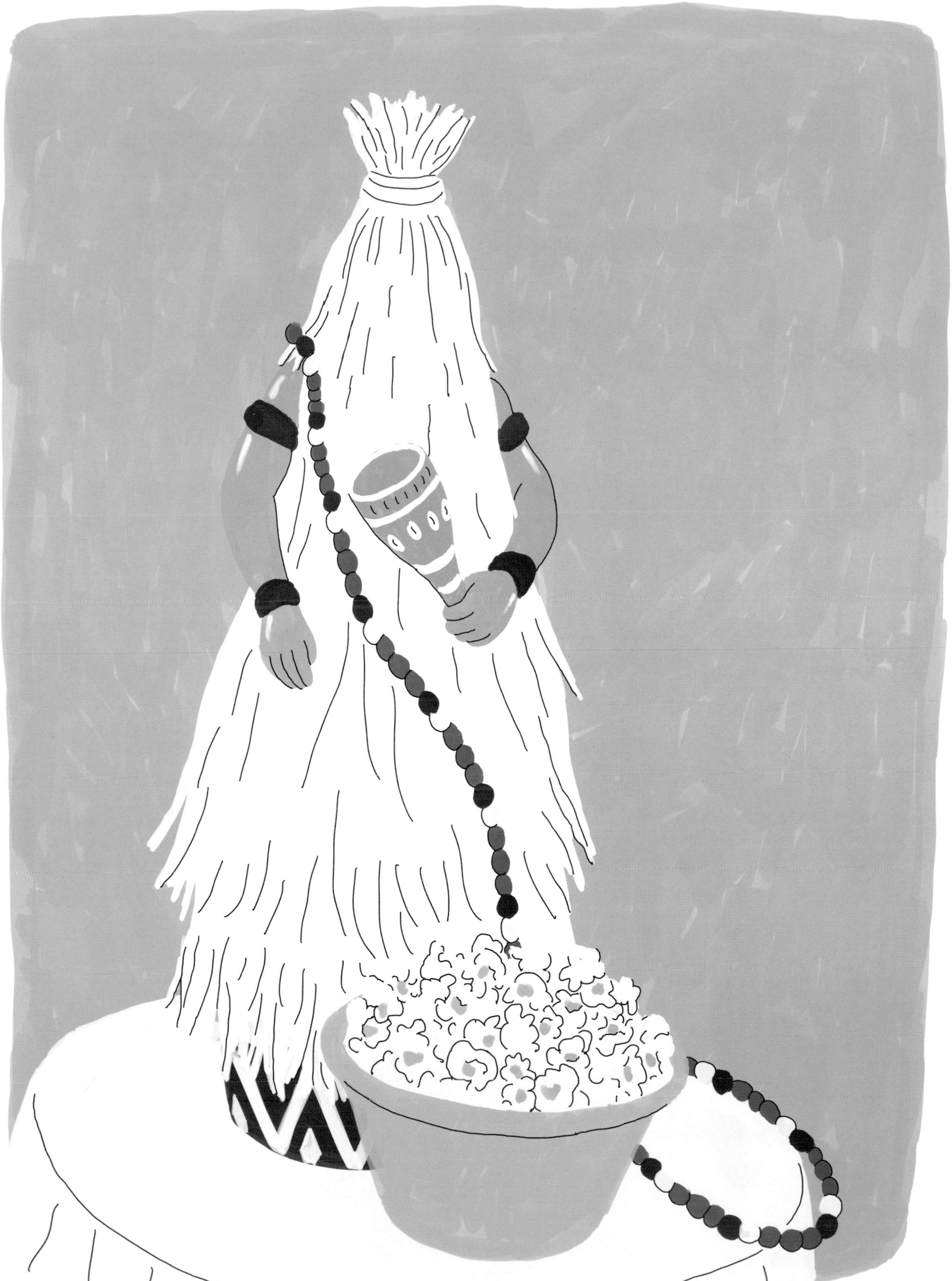

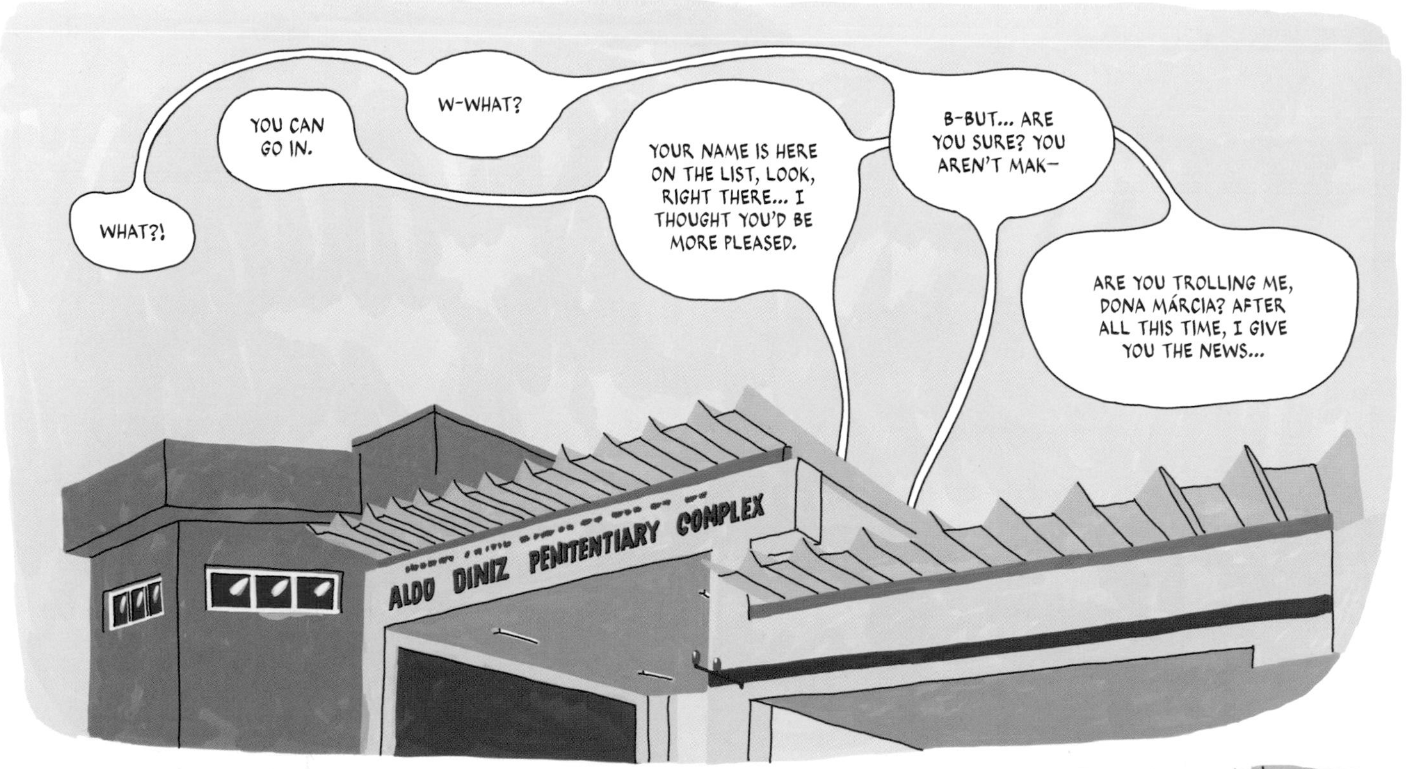
WHAT?!
YOU CAN GO IN.
W-WHAT?
YOUR NAME IS HERE ON THE LIST, LOOK, RIGHT THERE... I THOUGHT YOU'D BE MORE PLEASED.
B-BUT... ARE YOU SURE? YOU AREN'T MAK—
ARE YOU TROLLING ME, DONA MÁRCIA? AFTER ALL THIS TIME, I GIVE YOU THE NEWS...
ALDO DINIZ PENITENTIARY COMPLEX

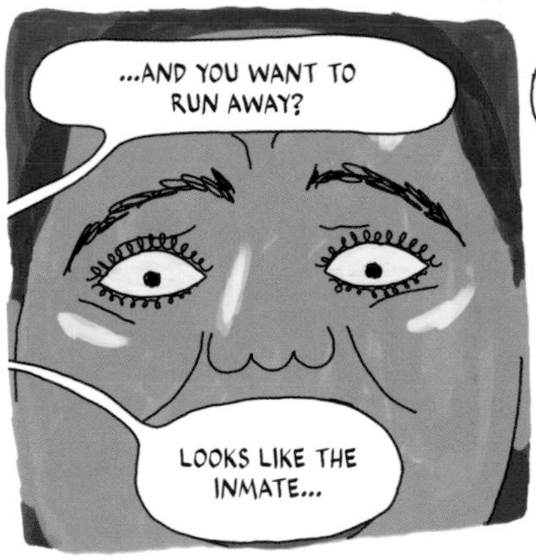
...AND YOU WANT TO RUN AWAY?
LOOKS LIKE THE INMATE...

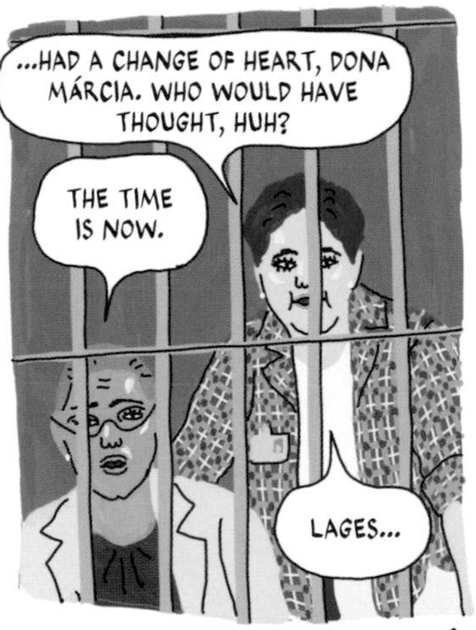
...HAD A CHANGE OF HEART, DONA MÁRCIA. WHO WOULD HAVE THOUGHT, HUH?
THE TIME IS NOW.
LAGES...

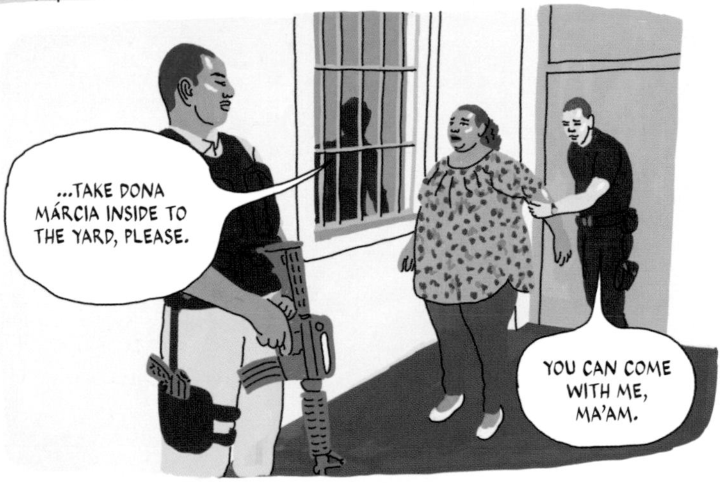
...TAKE DONA MÁRCIA INSIDE TO THE YARD, PLEASE.
YOU CAN COME WITH ME, MA'AM.

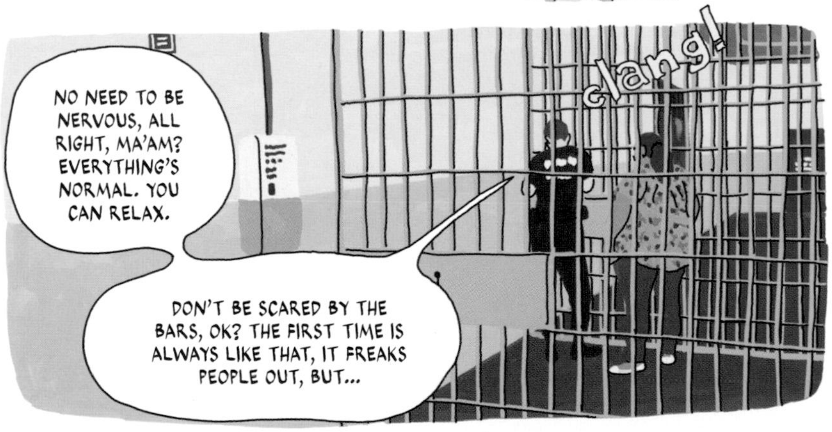
NO NEED TO BE NERVOUS, ALL RIGHT, MA'AM? EVERYTHING'S NORMAL. YOU CAN RELAX.
clang!
DON'T BE SCARED BY THE BARS, OK? THE FIRST TIME IS ALWAYS LIKE THAT, IT FREAKS PEOPLE OUT, BUT...

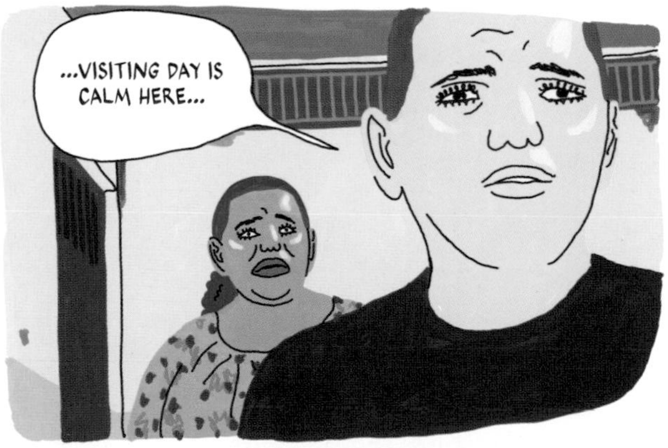
...VISITING DAY IS CALM HERE...

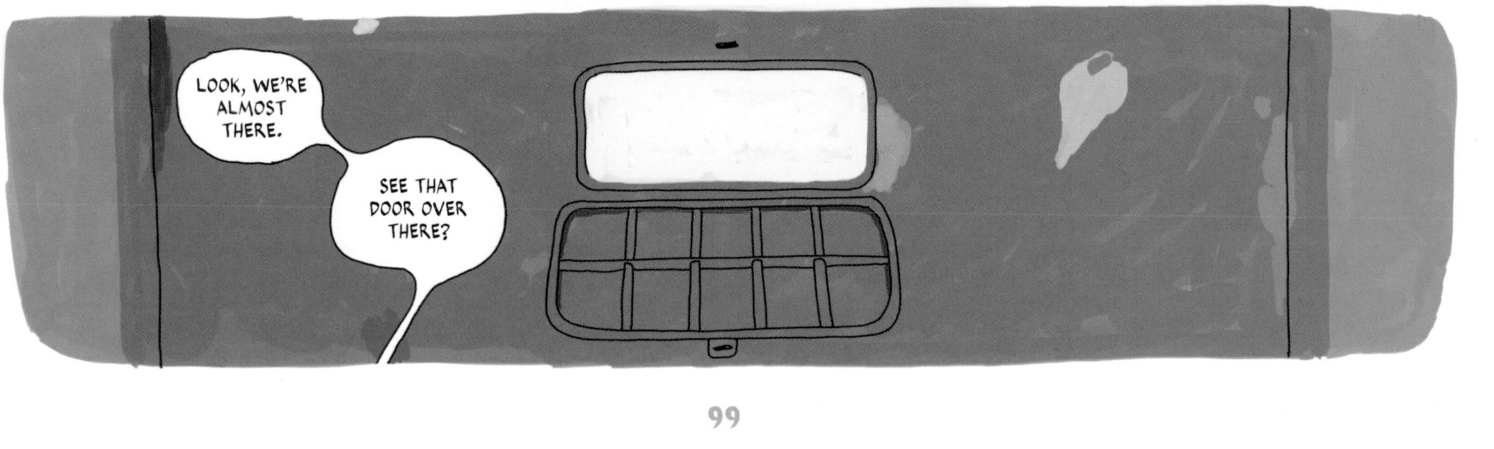
LOOK, WE'RE ALMOST THERE.
SEE THAT DOOR OVER THERE?

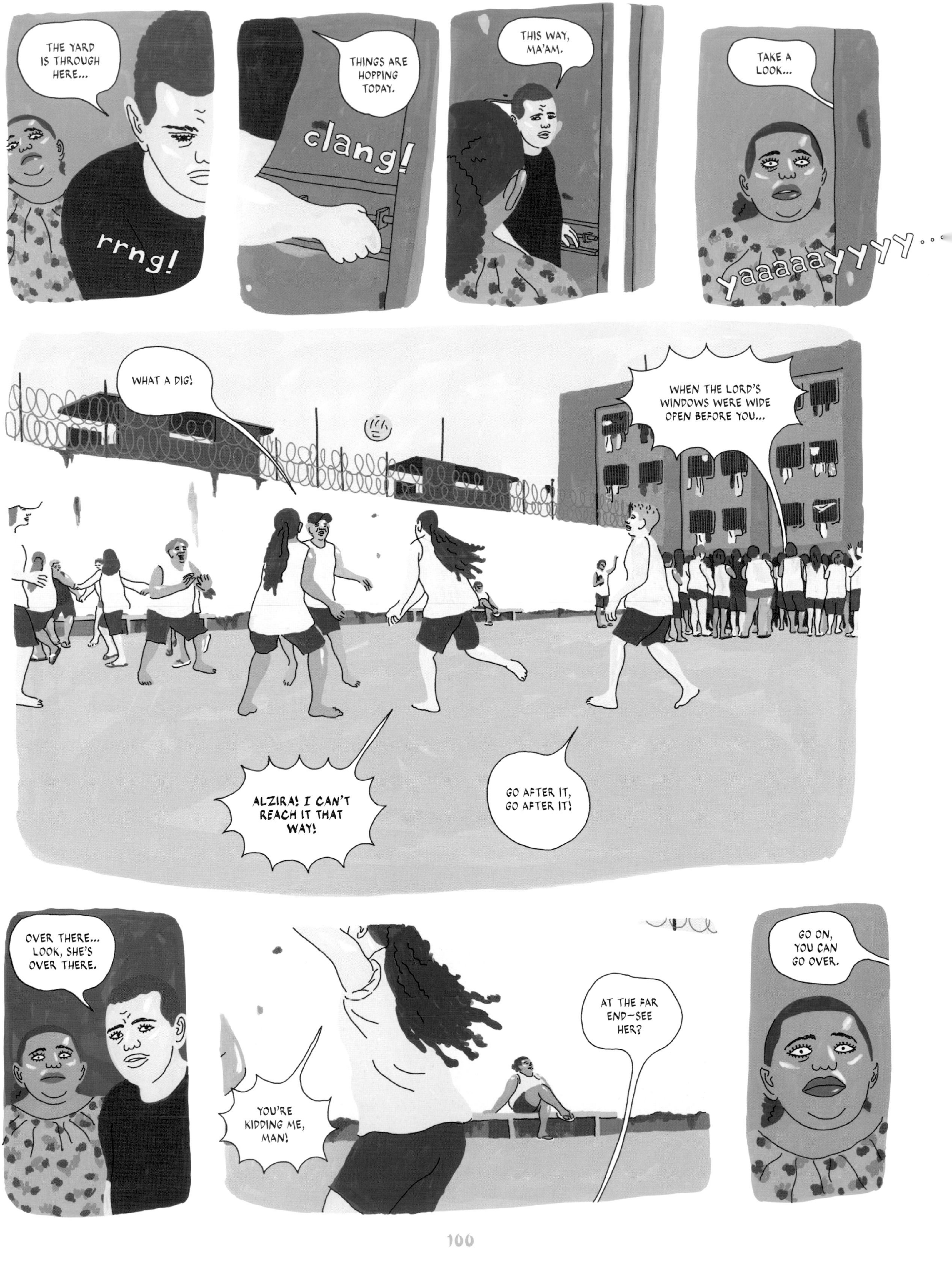
THE YARD IS THROUGH HERE...
rrng!
THINGS ARE HOPPING TODAY.
clang!
THIS WAY, MA'AM.
TAKE A LOOK...
yaaaaaYYYY...
WHAT A DIG!
WHEN THE LORD'S WINDOWS WERE WIDE OPEN BEFORE YOU...
ALZIRA! I CAN'T REACH IT THAT WAY!
GO AFTER IT, GO AFTER IT!
OVER THERE... LOOK, SHE'S OVER THERE.
YOU'RE KIDDING ME, MAN!
AT THE FAR END—SEE HER?
GO ON, YOU CAN GO OVER.

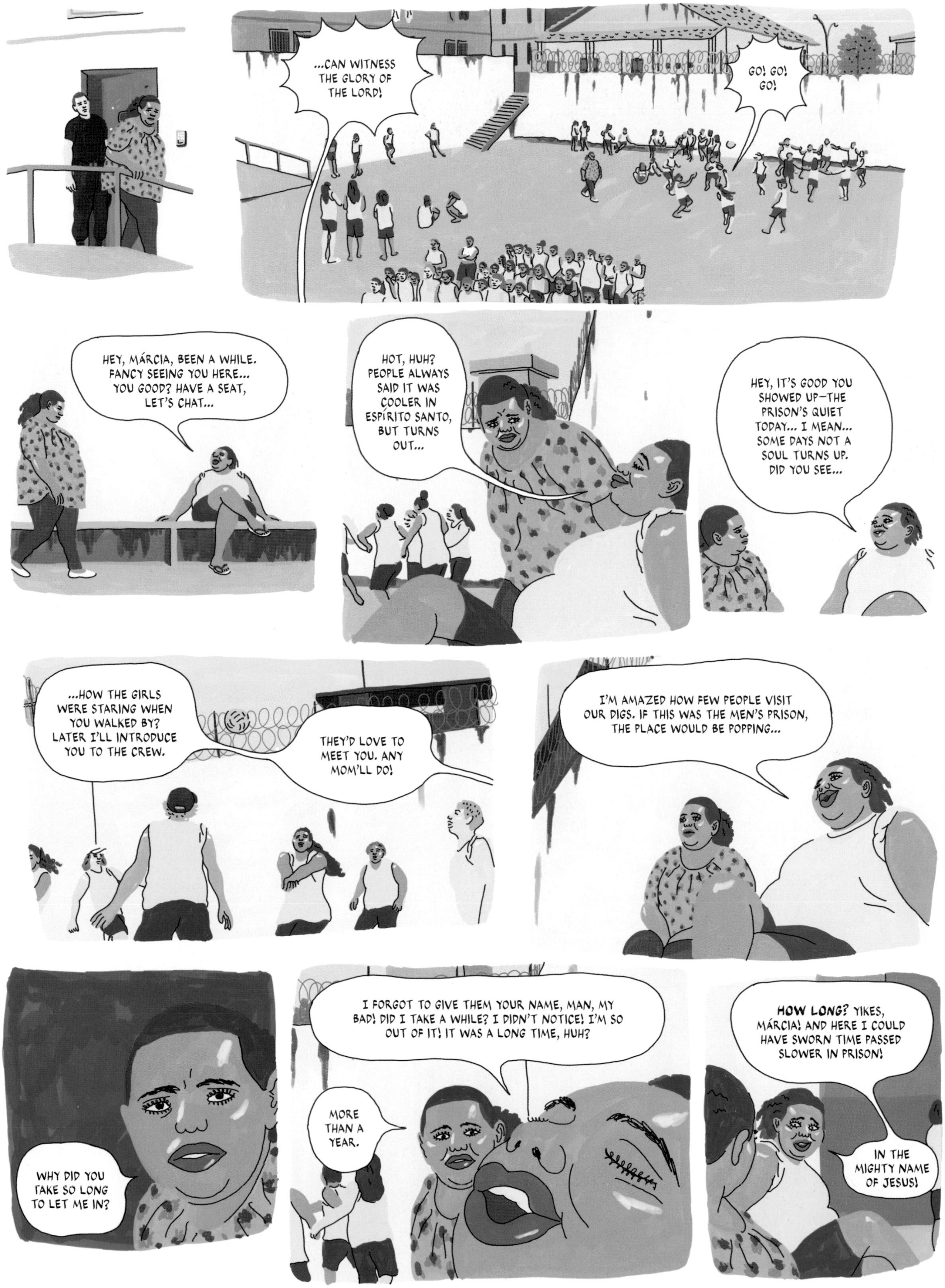

...CAN WITNESS THE GLORY OF THE LORD!
GO! GO! GO!
HEY, MÁRCIA, BEEN A WHILE. FANCY SEEING YOU HERE... YOU GOOD? HAVE A SEAT, LET'S CHAT...
HOT, HUH? PEOPLE ALWAYS SAID IT WAS COOLER IN ESPÍRITO SANTO, BUT TURNS OUT...
HEY, IT'S GOOD YOU SHOWED UP—THE PRISON'S QUIET TODAY... I MEAN... SOME DAYS NOT A SOUL TURNS UP. DID YOU SEE...
...HOW THE GIRLS WERE STARING WHEN YOU WALKED BY? LATER I'LL INTRODUCE YOU TO THE CREW.
THEY'D LOVE TO MEET YOU. ANY MOM'LL DO!
I'M AMAZED HOW FEW PEOPLE VISIT OUR DIGS. IF THIS WAS THE MEN'S PRISON, THE PLACE WOULD BE POPPING...
WHY DID YOU TAKE SO LONG TO LET ME IN?
I FORGOT TO GIVE THEM YOUR NAME, MAN, MY BAD! DID I TAKE A WHILE? I DIDN'T NOTICE! I'M SO OUT OF IT! IT WAS A LONG TIME, HUH?
MORE THAN A YEAR.
HOW LONG? YIKES, MÁRCIA! AND HERE I COULD HAVE SWORN TIME PASSED SLOWER IN PRISON!
IN THE MIGHTY NAME OF JESUS!

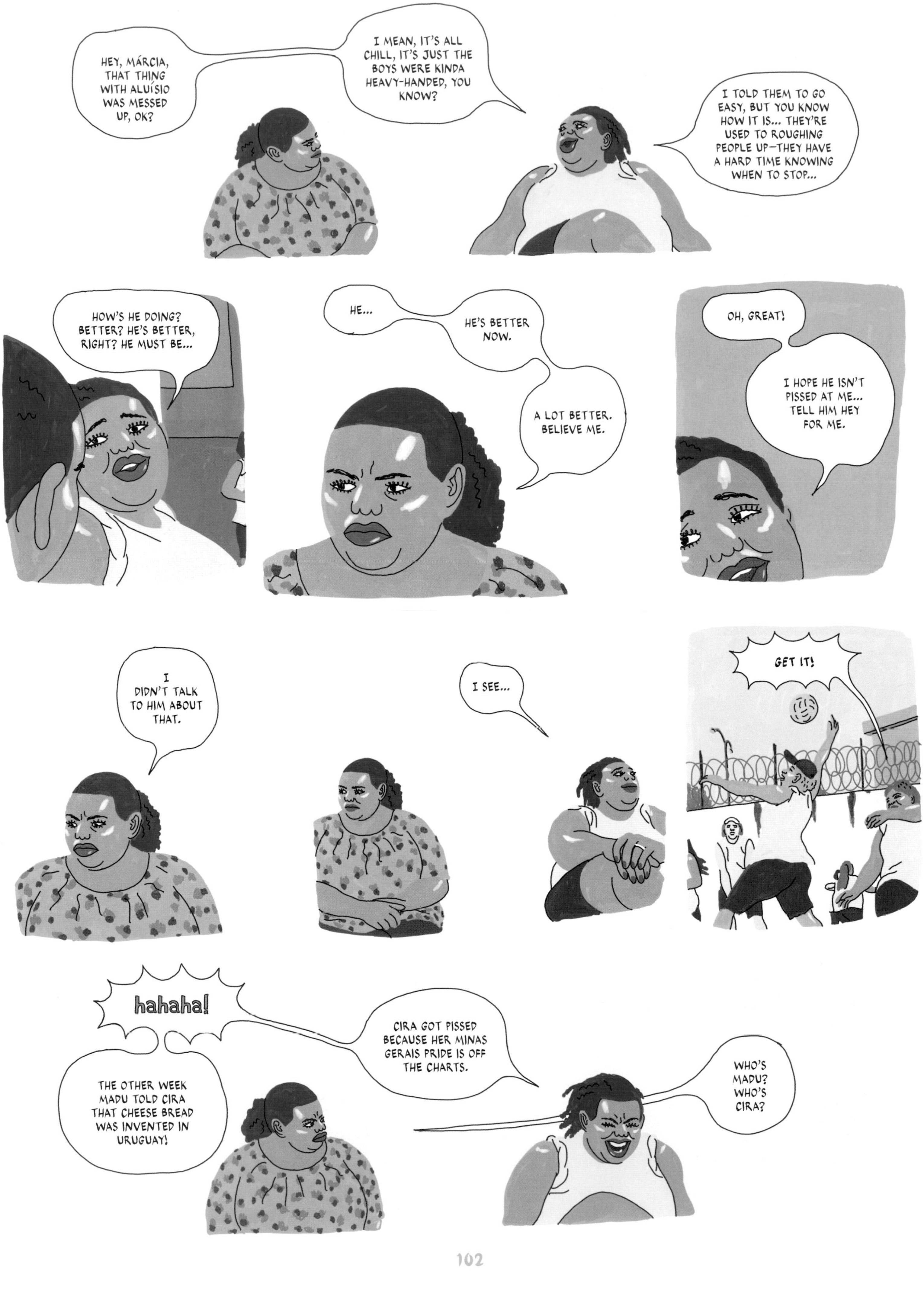
HEY, MÁRCIA, THAT THING WITH ALUÍSIO WAS MESSED UP, OK?
I MEAN, IT'S ALL CHILL, IT'S JUST THE BOYS WERE KINDA HEAVY-HANDED, YOU KNOW?
I TOLD THEM TO GO EASY, BUT YOU KNOW HOW IT IS... THEY'RE USED TO ROUGHING PEOPLE UP—THEY HAVE A HARD TIME KNOWING WHEN TO STOP...
HOW'S HE DOING? BETTER? HE'S BETTER, RIGHT? HE MUST BE...
HE...
HE'S BETTER NOW.
A LOT BETTER. BELIEVE ME.
OH, GREAT!
I HOPE HE ISN'T PISSED AT ME... TELL HIM HEY FOR ME.
I DIDN'T TALK TO HIM ABOUT THAT.
I SEE...
GET IT!
hahaha!
THE OTHER WEEK MADU TOLD CIRA THAT CHEESE BREAD WAS INVENTED IN URUGUAY!
CIRA GOT PISSED BECAUSE HER MINAS GERAIS PRIDE IS OFF THE CHARTS.
WHO'S MADU? WHO'S CIRA?

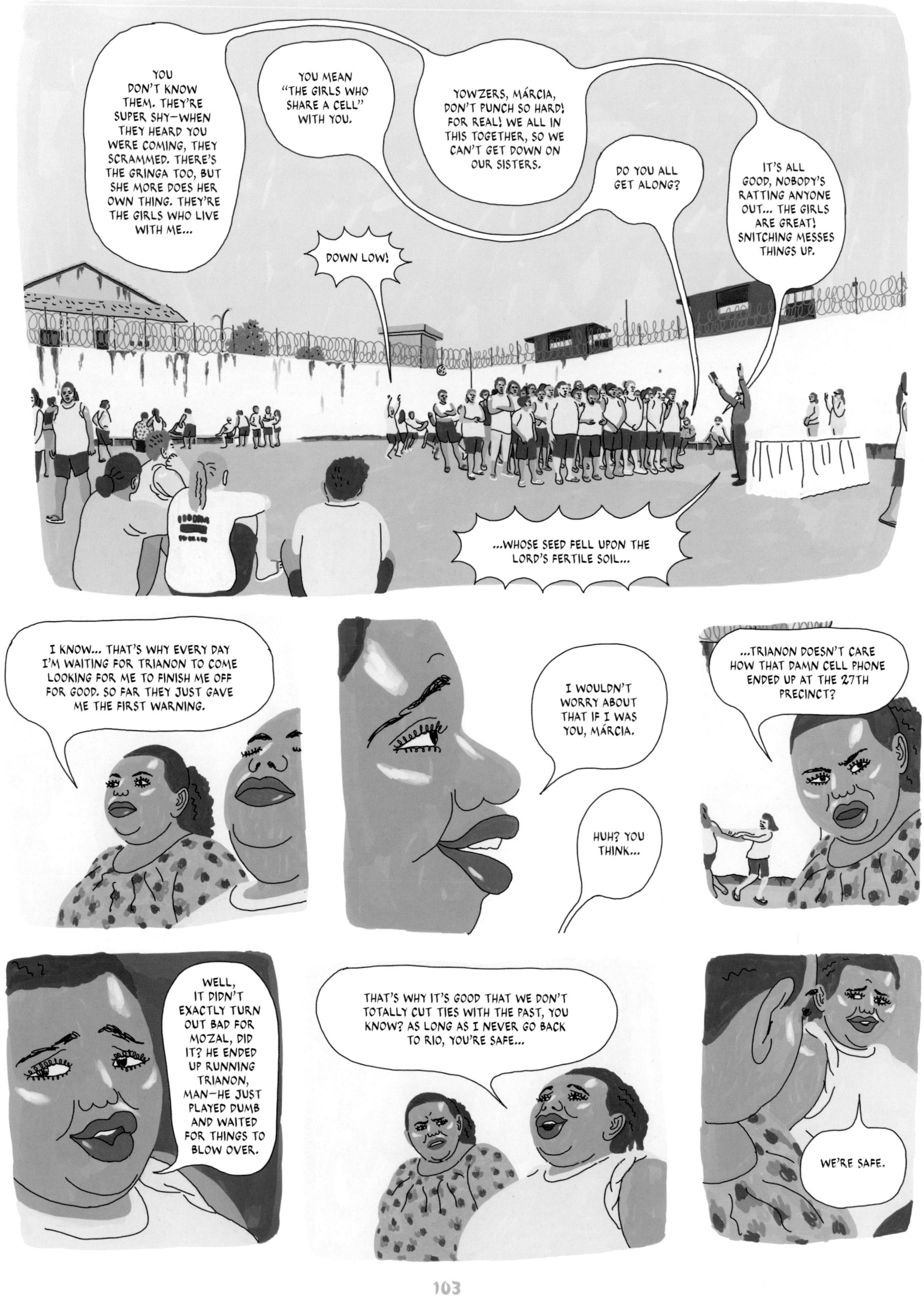
YOU DON'T KNOW THEM. THEY'RE SUPER SHY—WHEN THEY HEARD YOU WERE COMING, THEY SCRAMMED. THERE'S THE GRINGA TOO, BUT SHE MORE DOES HER OWN THING. THEY'RE THE GIRLS WHO LIVE WITH ME...
YOU MEAN "THE GIRLS WHO SHARE A CELL" WITH YOU.
YOWZERS, MÁRCIA, DON'T PUNCH SO HARD! FOR REAL! WE ALL IN THIS TOGETHER, SO WE CAN'T GET DOWN ON OUR SISTERS.
DO YOU ALL GET ALONG?
IT'S ALL GOOD, NOBODY'S RATTING ANYONE OUT... THE GIRLS ARE GREAT! SNITCHING MESSES THINGS UP.
DOWN LOW!
...WHOSE SEED FELL UPON THE LORD'S FERTILE SOIL...
I KNOW... THAT'S WHY EVERY DAY I'M WAITING FOR TRIANON TO COME LOOKING FOR ME TO FINISH ME OFF FOR GOOD. SO FAR THEY JUST GAVE ME THE FIRST WARNING.
I WOULDN'T WORRY ABOUT THAT IF I WAS YOU, MÁRCIA.
HUH? YOU THINK...
...TRIANON DOESN'T CARE HOW THAT DAMN CELL PHONE ENDED UP AT THE 27TH PRECINCT?
WELL, IT DIDN'T EXACTLY TURN OUT BAD FOR MOZAL, DID IT? HE ENDED UP RUNNING TRIANON, MAN—HE JUST PLAYED DUMB AND WAITED FOR THINGS TO BLOW OVER.
THAT'S WHY IT'S GOOD THAT WE DON'T TOTALLY CUT TIES WITH THE PAST, YOU KNOW? AS LONG AS I NEVER GO BACK TO RIO, YOU'RE SAFE...
WE'RE SAFE.

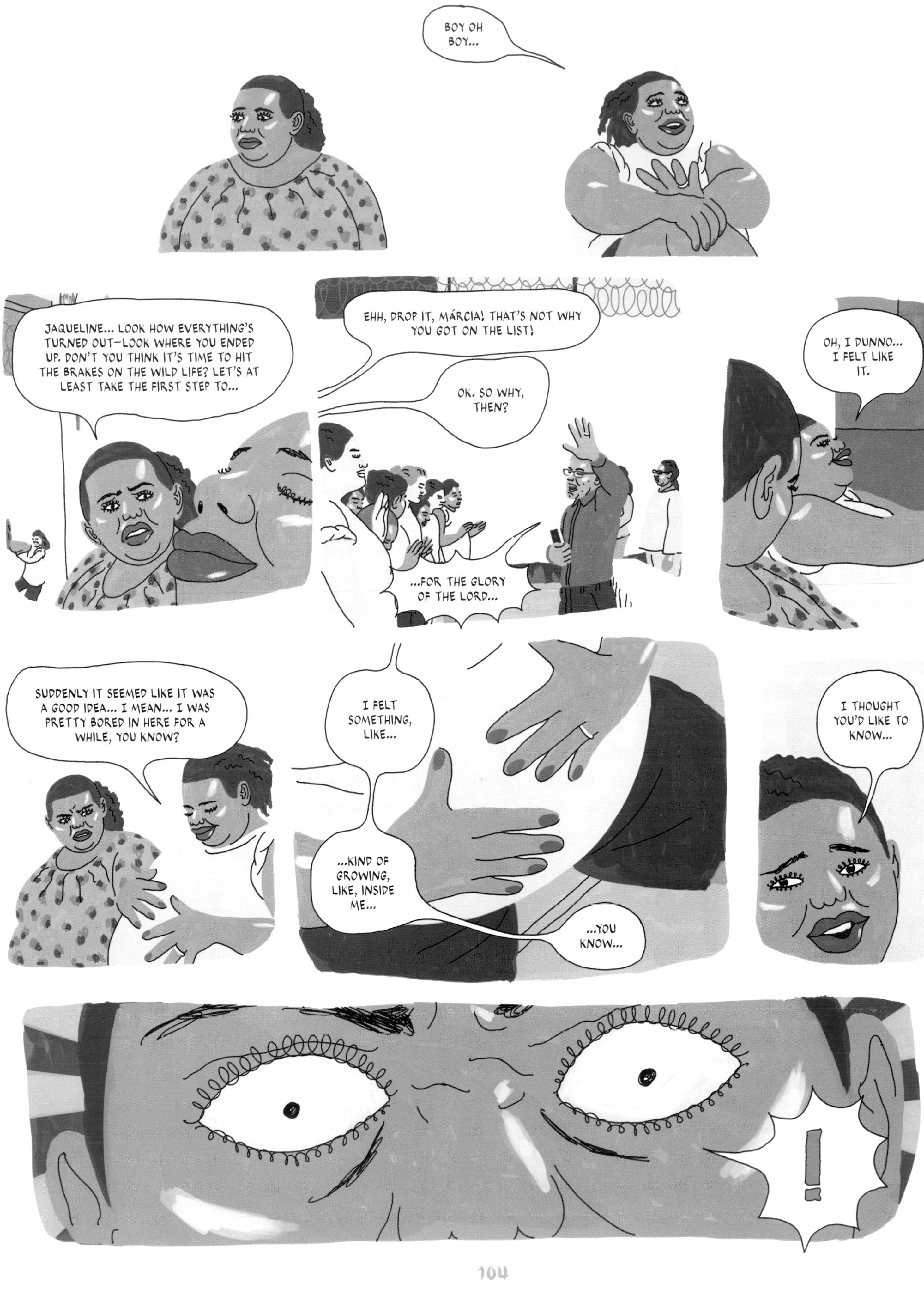

BOY OH BOY...
JAQUELINE... LOOK HOW EVERYTHING'S TURNED OUT—LOOK WHERE YOU ENDED UP. DON'T YOU THINK IT'S TIME TO HIT THE BRAKES ON THE WILD LIFE? LET'S AT LEAST TAKE THE FIRST STEP TO...
EHH, DROP IT, MÁRCIA! THAT'S NOT WHY YOU GOT ON THE LIST!
OK. SO WHY, THEN?
...FOR THE GLORY OF THE LORD...
OH, I DUNNO... I FELT LIKE IT.
SUDDENLY IT SEEMED LIKE IT WAS A GOOD IDEA... I MEAN... I WAS PRETTY BORED IN HERE FOR A WHILE, YOU KNOW?
I FELT SOMETHING, LIKE...
...KIND OF GROWING, LIKE, INSIDE ME...
...YOU KNOW...
I THOUGHT YOU'D LIKE TO KNOW...
!

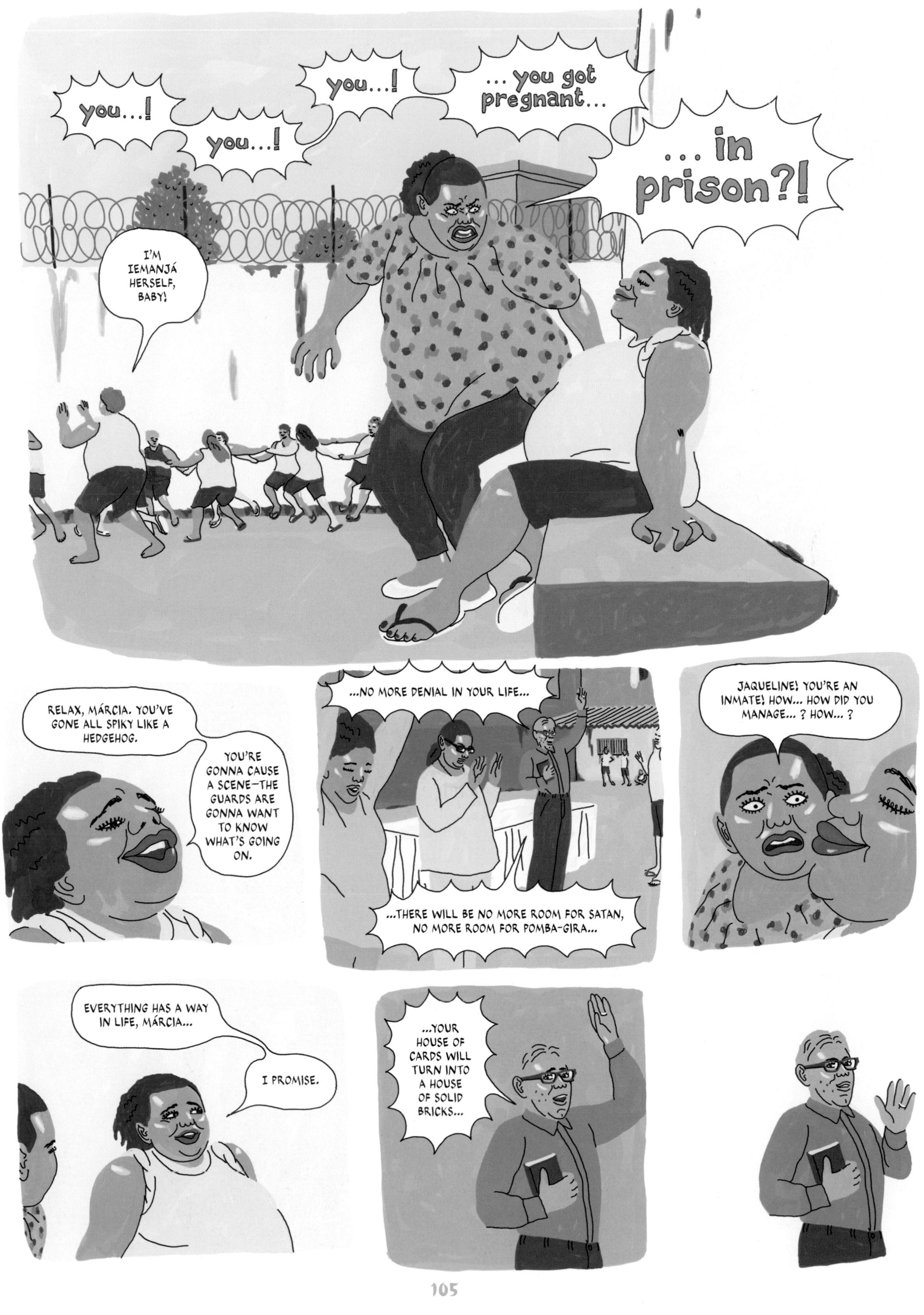
you...!
you...!
you...!
... you got pregnant...
... in prison?!
I'M IEMANJÁ HERSELF, BABY!
RELAX, MÁRCIA. YOU'VE GONE ALL SPIKY LIKE A HEDGEHOG.
YOU'RE GONNA CAUSE A SCENE—THE GUARDS ARE GONNA WANT TO KNOW WHAT'S GOING ON.
...NO MORE DENIAL IN YOUR LIFE...
...THERE WILL BE NO MORE ROOM FOR SATAN, NO MORE ROOM FOR POMBA-GIRA...
JAQUELINE! YOU'RE AN INMATE! HOW... HOW DID YOU MANAGE... ? HOW... ?
EVERYTHING HAS A WAY IN LIFE, MÁRCIA...
I PROMISE.
...YOUR HOUSE OF CARDS WILL TURN INTO A HOUSE OF SOLID BRICKS...

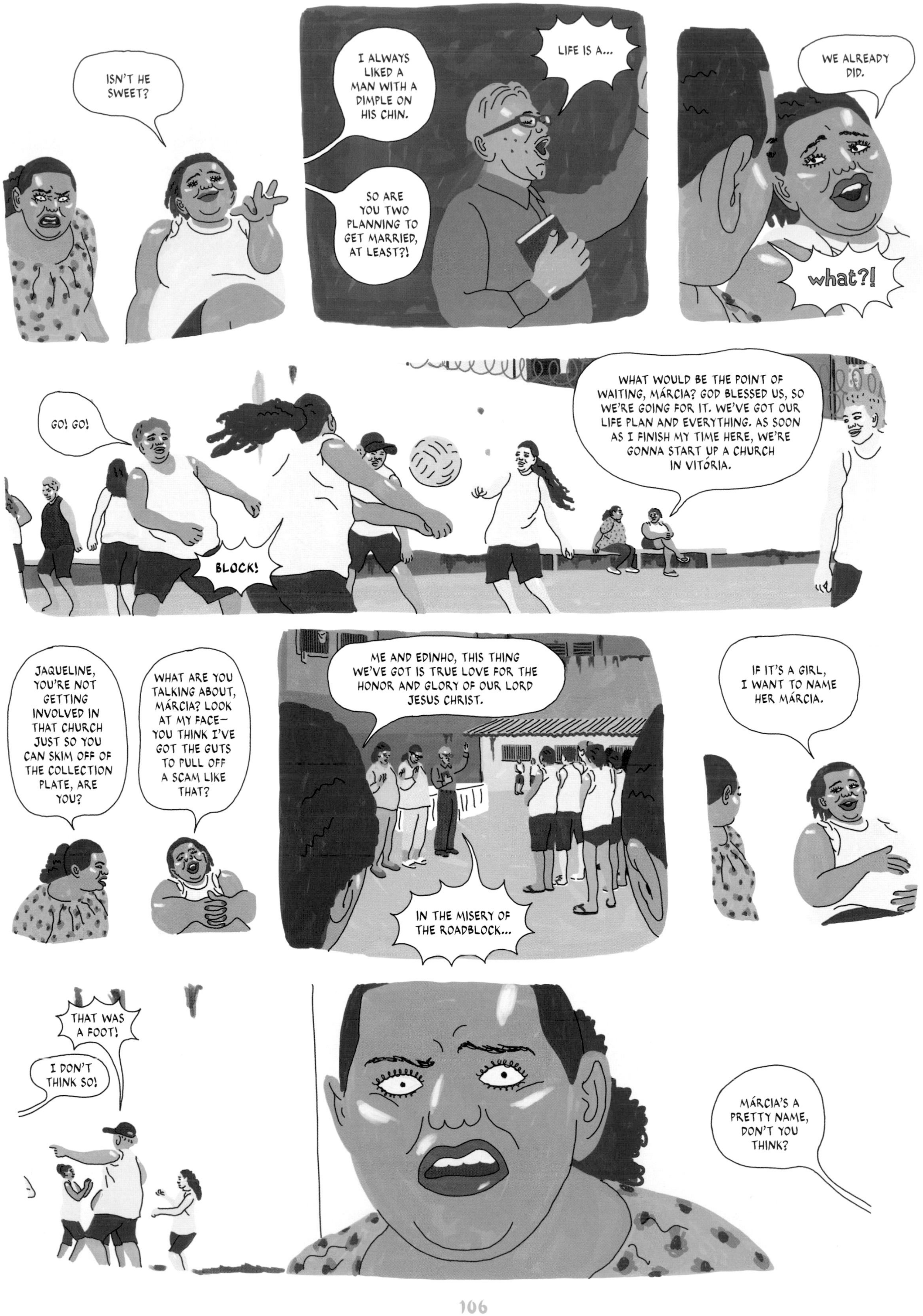
ISN'T HE SWEET?
I ALWAYS LIKED A MAN WITH A DIMPLE ON HIS CHIN.
LIFE IS A...
SO ARE YOU TWO PLANNING TO GET MARRIED, AT LEAST?!
WE ALREADY DID.
what?!
GO! GO!
BLOCK!
WHAT WOULD BE THE POINT OF WAITING, MÁRCIA? GOD BLESSED US, SO WE'RE GOING FOR IT. WE'VE GOT OUR LIFE PLAN AND EVERYTHING. AS SOON AS I FINISH MY TIME HERE, WE'RE GONNA START UP A CHURCH IN VITÓRIA.
JAQUELINE, YOU'RE NOT GETTING INVOLVED IN THAT CHURCH JUST SO YOU CAN SKIM OFF OF THE COLLECTION PLATE, ARE YOU?
WHAT ARE YOU TALKING ABOUT, MÁRCIA? LOOK AT MY FACE— YOU THINK I'VE GOT THE GUTS TO PULL OFF A SCAM LIKE THAT?
ME AND EDINHO, THIS THING WE'VE GOT IS TRUE LOVE FOR THE HONOR AND GLORY OF OUR LORD JESUS CHRIST.
IN THE MISERY OF THE ROADBLOCK...
IF IT'S A GIRL, I WANT TO NAME HER MÁRCIA.
THAT WAS A FOOT!
I DON'T THINK SO!
MÁRCIA'S A PRETTY NAME, DON'T YOU THINK?

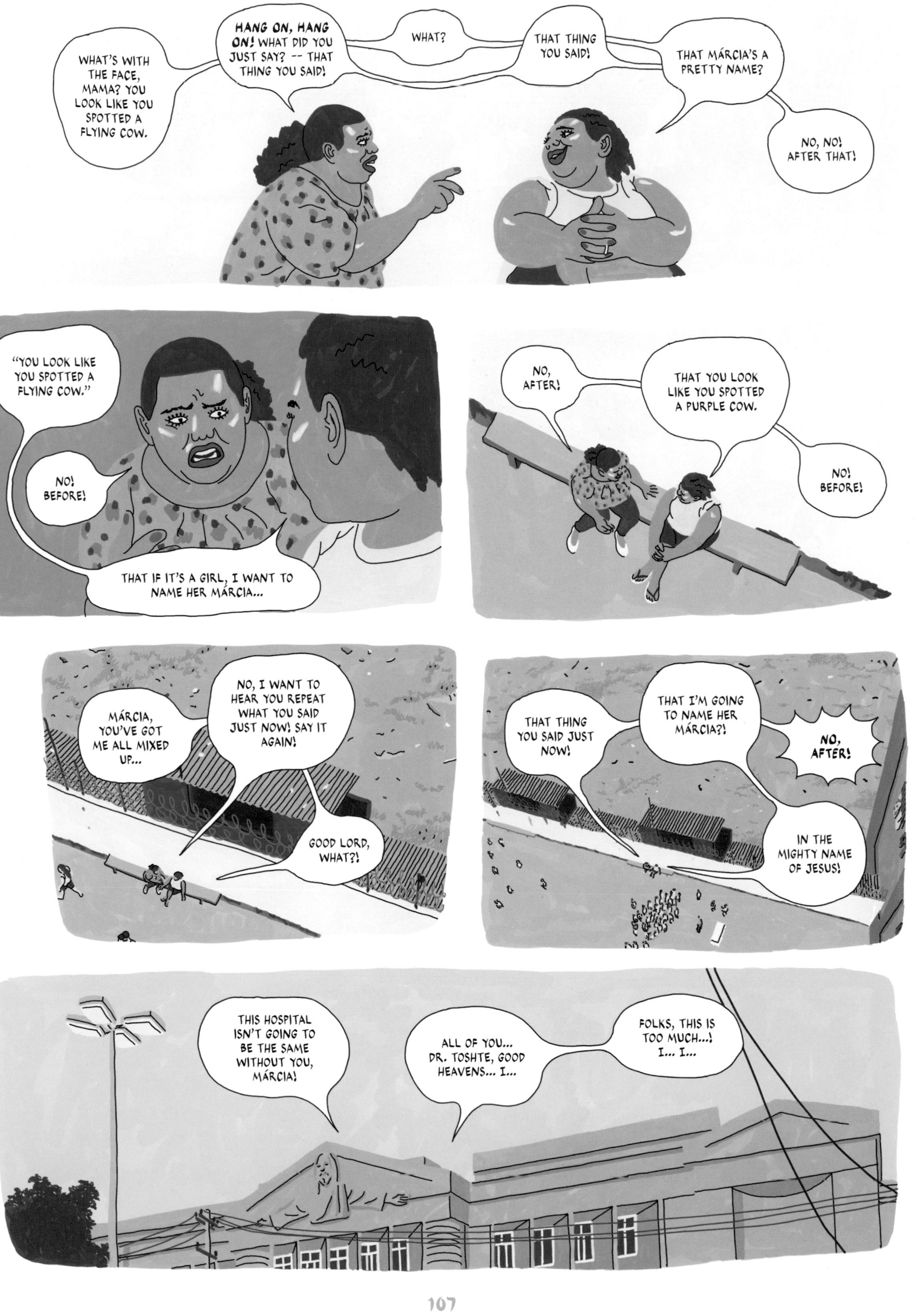
WHAT'S WITH THE FACE, MAMA? YOU LOOK LIKE YOU SPOTTED A FLYING COW.
HANG ON, HANG ON! WHAT DID YOU JUST SAY? -- THAT THING YOU SAID!
WHAT?
THAT THING YOU SAID!
THAT MÁRCIA'S A PRETTY NAME?
NO, NO! AFTER THAT!
"YOU LOOK LIKE YOU SPOTTED A FLYING COW."
NO! BEFORE!
THAT IF IT'S A GIRL, I WANT TO NAME HER MÁRCIA...
NO, AFTER!
THAT YOU LOOK LIKE YOU SPOTTED A PURPLE COW.
NO! BEFORE!
MÁRCIA, YOU'VE GOT ME ALL MIXED UP...
NO, I WANT TO HEAR YOU REPEAT WHAT YOU SAID JUST NOW! SAY IT AGAIN!
GOOD LORD, WHAT?!
THAT THING YOU SAID JUST NOW!
THAT I'M GOING TO NAME HER MÁRCIA?!
NO, AFTER!
IN THE MIGHTY NAME OF JESUS!
THIS HOSPITAL ISN'T GOING TO BE THE SAME WITHOUT YOU, MÁRCIA!
ALL OF YOU... DR. TOSHTE, GOOD HEAVENS... I...
FOLKS, THIS IS TOO MUCH...! I... I...

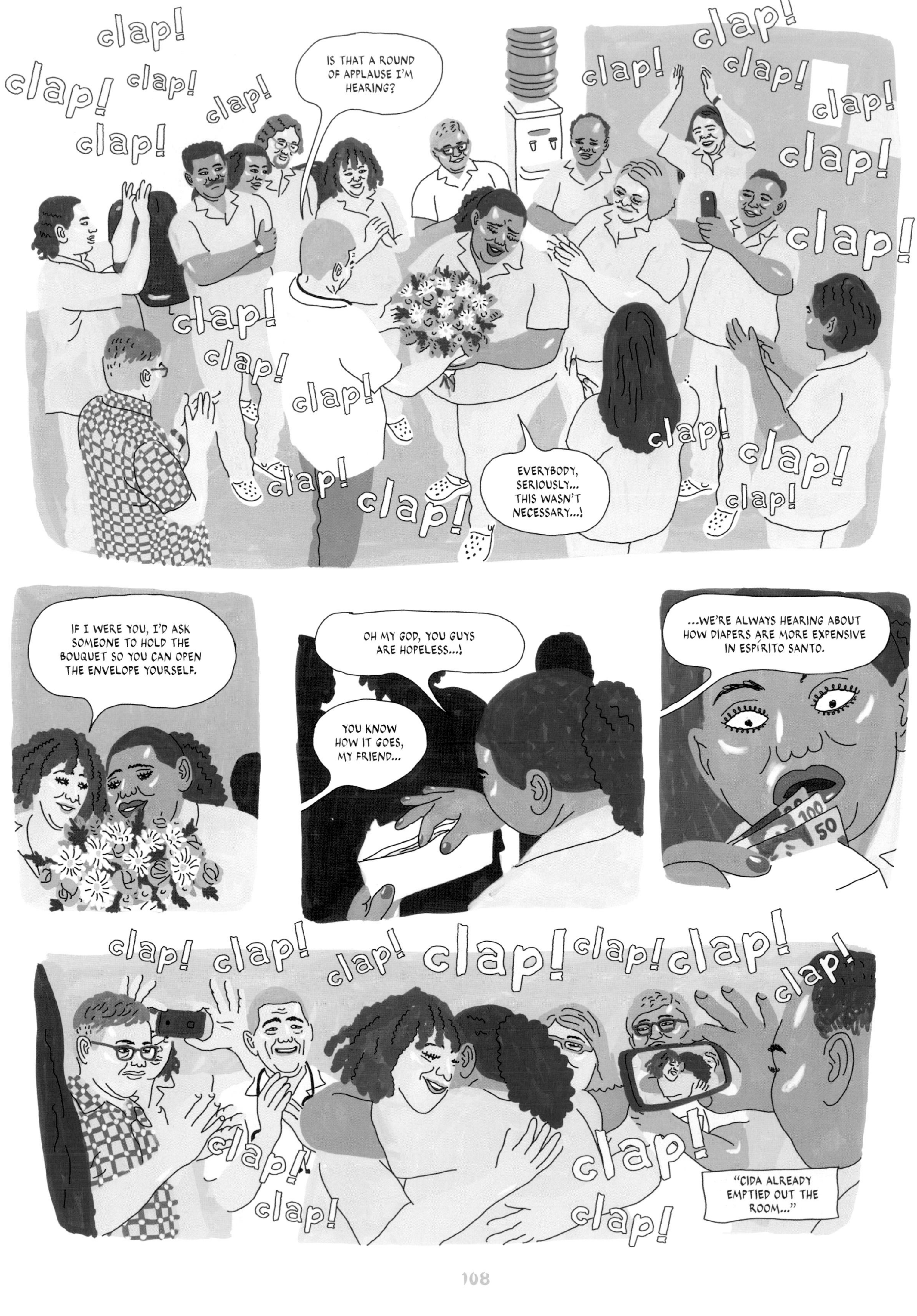
clap! clap! clap! clap! clap!
IS THAT A ROUND OF APPLAUSE I'M HEARING?
clap! clap! clap! clap! clap! clap!
clap! clap! clap!
EVERYBODY, SERIOUSLY... THIS WASN'T NECESSARY...!
clap! clap! clap! clap! clap!
IF I WERE YOU, I'D ASK SOMEONE TO HOLD THE BOUQUET SO YOU CAN OPEN THE ENVELOPE YOURSELF.
OH MY GOD, YOU GUYS ARE HOPELESS...!
YOU KNOW HOW IT GOES, MY FRIEND...
...WE'RE ALWAYS HEARING ABOUT HOW DIAPERS ARE MORE EXPENSIVE IN ESPÍRITO SANTO.
100
50
clap! clap! clap! clap! clap! clap! clap!
clap! clap! clap! clap!
"CIDA ALREADY EMPTIED OUT THE ROOM..."

...UH-HUH... SHE COULDN'T AFFORD TO RENT THE WHOLE HOUSE, SO I RENTED IT TO ONDINA, THAT GIRL WHO MOVED FROM SÃO LUÍS A LITTLE WHILE BACK. UH-HUH...

EXACTLY, JUST TO HOLD DOWN THE FORT FOR THE FIRST FEW MONTHS...

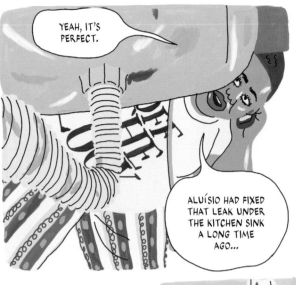

YEAH, IT'S PERFECT.

ALUÍSIO HAD FIXED THAT LEAK UNDER THE KITCHEN SINK A LONG TIME AGO...

MM-HMM. SOLD IT. I SOLD ALL THE FURNITURE.

EXACTLY.

YEAH.

YUP, SO I CAN BE CLOSER, YOU KNOW?

plec...

plec...

plec...

NOW THAT THEY'VE GOT A LITTLE ONE ON THE WAY, MOM AND DAD CAN'T HANDLE THEIR FIRST RODEO ALL BY THEMSELVES.

THEY NEED A STRONG ARM TO LEAN ON. THAT'LL BE EASIER IF I'M CLOSER. HA HA...

YOU'RE A GOOF, BABY. I DID MOST OF THE MOVE A LITTLE AT A TIME. I LIKE TRAVELING FREE AND UNENCUMBERED!

YEAH... MM-HMM... YEAH. SURE... NO, I DON'T WANT A RIDE TO THE BUS STATION! NO MA'AM, NO WAY, I CAN'T STAND GOODBYES!

I ALREADY SHOOED THEM OFF AT THE HOSPITAL.

THE GIRLS GAVE ME THAT SAME CRAP ABOUT LET US TAKE YOU TO THE BUS STATION, LET US TAKE YOU TO THE BUS STATION, AND I SAID, "WHOA THERE, HANG ON, YOU'RE NOT TAKING ME ANYWHERE!"

THEN YOU GET ALL THE SNIFFLING AND SOBBING, EVERYBODY BOOHOOING, NO THANK YOU...

YOU CAN KEEP IT!

I'M GOING TO SLINK OUT OF HERE ON THE DOWN-LOW.

ALL RIGHT... ALL RIGHT, HONEY... BYE-BYE... I PROMISE I'LL HAVE THAT BEER WITH YOU ONE DAY. HA HA... YES, I PROMISE! HA HA... BYE. KISSES.

clack...

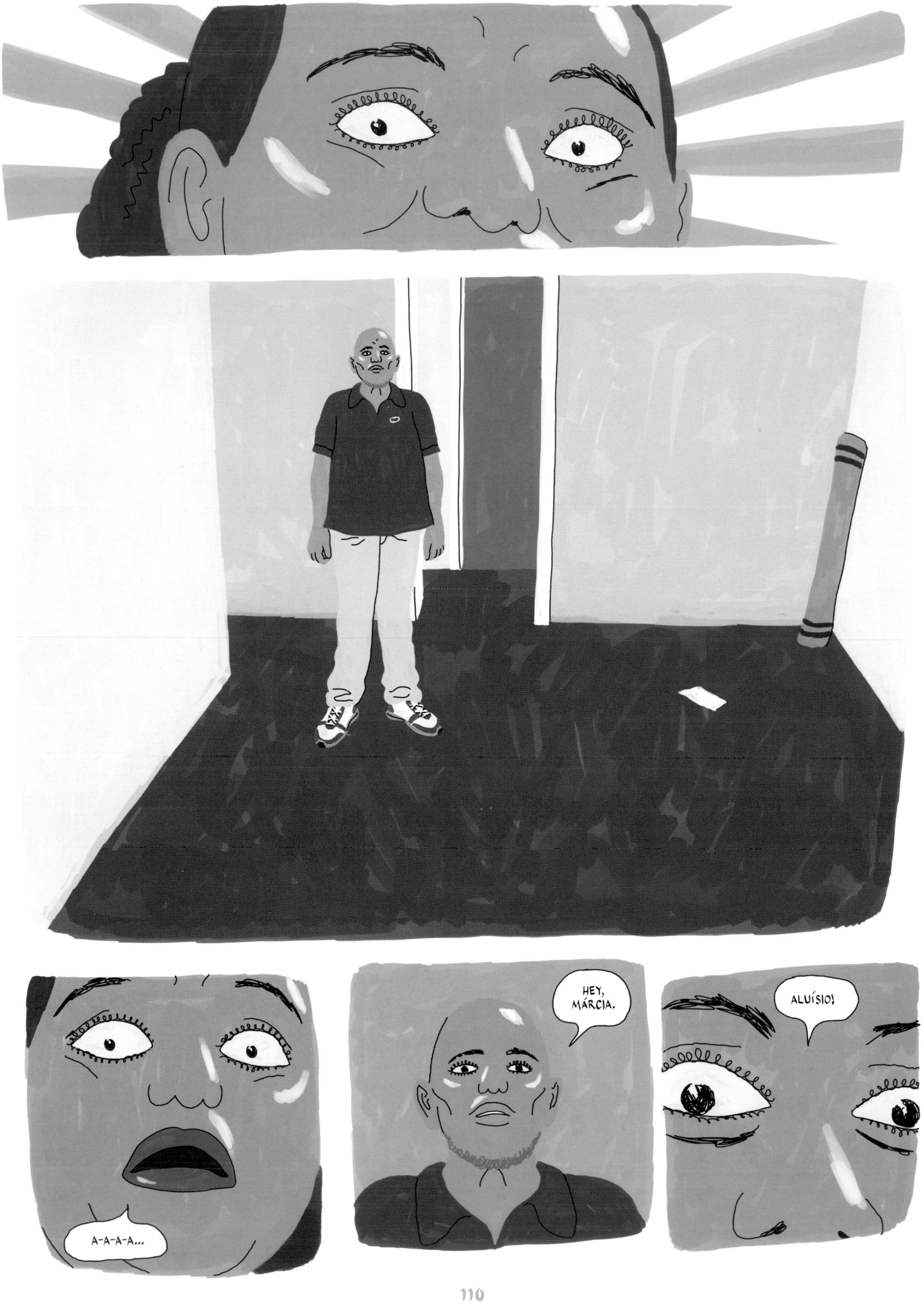
A-A-A-A...
HEY, MÁRCIA.
ALUÍSIO!

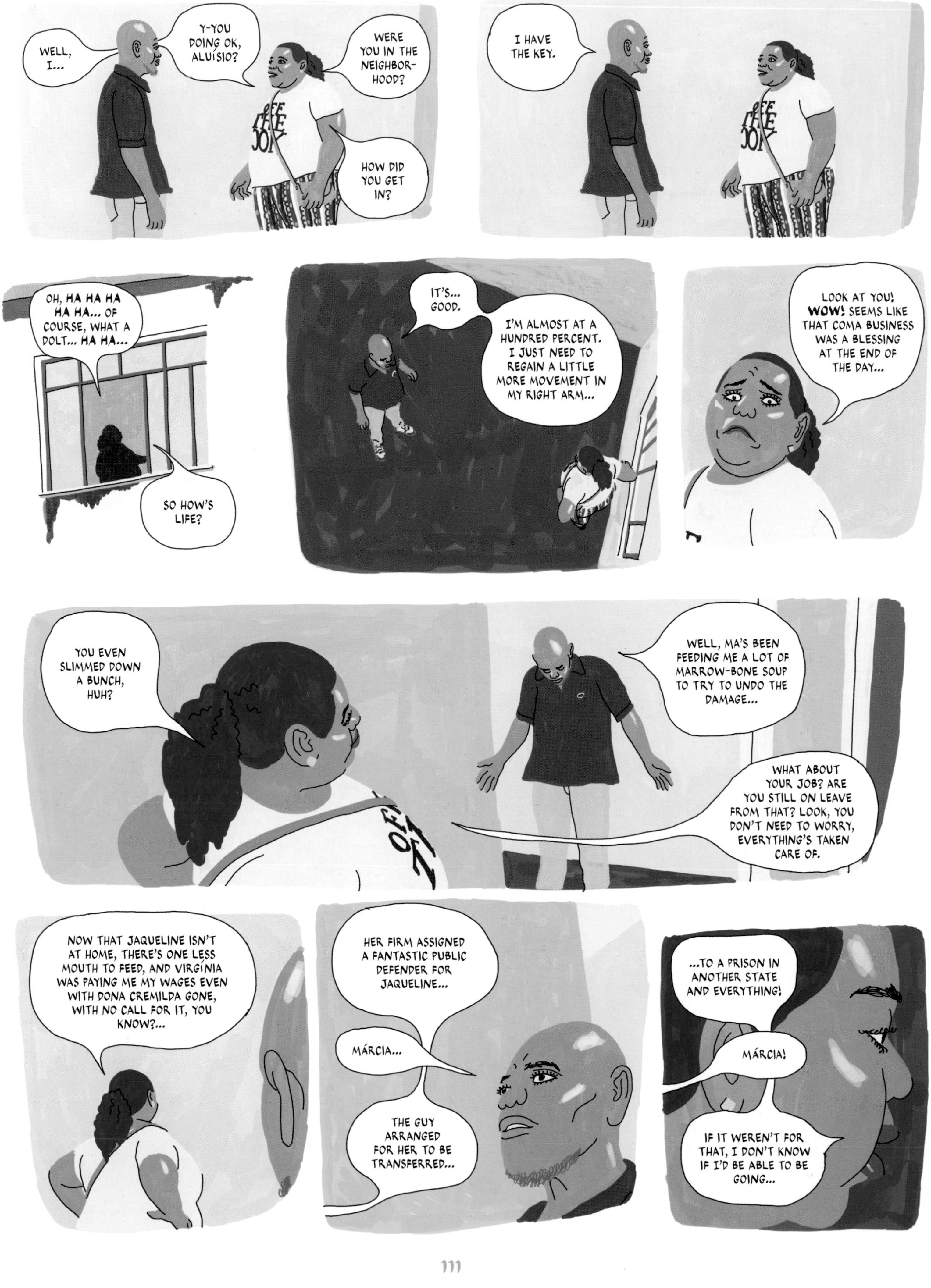
WELL, I...
Y-YOU DOING OK, ALUÍSIO?
WERE YOU IN THE NEIGHBOR-HOOD?
HOW DID YOU GET IN?
I HAVE THE KEY.
OH, HA HA HA HA HA... OF COURSE, WHAT A DOLT... HA HA...
SO HOW'S LIFE?
IT'S... GOOD.
I'M ALMOST AT A HUNDRED PERCENT. I JUST NEED TO REGAIN A LITTLE MORE MOVEMENT IN MY RIGHT ARM...
LOOK AT YOU! WOW! SEEMS LIKE THAT COMA BUSINESS WAS A BLESSING AT THE END OF THE DAY...
YOU EVEN SLIMMED DOWN A BUNCH, HUH?
WELL, MA'S BEEN FEEDING ME A LOT OF MARROW-BONE SOUP TO TRY TO UNDO THE DAMAGE...
WHAT ABOUT YOUR JOB? ARE YOU STILL ON LEAVE FROM THAT? LOOK, YOU DON'T NEED TO WORRY, EVERYTHING'S TAKEN CARE OF.
NOW THAT JAQUELINE ISN'T AT HOME, THERE'S ONE LESS MOUTH TO FEED, AND VIRGÍNIA WAS PAYING ME MY WAGES EVEN WITH DONA CREMILDA GONE, WITH NO CALL FOR IT, YOU KNOW?...
HER FIRM ASSIGNED A FANTASTIC PUBLIC DEFENDER FOR JAQUELINE...
MÁRCIA...
THE GUY ARRANGED FOR HER TO BE TRANSFERRED...
...TO A PRISON IN ANOTHER STATE AND EVERYTHING!
MÁRCIA!
IF IT WEREN'T FOR THAT, I DON'T KNOW IF I'D BE ABLE TO BE GOING...

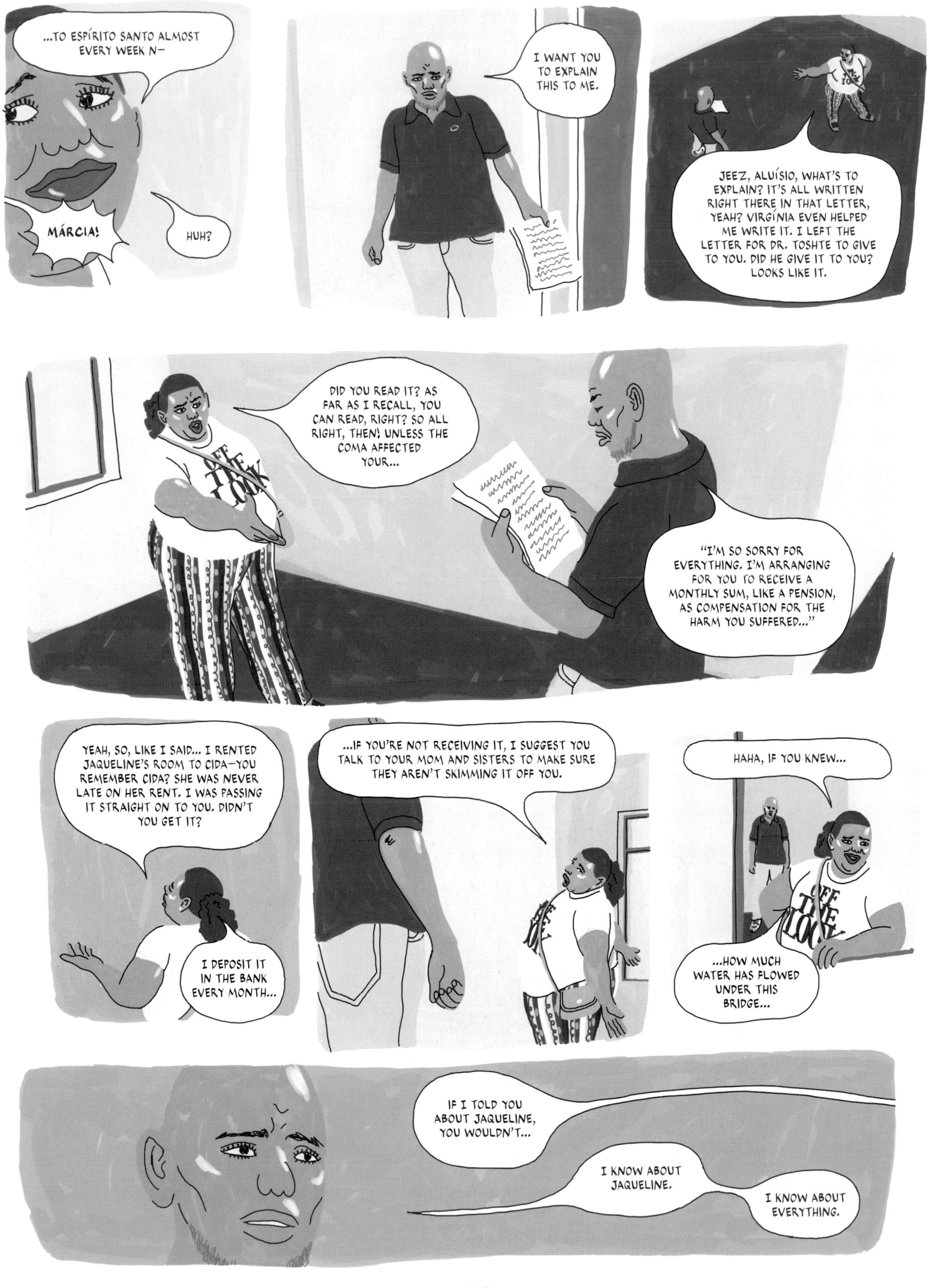

...TO ESPÍRITO SANTO ALMOST EVERY WEEK N—
MÁRCIA!
HUH?
I WANT YOU TO EXPLAIN THIS TO ME.
JEEZ, ALUÍSIO, WHAT'S TO EXPLAIN? IT'S ALL WRITTEN RIGHT THERE IN THAT LETTER, YEAH? VIRGÍNIA EVEN HELPED ME WRITE IT. I LEFT THE LETTER FOR DR. TOSHTE TO GIVE TO YOU. DID HE GIVE IT TO YOU? LOOKS LIKE IT.
DID YOU READ IT? AS FAR AS I RECALL, YOU CAN READ, RIGHT? SO ALL RIGHT, THEN! UNLESS THE COMA AFFECTED YOUR...
"I'M SO SORRY FOR EVERYTHING. I'M ARRANGING FOR YOU TO RECEIVE A MONTHLY SUM, LIKE A PENSION, AS COMPENSATION FOR THE HARM YOU SUFFERED..."
YEAH, SO, LIKE I SAID... I RENTED JAQUELINE'S ROOM TO CIDA—YOU REMEMBER CIDA? SHE WAS NEVER LATE ON HER RENT. I WAS PASSING IT STRAIGHT ON TO YOU. DIDN'T YOU GET IT?
I DEPOSIT IT IN THE BANK EVERY MONTH...
...IF YOU'RE NOT RECEIVING IT, I SUGGEST YOU TALK TO YOUR MOM AND SISTERS TO MAKE SURE THEY AREN'T SKIMMING IT OFF YOU.
HAHA, IF YOU KNEW...
...HOW MUCH WATER HAS FLOWED UNDER THIS BRIDGE...
IF I TOLD YOU ABOUT JAQUELINE, YOU WOULDN'T...
I KNOW ABOUT JAQUELINE.
I KNOW ABOUT EVERYTHING.

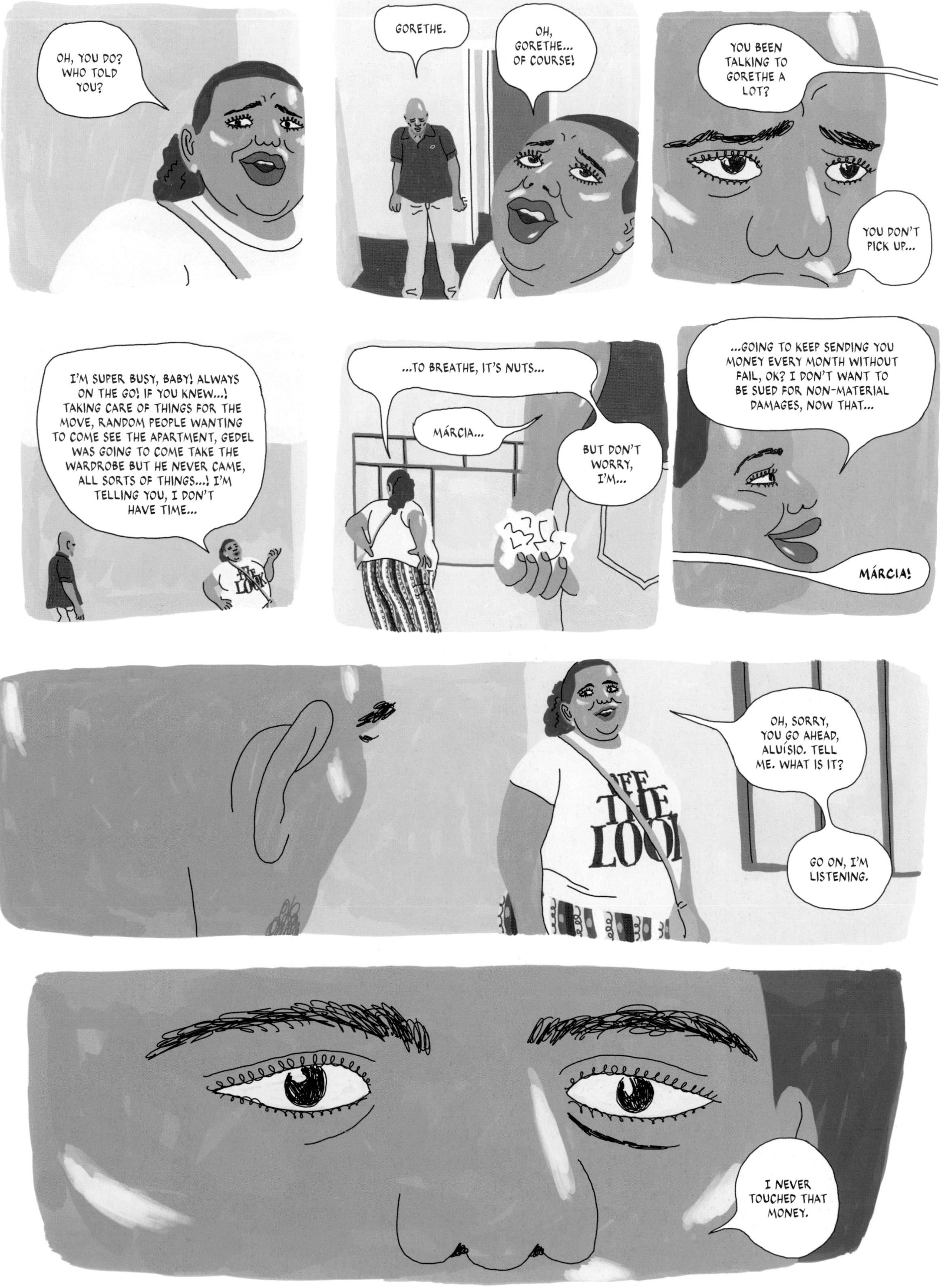
OH, YOU DO? WHO TOLD YOU?
GORETHE.
OH, GORETHE... OF COURSE!
YOU BEEN TALKING TO GORETHE A LOT?
YOU DON'T PICK UP...
I'M SUPER BUSY, BABY! ALWAYS ON THE GO! IF YOU KNEW...! TAKING CARE OF THINGS FOR THE MOVE, RANDOM PEOPLE WANTING TO COME SEE THE APARTMENT, GEDEL WAS GOING TO COME TAKE THE WARDROBE BUT HE NEVER CAME, ALL SORTS OF THINGS...! I'M TELLING YOU, I DON'T HAVE TIME...
...TO BREATHE, IT'S NUTS...
MÁRCIA...
BUT DON'T WORRY, I'M...
...GOING TO KEEP SENDING YOU MONEY EVERY MONTH WITHOUT FAIL, OK? I DON'T WANT TO BE SUED FOR NON-MATERIAL DAMAGES, NOW THAT...
MÁRCIA!
OH, SORRY, YOU GO AHEAD, ALUÍSIO. TELL ME. WHAT IS IT?
GO ON, I'M LISTENING.
I NEVER TOUCHED THAT MONEY.

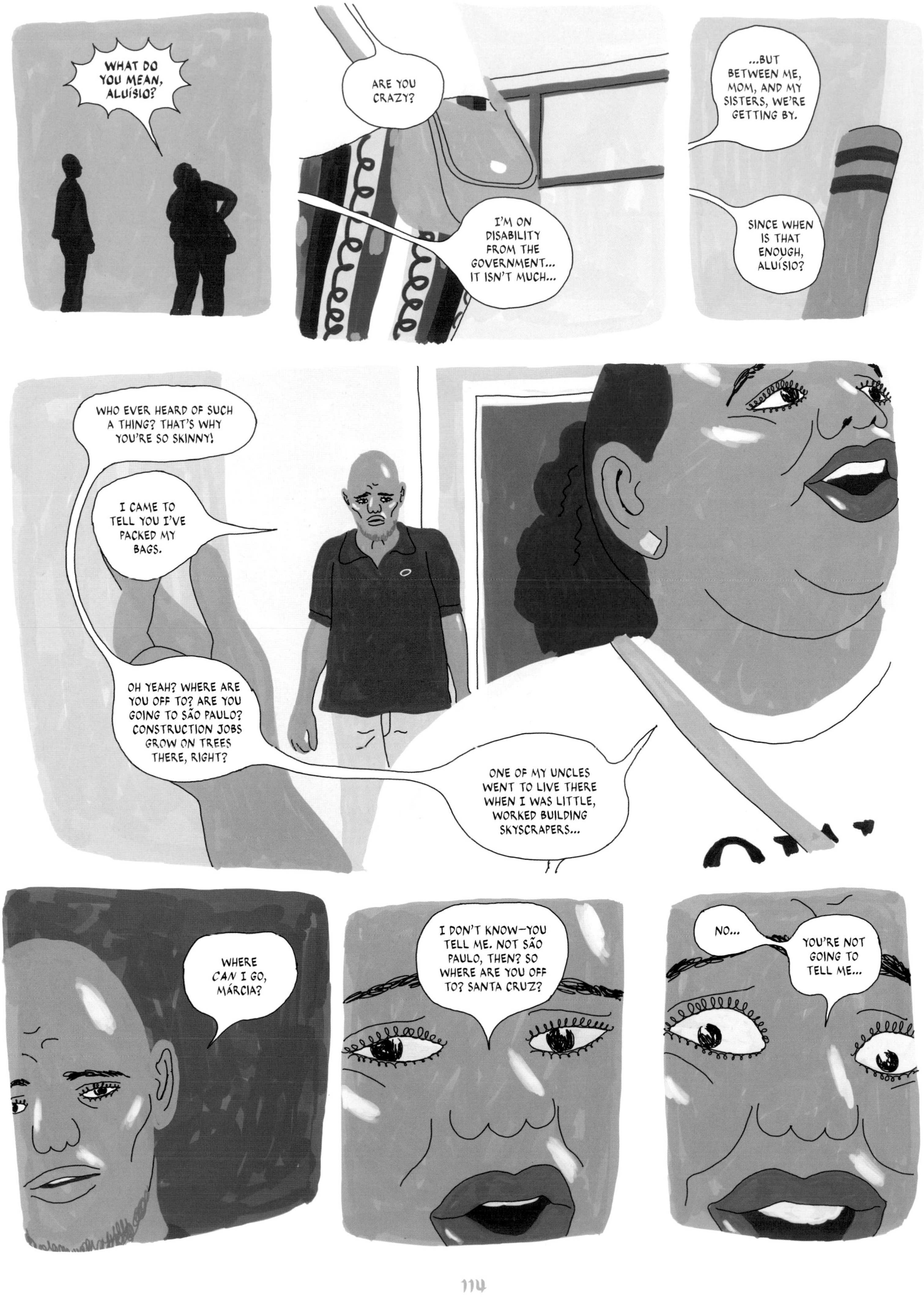
WHAT DO YOU MEAN, ALUÍSIO?
ARE YOU CRAZY?
I'M ON DISABILITY FROM THE GOVERNMENT... IT ISN'T MUCH...
...BUT BETWEEN ME, MOM, AND MY SISTERS, WE'RE GETTING BY.
SINCE WHEN IS THAT ENOUGH, ALUÍSIO?
WHO EVER HEARD OF SUCH A THING? THAT'S WHY YOU'RE SO SKINNY!
I CAME TO TELL YOU I'VE PACKED MY BAGS.
OH YEAH? WHERE ARE YOU OFF TO? ARE YOU GOING TO SÃO PAULO? CONSTRUCTION JOBS GROW ON TREES THERE, RIGHT?
ONE OF MY UNCLES WENT TO LIVE THERE WHEN I WAS LITTLE, WORKED BUILDING SKYSCRAPERS...
WHERE *CAN* I GO, MÁRCIA?
I DON'T KNOW—YOU TELL ME. NOT SÃO PAULO, THEN? SO WHERE ARE YOU OFF TO? SANTA CRUZ?
NO...
YOU'RE NOT GOING TO TELL ME...

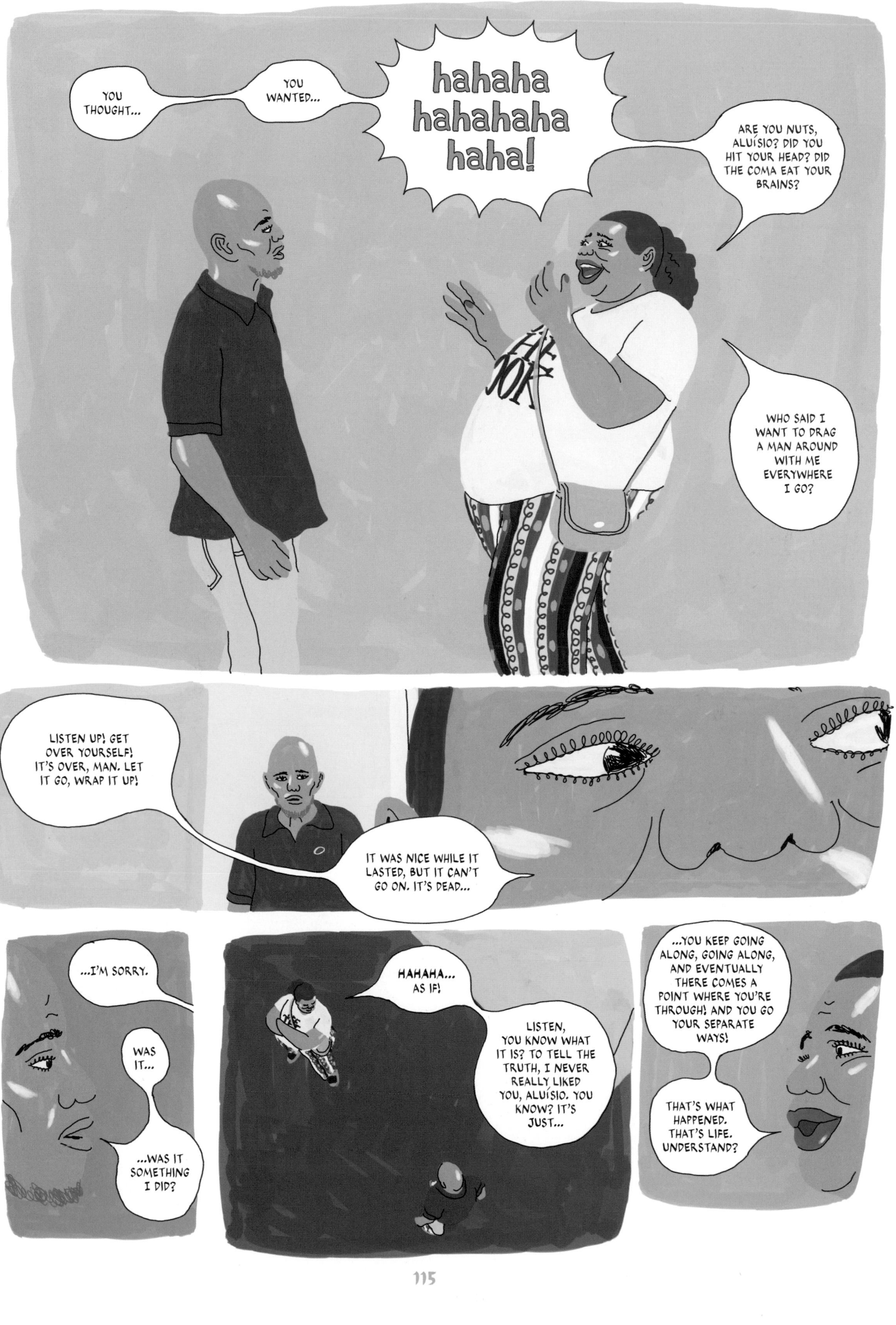
YOU THOUGHT...
YOU WANTED...
hahaha hahahaha haha!
ARE YOU NUTS, ALUÍSIO? DID YOU HIT YOUR HEAD? DID THE COMA EAT YOUR BRAINS?
WHO SAID I WANT TO DRAG A MAN AROUND WITH ME EVERYWHERE I GO?
LISTEN UP! GET OVER YOURSELF! IT'S OVER, MAN. LET IT GO, WRAP IT UP!
IT WAS NICE WHILE IT LASTED, BUT IT CAN'T GO ON. IT'S DEAD...
...I'M SORRY.
WAS IT...
...WAS IT SOMETHING I DID?
HAHAHA... AS IF!
LISTEN, YOU KNOW WHAT IT IS? TO TELL THE TRUTH, I NEVER REALLY LIKED YOU, ALUÍSIO. YOU KNOW? IT'S JUST...
...YOU KEEP GOING ALONG, GOING ALONG, AND EVENTUALLY THERE COMES A POINT WHERE YOU'RE THROUGH! AND YOU GO YOUR SEPARATE WAYS!
THAT'S WHAT HAPPENED. THAT'S LIFE. UNDERSTAND?

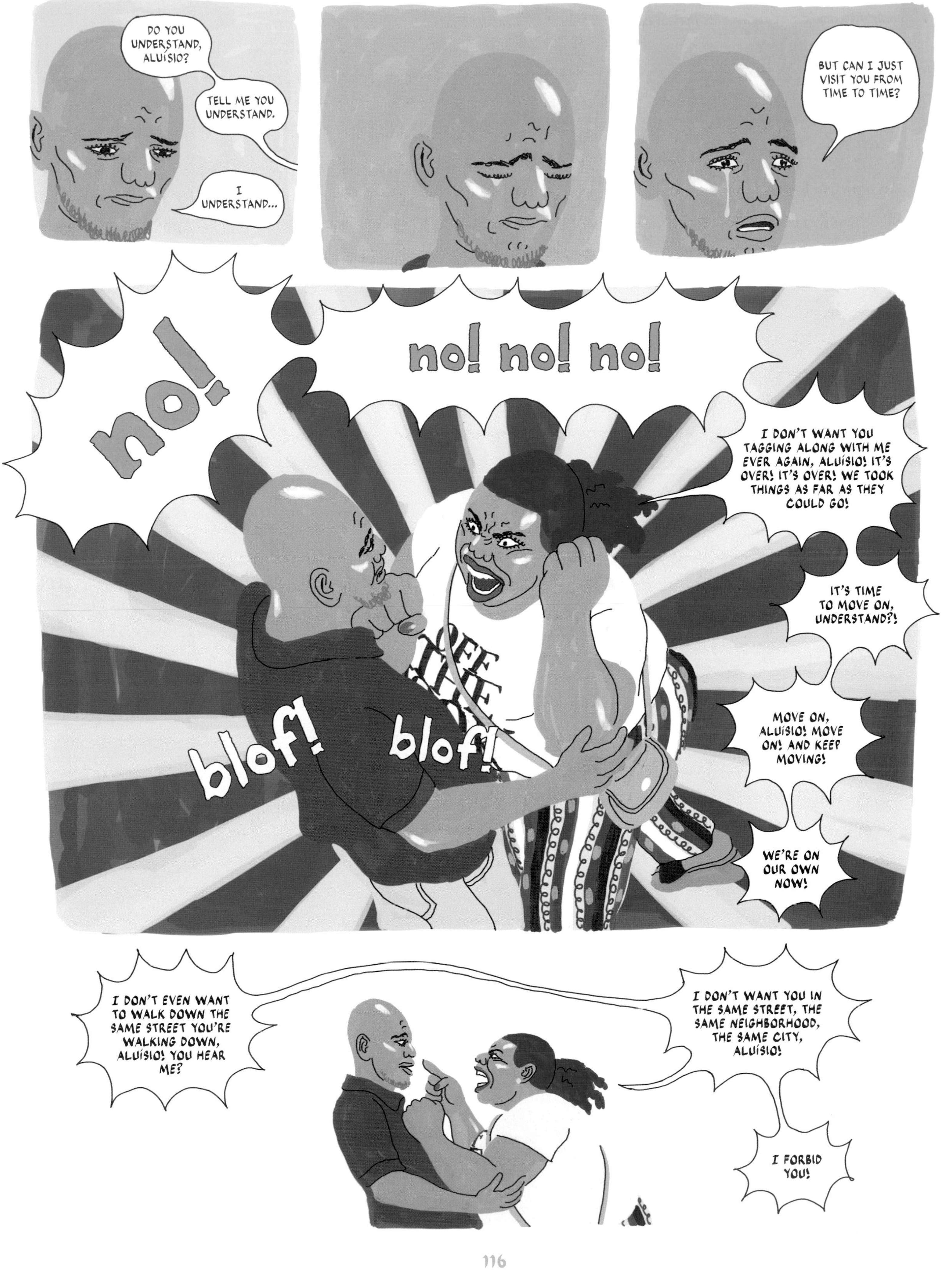
DO YOU UNDERSTAND, ALUÍSIO?
TELL ME YOU UNDERSTAND.
I UNDERSTAND...
BUT CAN I JUST VISIT YOU FROM TIME TO TIME?
no!
no! no! no!
I DON'T WANT YOU TAGGING ALONG WITH ME EVER AGAIN, ALUÍSIO! IT'S OVER! IT'S OVER! WE TOOK THINGS AS FAR AS THEY COULD GO!
IT'S TIME TO MOVE ON, UNDERSTAND?!
blof! blof!
MOVE ON, ALUÍSIO! MOVE ON! AND KEEP MOVING!
WE'RE ON OUR OWN NOW!
I DON'T EVEN WANT TO WALK DOWN THE SAME STREET YOU'RE WALKING DOWN, ALUÍSIO! YOU HEAR ME?
I DON'T WANT YOU IN THE SAME STREET, THE SAME NEIGHBORHOOD, THE SAME CITY, ALUÍSIO!
I FORBID YOU!

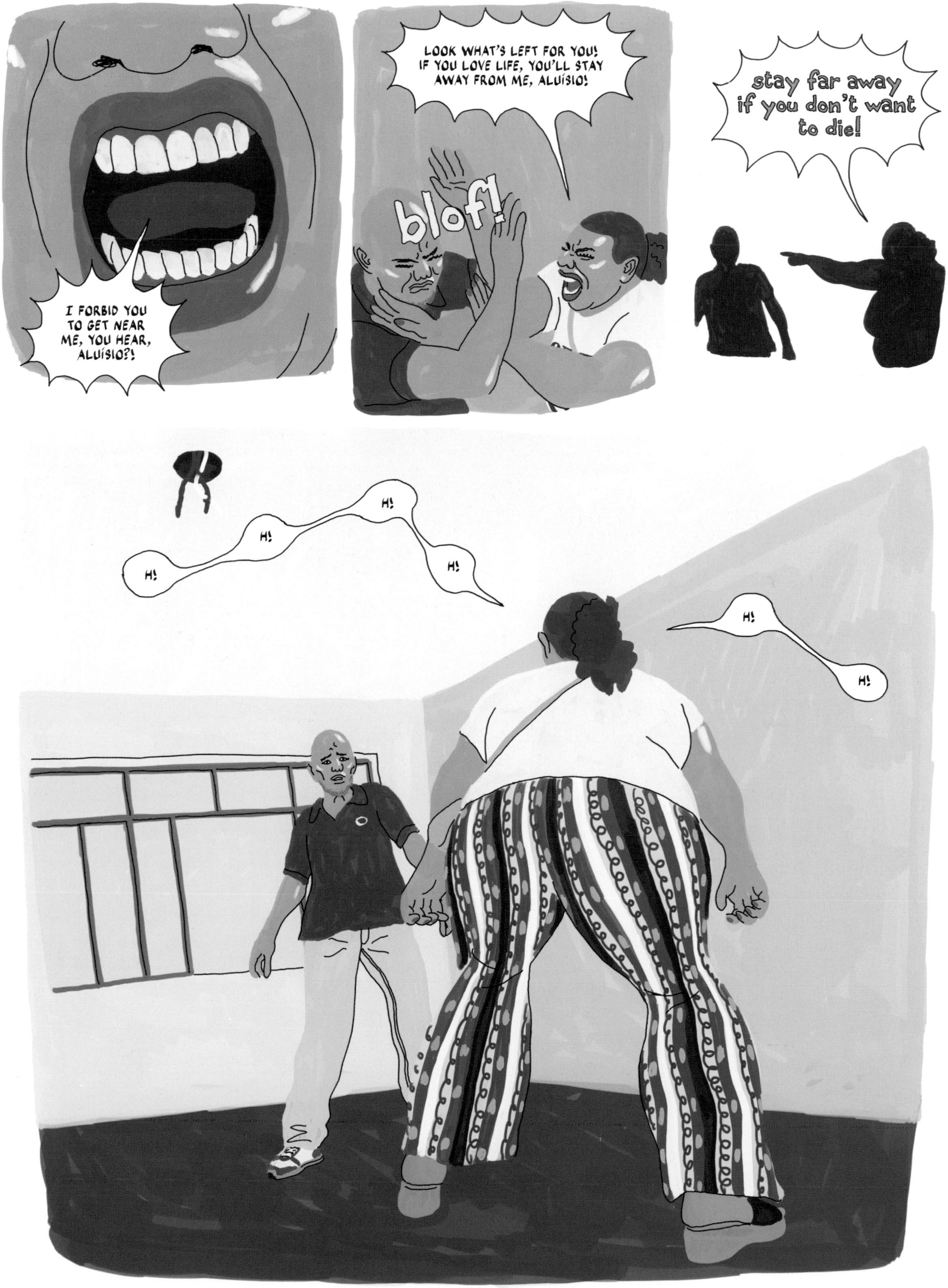
I FORBID YOU TO GET NEAR ME, YOU HEAR, ALUÍSIO?!
LOOK WHAT'S LEFT FOR YOU! IF YOU LOVE LIFE, YOU'LL STAY AWAY FROM ME, ALUÍSIO!
blof!
stay far away if you don't want to die!
H!
H!
H!
H!
H!
H!

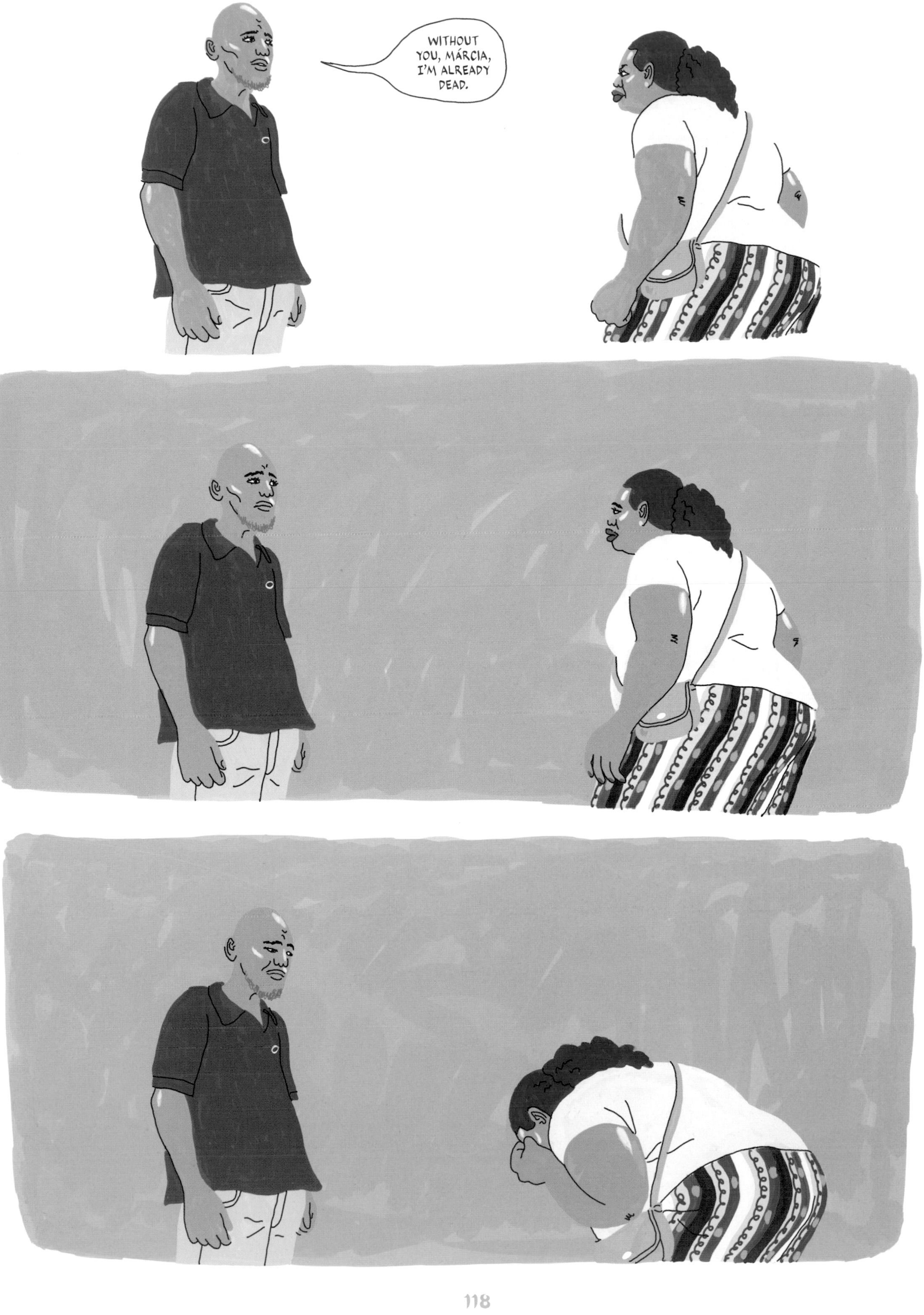
WITHOUT YOU, MÁRCIA, I'M ALREADY DEAD.

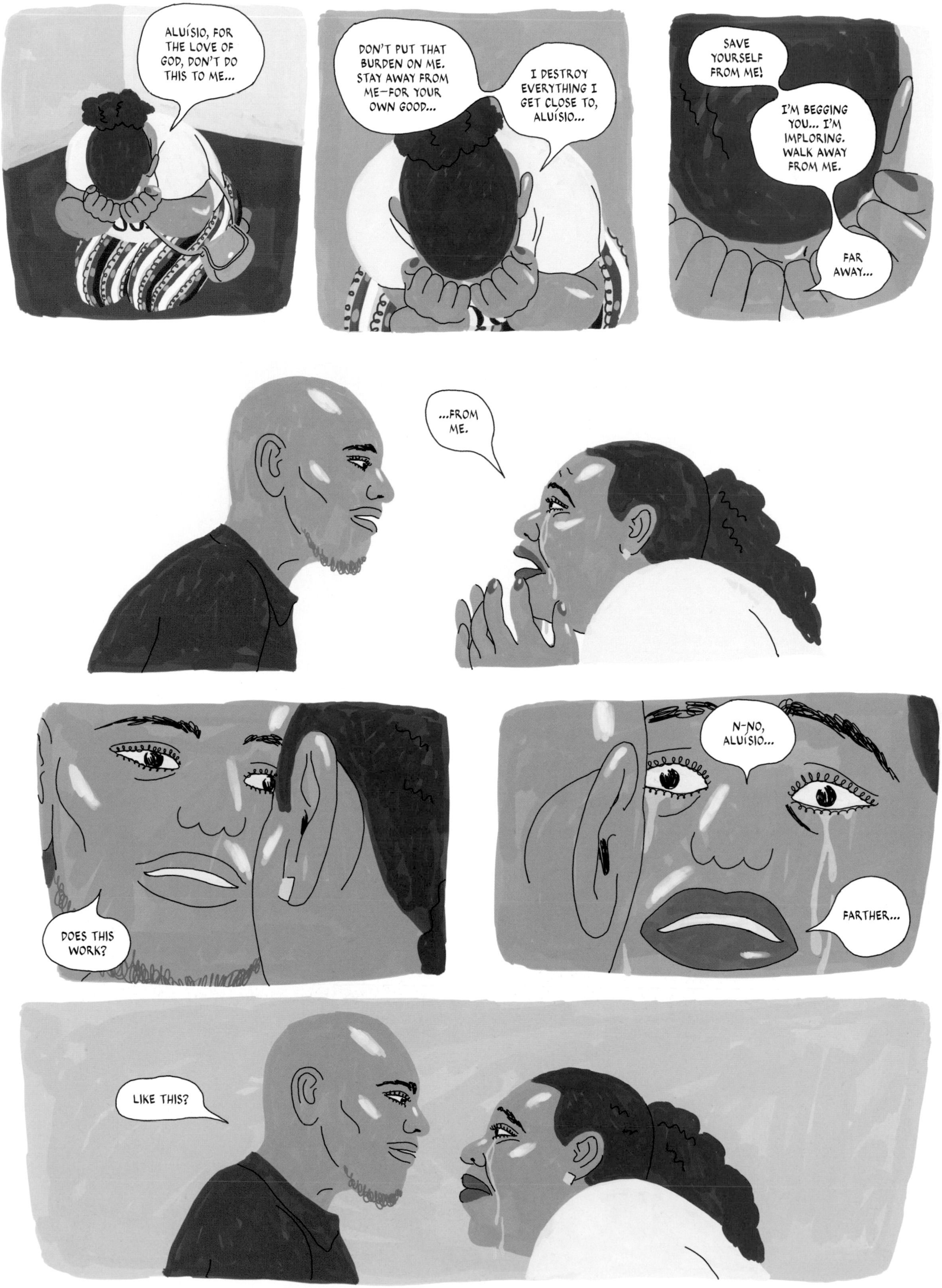
ALUÍSIO, FOR THE LOVE OF GOD, DON'T DO THIS TO ME...
DON'T PUT THAT BURDEN ON ME. STAY AWAY FROM ME—FOR YOUR OWN GOOD...
I DESTROY EVERYTHING I GET CLOSE TO, ALUÍSIO...
SAVE YOURSELF FROM ME!
I'M BEGGING YOU... I'M IMPLORING. WALK AWAY FROM ME.
FAR AWAY...
...FROM ME.
DOES THIS WORK?
N-NO, ALUÍSIO...
FARTHER...
LIKE THIS?

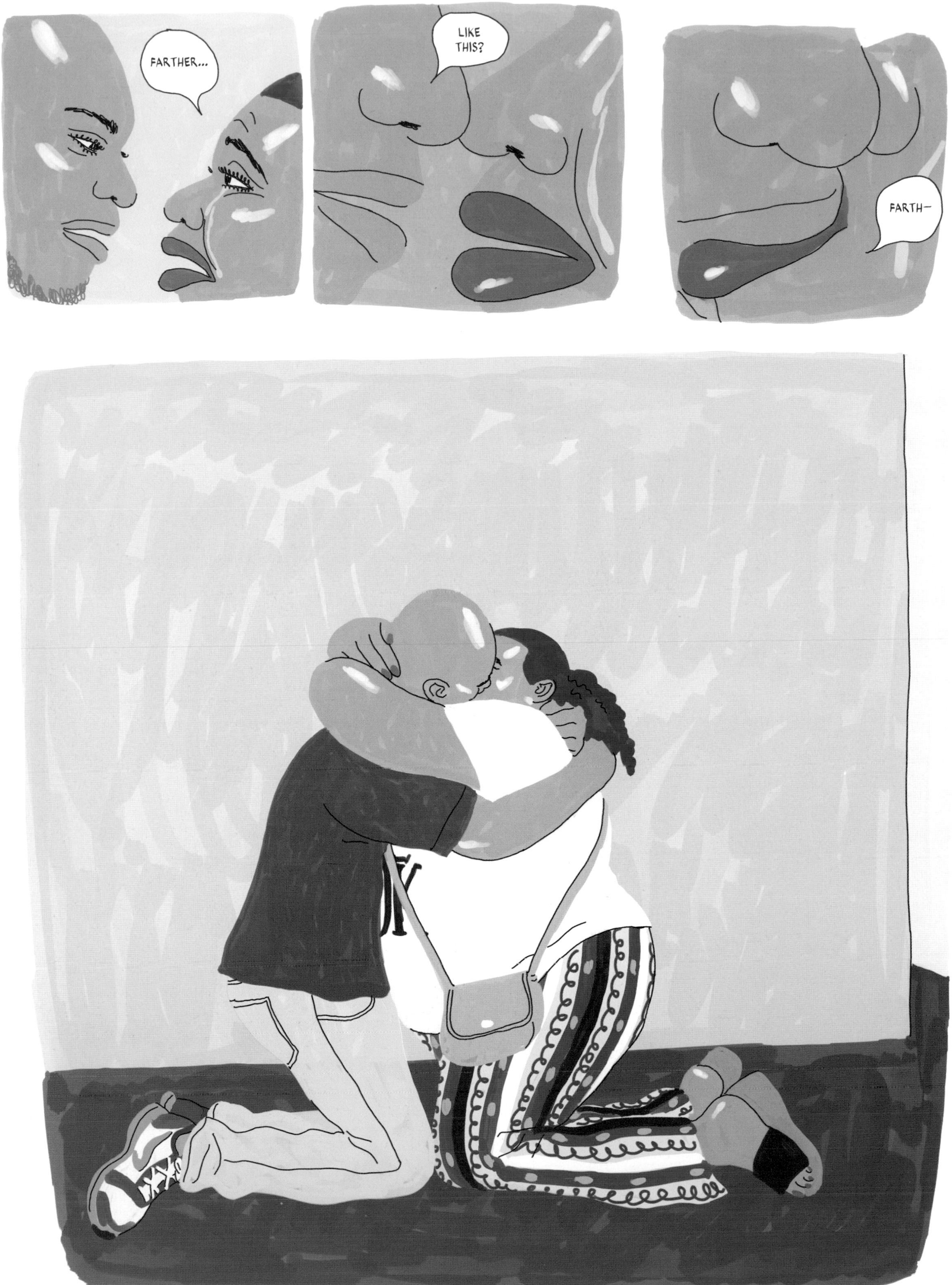
FARTHER...
LIKE THIS?
FARTH—

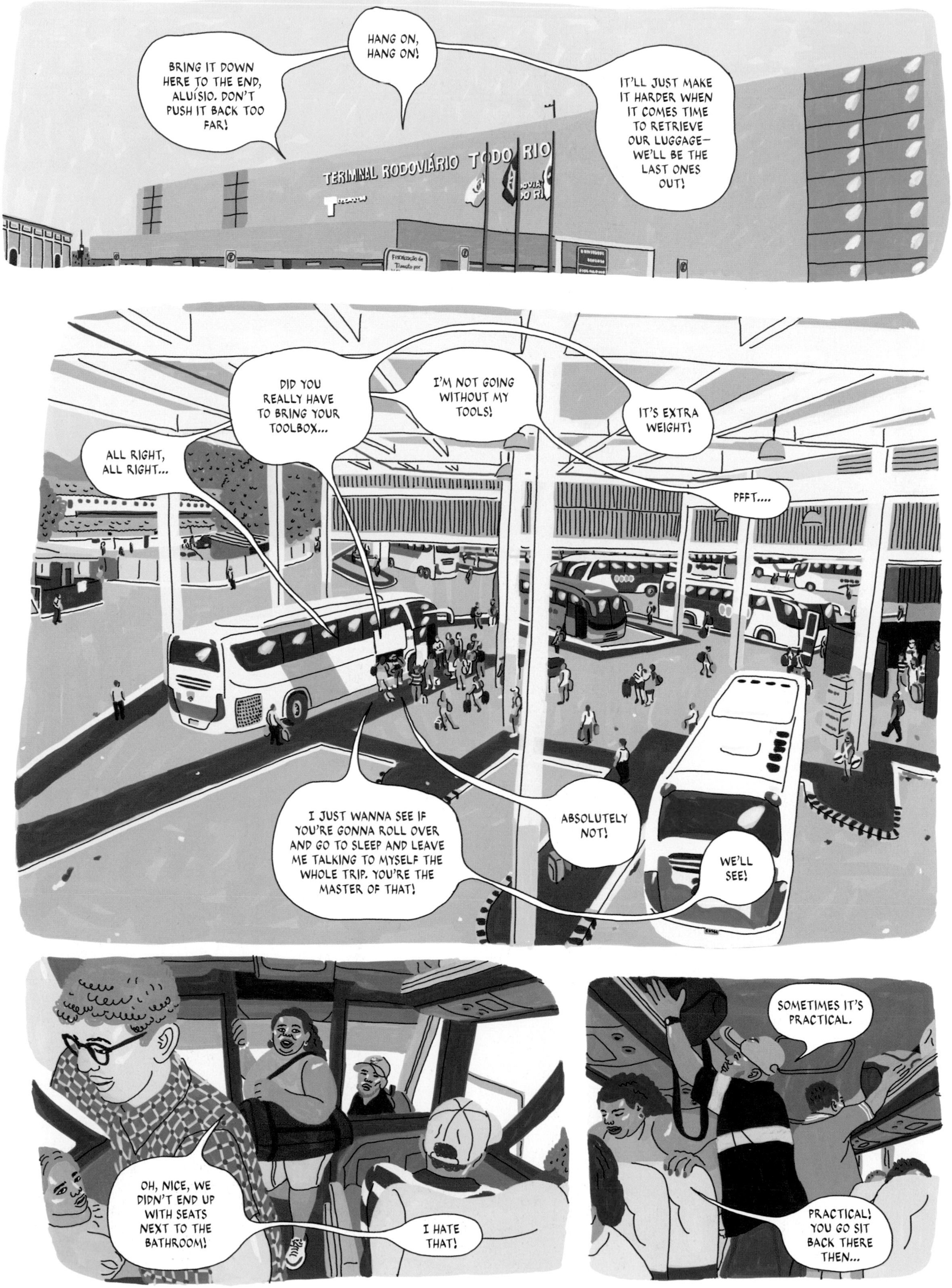
BRING IT DOWN HERE TO THE END, ALUÍSIO. DON'T PUSH IT BACK TOO FAR!
HANG ON, HANG ON!
IT'LL JUST MAKE IT HARDER WHEN IT COMES TIME TO RETRIEVE OUR LUGGAGE— WE'LL BE THE LAST ONES OUT!
TERMINAL RODOVIÁRIO TODO RIO
ALL RIGHT, ALL RIGHT...
DID YOU REALLY HAVE TO BRING YOUR TOOLBOX...
I'M NOT GOING WITHOUT MY TOOLS!
IT'S EXTRA WEIGHT!
PFFT....
I JUST WANNA SEE IF YOU'RE GONNA ROLL OVER AND GO TO SLEEP AND LEAVE ME TALKING TO MYSELF THE WHOLE TRIP. YOU'RE THE MASTER OF THAT!
ABSOLUTELY NOT!
WE'LL SEE!
OH, NICE, WE DIDN'T END UP WITH SEATS NEXT TO THE BATHROOM!
I HATE THAT!
SOMETIMES IT'S PRACTICAL.
PRACTICAL! YOU GO SIT BACK THERE THEN...

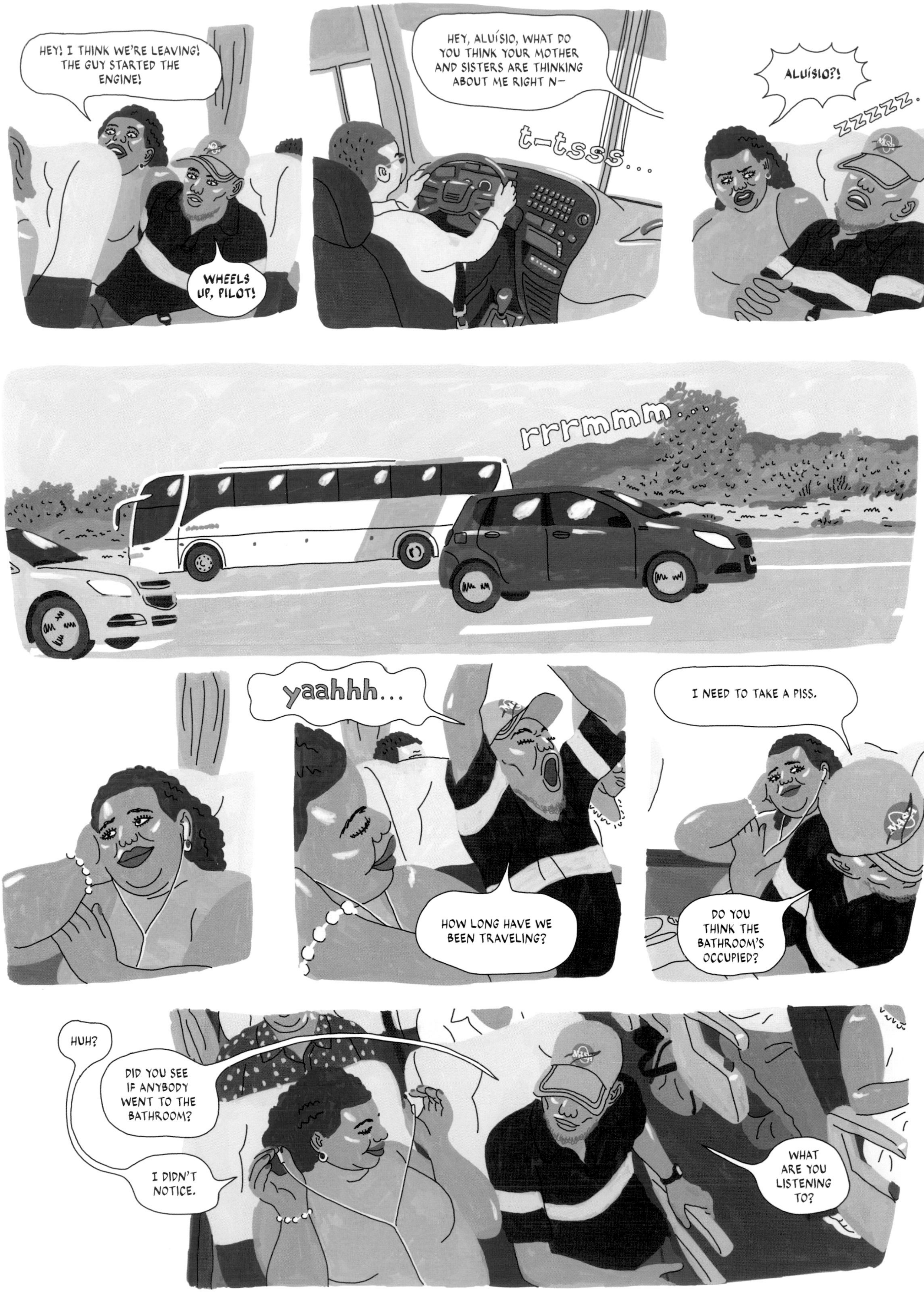
HEY! I THINK WE'RE LEAVING! THE GUY STARTED THE ENGINE!
WHEELS UP, PILOT!
HEY, ALUÍSIO, WHAT DO YOU THINK YOUR MOTHER AND SISTERS ARE THINKING ABOUT ME RIGHT N–
t-tsss...
ALUÍSIO?!
zzzzzz...
rrrmmm...
yaahhh...
HOW LONG HAVE WE BEEN TRAVELING?
I NEED TO TAKE A PISS.
DO YOU THINK THE BATHROOM'S OCCUPIED?
HUH?
DID YOU SEE IF ANYBODY WENT TO THE BATHROOM?
I DIDN'T NOTICE.
WHAT ARE YOU LISTENING TO?

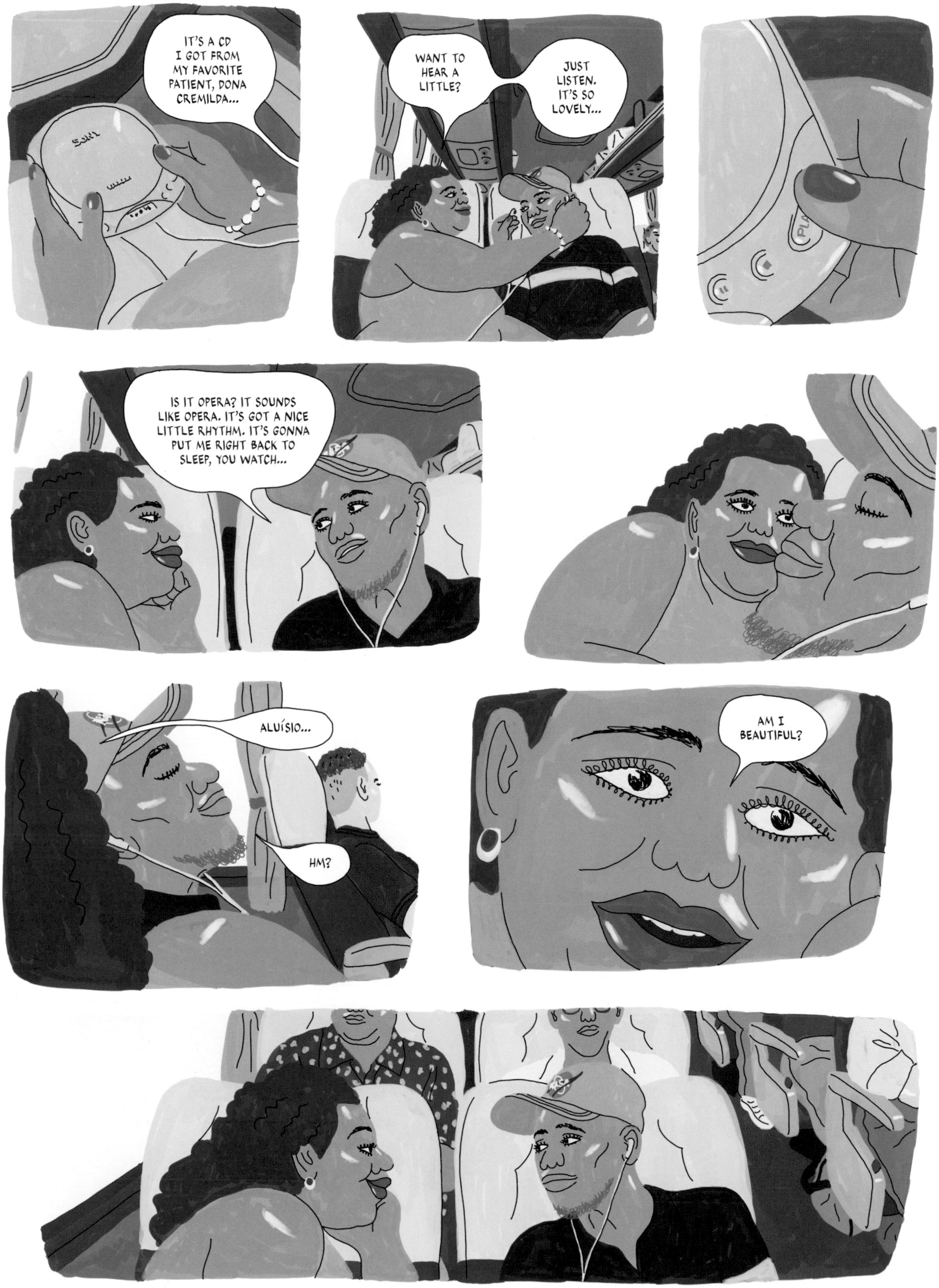
IT'S A CD I GOT FROM MY FAVORITE PATIENT, DONA CREMILDA...
SONY
WANT TO HEAR A LITTLE?
JUST LISTEN. IT'S SO LOVELY...
IS IT OPERA? IT SOUNDS LIKE OPERA. IT'S GOT A NICE LITTLE RHYTHM. IT'S GONNA PUT ME RIGHT BACK TO SLEEP, YOU WATCH...
ALUÍSIO...
HM?
AM I BEAUTIFUL?

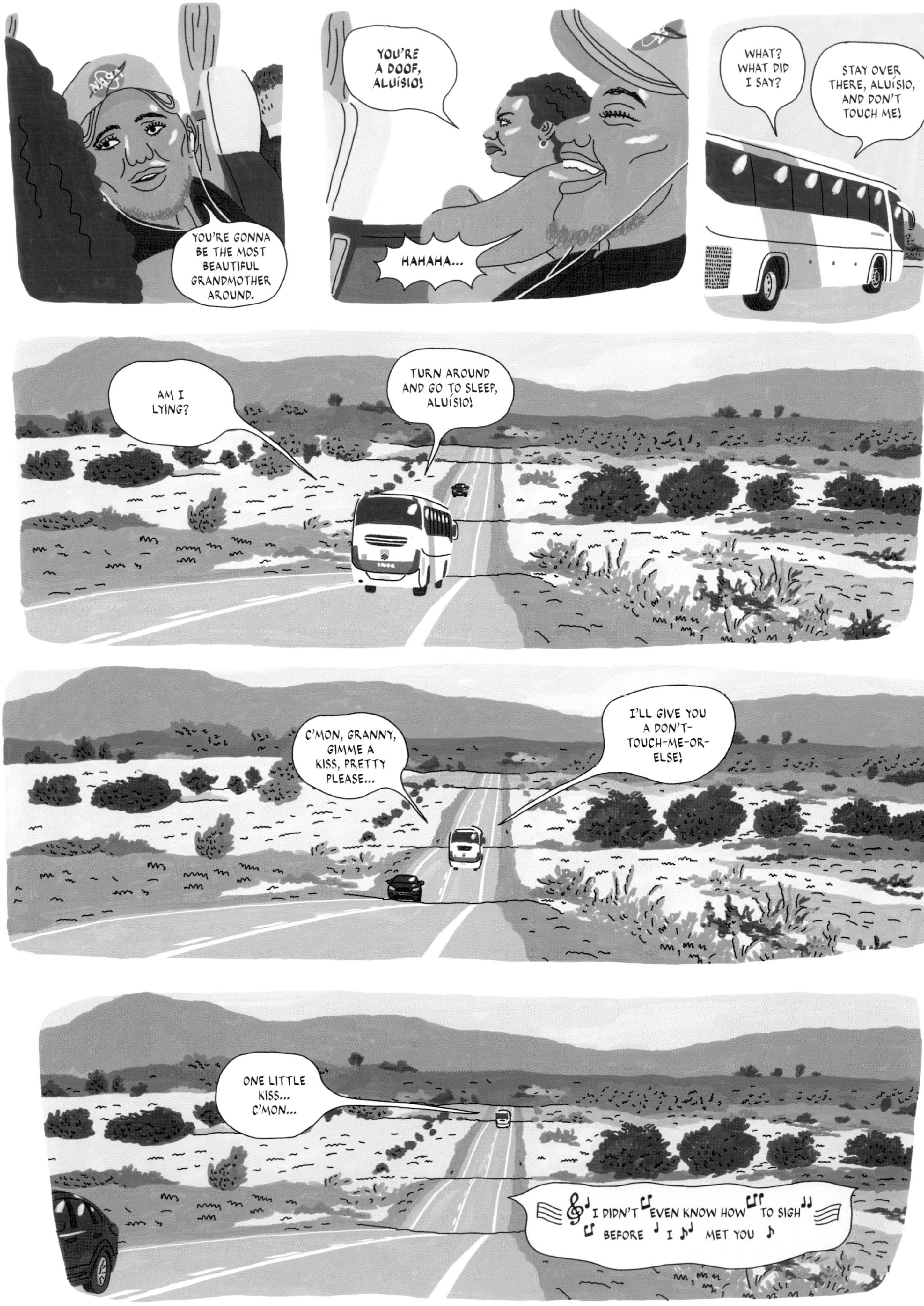
YOU'RE GONNA BE THE MOST BEAUTIFUL GRANDMOTHER AROUND.
YOU'RE A DOOF, ALUÍSIO!
HAHAHA...
WHAT? WHAT DID I SAY?
STAY OVER THERE, ALUÍSIO, AND DON'T TOUCH ME!
AM I LYING?
TURN AROUND AND GO TO SLEEP, ALUÍSIO!
C'MON, GRANNY, GIMME A KISS, PRETTY PLEASE...
I'LL GIVE YOU A DON'T-TOUCH-ME-OR-ELSE!
ONE LITTLE KISS... C'MON...
I DIDN'T EVEN KNOW HOW TO SIGH BEFORE I MET YOU

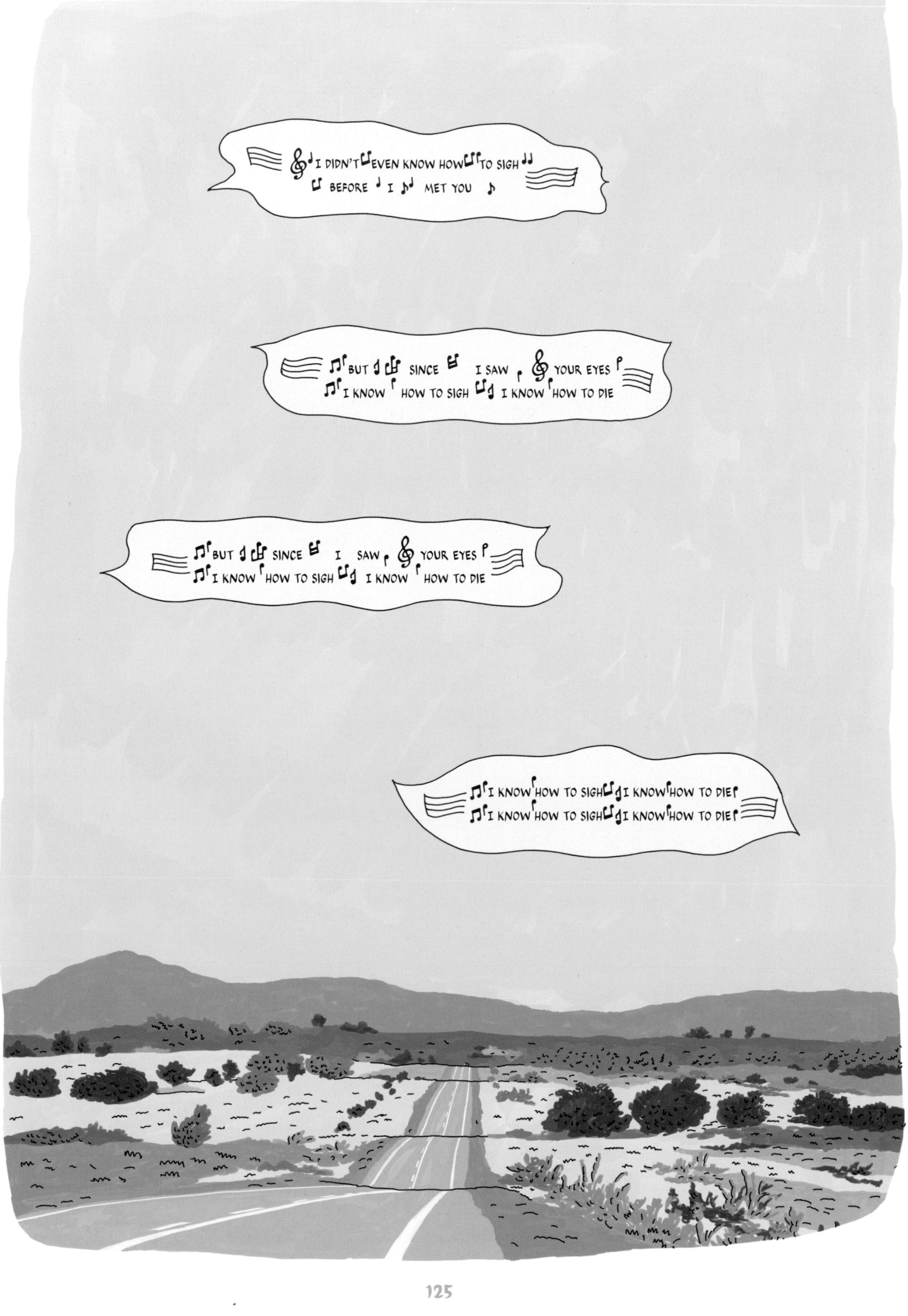
I DIDN'T EVEN KNOW HOW TO SIGH BEFORE I MET YOU
BUT SINCE I SAW YOUR EYES I KNOW HOW TO SIGH I KNOW HOW TO DIE
BUT SINCE I SAW YOUR EYES I KNOW HOW TO SIGH I KNOW HOW TO DIE
I KNOW HOW TO SIGH I KNOW HOW TO DIE I KNOW HOW TO SIGH I KNOW HOW TO DIE

Notes

PAGE 10, PANEL 5: SONG CREDIT: EDMUNDO ROSA SOUTO/DANILO CANDIDO TOSTES CAYMMI/PAULO FILHO, "ANDANÇA" ©WARNER CHAPPELL MUSIC, INC., SONY/ATV MUSIC PUBLISHING LLC.

PAGE 17, PANEL 4: BAILES FUNK: APPEARING IN THE 1970S, THESE GATHERINGS ATTRACTED THOUSANDS OF PARTIERS IN THE FAVELAS OF RIO. THESE PARTIES WERE THE BACKDROP FOR THE EVOLUTION OF FUNK CARIOCA, A MUSICAL STYLE INFLUENCED BY MIAMI BASS AND FREESTYLE RAP.

PAGE 37, PANEL 1: SONG CREDIT: ANONYMOUS, "ESCUTA, FORMOSA MÁRCIA" ("LISTEN, BEAUTIFUL MÁRCIA"), MODINHA COLLECTED BY SPIX AND MARTIUS IN REISE IN BRASILIEN, MUNICH, 1823.

PAGE 50, PANEL 1: MILITIAS FORMED IN THE FAVELAS OF RIO DE JANEIRO IN THE EARLY 2000S. THEY WERE FORMED NOTABLY BY POLICE OFFICERS AND SOLDIERS. AT FIRST, THE MILITIAS' OFFICIAL GOALS WERE TO PROTECT THE POPULATION AND TO COMBAT DRUG TRAFFICKING, SOMETIMES RECEIVING SUPPORT FROM THE AUTHORITIES. BUT GRADUALLY THESE PARAMILITARY GROUPS, IN TURN, BECAME VIOLENT, CRIMINAL ORGANIZATIONS, INVOLVED IN A WIDE RANGE OF ILLEGAL ACTIVITIES, SOMETIMES IN COLLUSION WITH CORRUPT POLITICIANS.

PAGE 67, PANEL 3: IN AFRO-BRAZILIAN RELIGIONS, OMOLU, A GOD WITH ORIGINS IN THE YORUBA PANTHEON, IS SEEN AS THE PROTECTOR OF HEALTH. IN SYNCRETIC BELIEFS, HE IS ASSOCIATED WITH THE CATHOLIC SAINT LAZARUS.

PAGE 105, PANEL 3: IN THE AFRO-BRAZILIAN RELIGION OF UMBANDA, POMBA-GIRA IS A FEMININE ENTITY FROM BANTU MYTHOLOGY, WHO IS LUSTFUL, EXUBERANT, INSOLENT, AND OFTEN ASSOCIATED WITH DEMONIC TRAITS. TODAY, FOLLOWERS OF AFRO-BRAZILIAN RELIGIONS ARE MISUNDERSTOOD, AND EVEN PERSECUTED BY A LARGE PORTION OF THE NEO-PENTECOSTALS.

PAGE 106, PANEL 6: TRANCA RUA BELONGS TO THE GROUP OF SPIRITS KNOWN AS EXUS AND CULTURALLY LINKED TO THE DEVIL IN THE AFRO-BRAZILIAN RELIGION OF UMBANDA. TRANCA RUA IS THE SPIRIT CHARGED WITH OPENING OR CLOSING THE PATHS TAKEN BY HUMAN BEINGS DURING THEIR EXISTENCE.

About

MARCELLO QUINTANILHA WAS BORN IN 1971 IN NITERÓI, BRAZIL. A SELF-TAUGHT ARTIST, HE BEGAN PUBLISHING AS A TEENAGER IN THE 1980S, DRAWING HORROR AND MARTIAL ARTS COMICS UNDER THE PSEUDONYM MARCELLO GAÚ. SINCE THE 1990S, HE HAS WORKED IN ANIMATION AND FOR A VARIETY OF PRESS OUTLETS INTERNATIONALLY, INCLUDING *O ESTADO DE SÃO PAULO, BRAVO, LE MONDE, INTERNAZIONALE, ART REVIEW, LA VANGUARDIA, LE 1,* AND *EL PAÍS.*

IN 1999 HE PUBLISHED HIS FIRST GRAPHIC NOVEL, *FEALDADE DE FABIANO GORILA.* THREE YEARS LATER, HE MOVED TO BARCELONA, WHERE HE STARTED DRAWING *OXFORD'S SEPT BALLES* SERIES, WRITTEN BY JORGE ZENTNER AND MONTECARLO. AT THE SAME TIME, HIS GRAPHIC NOVELS *SALVADOR* (2005), *SÁBADO DOS MEUS AMORES* (2009), *ALMAS PÚBLICAS* (2011) AND *O ATENEU* (2012) WERE PUBLISHED IN BRAZIL.

TUNGSTÊNIO, PUBLISHED BY VENETA IN 2014, WON SEVERAL AWARDS, THE MOST IMPORTANT BEING THE FAUVE POLAR SNCF AT ANGOULÊME (AWARDED EVERY YEAR TO THE BEST GRAPHIC CRIME NOVEL RELEASED IN FRANCE). IN 2018, A MOVIE ADAPTATION OF THE GRAPHIC NOVEL, DIRECTED BY HEITOR DHALIA, WAS RELEASED IN BRAZIL. *TALCO DE VIDRO* WAS PUBLISHED IN 2015 TO ENTHUSIASTIC ACCLAIM FROM READERS AND CRITICS. IN 2016, HINÁRIO NACIONAL WAS AWARDED A PRÊMIO JABUTI, BRAZIL'S MOST PRESTIGIOUS PUBLISHING AWARD. IT WAS FOLLOWED BY *TODOS OS SANTOS* (2018), *LUZES DE NITERÓI* (2019), AND, IN 2020, QUINTANILHA'S FIRST NOVEL, *DESERAMA.*

LISTEN, BEAUTIFUL MÁRCIA IS QUINTANILHA'S FIRST GRAPHIC NOVEL TRANSLATED INTO ENGLISH. INITIALLY RELEASED IN FRANCE IN 2021 AS *ÉCOUTE, JOLIE MÁRCIA,* IT GARNERED THE COVETED FAUVE D'OR PRIZE AT THE 2022 ANGOULÊME FESTIVAL FOR BEST GRAPHIC NOVEL OF THE YEAR.

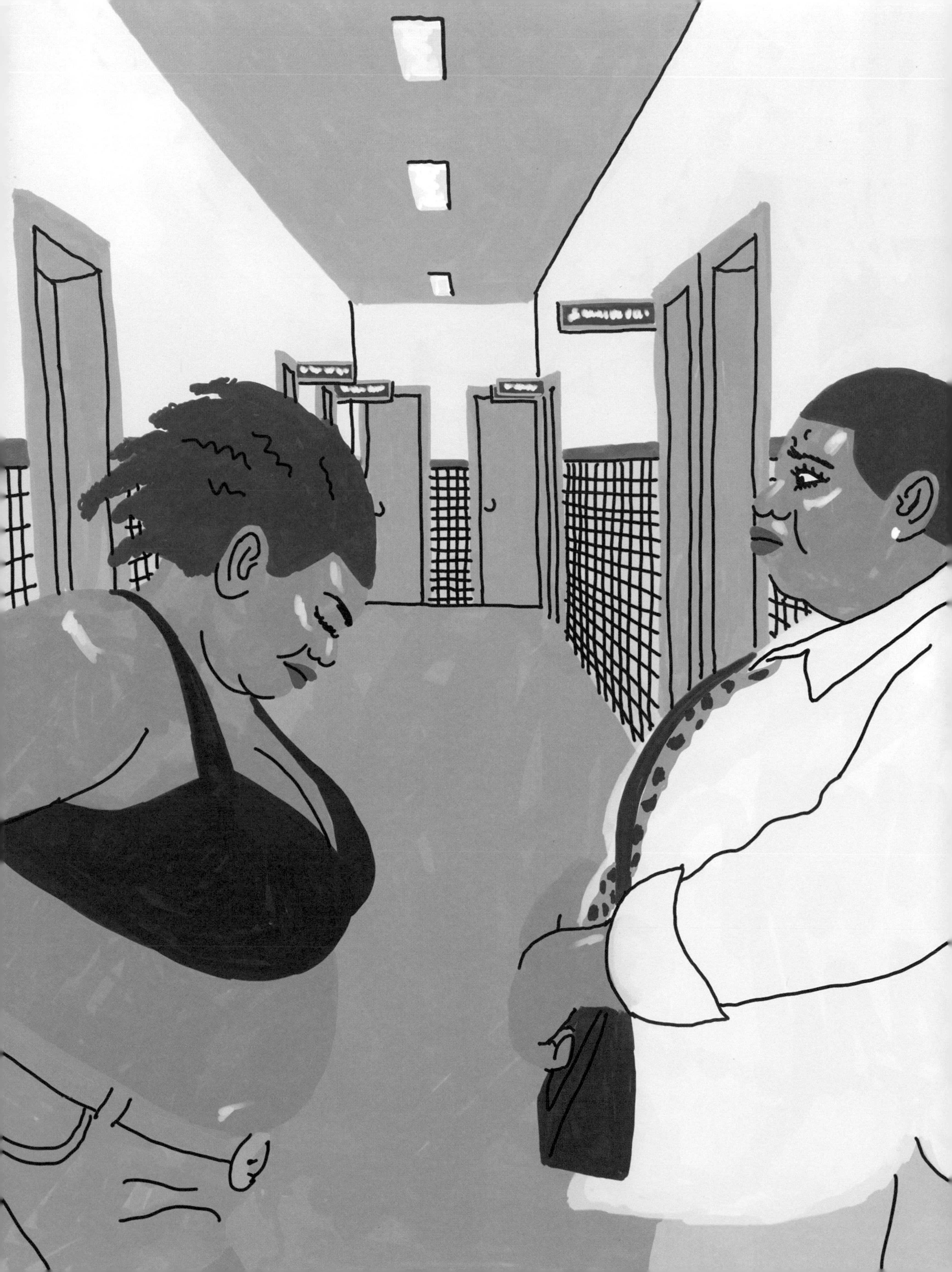